Psychotherapy
A critical examination

Keith Tudor

First published 2018

PCCS Books Ltd
Wyastone Business Park
Wyastone Leys
Monmouth
NP25 3SR
UK

Tel +44 (0)1600 891509
contact@pccs-books.co.uk
www.pccs-books.co.uk

© Keith Tudor 2018

All rights reserved.
No part of this publication may be reproduced, stored in a retrieval system, transmitted or utilised in any form by any means, electronic, mechanical, photocopying or recording or otherwise without permission in writing from the publishers.

The author has asserted his right to be identified as the author of this work in accordance with the Copyright, Designs and Patents Act 1988.

Psychotherapy: a critical examination

British Library Cataloguing in Publication Data.
A catalogue record for this book is available from the British Library.

ISBN 978 1 906254 61 2

Cover designed in the UK by Old Dog Graphics
Printed in the UK by ImprintDigital, Exeter

'The key defining feature of a healthily mature profession, or field of professional activity, is that it be sufficiently sturdy and reflexive not only to withstand but to grow through and thrive upon fearless engagement with its core theoretical assumptions and real-world practices. Keith Tudor's remarkable *tour de force* marks a historical turning point in the evolution of the psy therapies, with the field now sufficiently robust to positively welcome the depth of critical engagement articulated in these pages – an engagement that the field's further development and deepening necessitates. I can think of few if any current psy writers who could have fulfilled this vital task as efficiently and thoroughly as Keith Tudor. Someone *had* to write this book, and the field should be eternally grateful that Tudor has done so. No therapist can afford not to read this book.'

Dr Richard House, chartered psychologist, left-green political activist and writer

'This important book teaches clinicians to think carefully and to question everything about psychotherapy: its doctrines, its institutional training, its assumptions, its practices, its aims, its views of the human. Keith Tudor is training us to be practising philosophers, for the benefit of those whom we serve. A valuable and challenging read.'

Donna Orange, Assistant Clinical Professor (Adjunct) and Consultant/Supervisor for the New York University post-doctoral program in psychotherapy and psychoanalysis

'This outstanding, well-written book provides new perspectives and provocative quotes for those interested in critically questioning psychotherapeutic practices, theories, research, trainings and ways of questioning questioning itself.'

Professor Del Loewenthal, University of Roehampton

CONTENTS

	Series foreword, Ian Parker	v
	Acknowledgements	vii
	Abbreviations and acronyms used in the text	ix
	Introduction	1
1	Being critical	11
2	Psyche and therapy	42
3	Methods, practice and praxis	78
4	Theory	113
5	Personal therapy and supervision	141
6	Psychotherapy research	173
7	Education, training and sustaining professional development	207
8	Discipline, profession and social criticism	242
	Name index	265
	Subject index	271

SERIES FOREWORD

The value of critique

'Critique' is the crux of good academic work, and functions as the hinge-point between scholarship, professional activity and practice. Each theory is only as strong as its capacity to withstand sustained critical examination of the assumptions it makes about the world, and so each of these books has been constructed in such a way as to anticipate what would be made of their arguments by the most searching reader.

A founding premise of each book is that learning about a field of professional activity must also be to understand how theory and practice are linked together, and so the role of 'critique' in this process of linking ideas is to question what the impact will be of those ideas on the lives of people outside the classroom. To 'critically examine' an argument is a way of constructing a new practice which will help us understand the world and change it.

Ian Parker
Professor of Psychology
Discourse Unit
Manchester Metropolitan University

Acknowledgements

This is the third in a series of books that offers a critical examination of what are broadly referred to as the psychological or 'psy' disciplines and their professions: counselling and counselling psychology (combined), and clinical psychology. This volume has the benefit of being third and, as such, being able to draw on, refer to and, to some extent, respond to the first two, much as I, as the youngest of three sons, had the benefit – and the challenge – of two older brothers. From my elder brother, Roland, I first learned the discourse of rough-and-tumble, which helped prepare me for the rough-and-tumble of life, debate and criticism, and it is to him that I dedicate this book with affection and love.

I began writing this book some time ago, when I had the benefit of some research and study leave, some of which I spent in the UK. During that time, I stayed with a good friend of mine, John Fox, who not only lent me his study and various books on early radical and critical perspectives on therapy, but also, as ever, looked after me generously.

During the writing of this book, two of my close colleagues and friends died: Evan Sherrard (1934–2016) and Claude Steiner (1935–2017). Both were critics, albeit in very different ways, and both were supportive of my critical perspective on psychotherapy. While I miss each of them, my mourning has been assuaged by my continuing dialogue with them as I have written this book. Finally, in these more personal acknowledgements, I want to thank my wife, Louise Embleton Tudor, who is, I would say, my kindest and most robust critic. As I have known her for more than half my life, she has been instrumental in my development – not least as a critic, but also as a colleague, co-worker, life partner, parent and advocate.

I am grateful to Craig Newnes for inviting me to take on the task of critically examining psychotherapy. Sigmund Freud famously referred to psychotherapy as 'the impossible profession';

120 years later, there have been times when this book has felt like the impossible book about the impossible profession, given the breadth and depth of this field, discipline, practice and profession. I am grateful both to Craig and to my colleagues and friends at PCCS Books, especially Pete Sanders, Maggie Taylor-Sanders, Heather Allen and Catherine Jackson, for their patience with regard to the production of this particular volume, as well as for their interest and support over the years.

I also wish to acknowledge my employer, the Auckland University of Technology (AUT), for its support of me, my research and my writing, and especially the School of Public Health & Psychosocial Studies and its funding of a research assistant, Brigitte Viljoen, who has provided invaluable assistance in the writing of this book, and whom I thank for her responsiveness and thoroughness, as well as her interest in this subject. Although I have quite a range of experience in the field of psychotherapy (as I detail in the Introduction), when I lived and worked in the UK I primarily identified with(in) humanistic psychotherapy. Since emigrating to Aotearoa New Zealand, my experience has widened, both with regard to indigenous perspectives on psychotherapy and, indeed, life, and as a result of more direct and regular contact with colleagues informed by psychodynamic perspectives on and in psychotherapy. For this, I am grateful to *tangata whenua* (the first peoples of the land) for their welcome to me and my family, and for their continuing support, and to my colleagues and friends in the Discipline of Psychotherapy at AUT, as well as in the wider psychotherapy community in this country.

Finally, as I appreciate the benefit of the rigour of peer review, in addition to Craig and Louise for their comments on the manuscript as a whole, I am grateful to a number of colleagues – Giles Barrow, Dr Heather Came, Dr Paula Collens, Dr Gottfried Heuer, Dr Peter Jenkins, Professor Del Loewenthal, Associate Professor Dave Nicholls and Professor Liz Smythe – for their feedback and specific comments on individual chapters. I am also very appreciative of the generous endorsements of the book from Richard House, Del Loewenthal and Donna Orange.

Abbreviations and acronyms used in the text

APA	American Psychological Association
AUT	Auckland University of Technology
BACP	British Association for Counselling and Psychotherapy
CBT	cognitive behavioural therapy
CEC	UKCP Constructivist and Existentialist College
CFCST	UKCP College for Family, Couple and Systemic Therapy
CHP	UKCP College for Hypno-Psychotherapists
CMP	UKCP College of Medical Psychotherapists
CPC	UKCP Cognitive Psychotherapies College
CPD	continuing professional development
CPJA	Council for Psychoanalysis & Jungian Analysis
CSRP	UKCP College for Sexual and Relationship Psychotherapy
CTA	certified transactional analyst
EATA	European Association for Transactional Analysis
EBP	evidence-based practice
EST	empirically-supported treatment
HIPC	UKCP Humanistic & Integrative Psychotherapy College
IAPT	Improving Access to Psychological Therapies
IPA	International Psychoanalytic Association
ITA	Institute of Transactional Analysis (UK)
ITAA	International Transactional Analysis Association
NZAP	New Zealand Association of Psychotherapists
PBANZ	Psychotherapists Board of Aotearoa New Zealand
PCIPC	UKCP Psychotherapeutic Counselling and Intersubjective Psychotherapy College
PTSTA	provisional teaching and supervising transactional analyst
RCT	randomised controlled trial

SCPD	sustaining and continuing professional development
TA	transactional analysis
TSTA	teaching and supervising transactional analyst
UKCP	United Kingdom Council for Psychotherapy
UTC	UKCP Universities Training College

INTRODUCTION

O gentle lady, do not put me to't;
For I am nothing, if not critical.
(Shakespeare, *Othello*)[1]

In the early 1980s, for various personal and professional reasons, I decided to have some personal therapy. I was, at the time, working as a youth counsellor and researcher, living in a collective house and being a political activist. This was the beginning of a journey in and with psychotherapy that continues to this day, and has encompassed my own experience as a client of different theoretical approaches to therapy – namely, gestalt therapy, transactional analysis (TA), integrative therapy, Jungian analysis, psychoanalytic psychotherapy and Hakomi – as well as different forms of therapy – individual, group, couple, family and filial.

I undertook my first training in 1984/1985, in gestalt therapy, and subsequently completed a training in transactional analysis (1987–1994). In addition, I have undertaken extensive further professional development in person-centred psychology and have also completed a number of short courses, including one on Kleinian psychoanalysis. I have been a member of a number of professional organisations,[2] and am currently a full member of the United Kingdom Council for Psychotherapy (UKCP) (in its Humanistic and Integrative Psychotherapy College), and a provisional member of the New Zealand Association of

Psychotherapists (NZAP), working towards full membership on He Ara, a pathway that has been developed by Māori colleagues. Following my clinical qualification, I undertook further training as a teacher and supervisor, and, since 2004, have been a teaching and supervising transactional analyst (TSTA), accredited by the International Transactional Analysis Association. As a practitioner in Aotearoa New Zealand, I identify as a transactional analyst (the politics of which I discuss in Chapter 8). I worked as an independent academic for a number of years in the UK, and have, since 2009, been an employed academic at Auckland University of Technology (AUT), and in 2015 was appointed Professor of Psychotherapy.

I offer this brief sketch of my association and involvement in psychotherapy as I think that all theory is autobiographical – or, rather, that our association with, espousal of and contribution to theory is strongly influenced by our autobiography – so, in that spirit, I offer some further autobiographical details by way of an introduction to being critical (in Chapter 1).

The task has not been – and is not – without its complexities. As far as psychotherapy is concerned:

- there is no single, agreed definition of psychotherapy, and the term now encompasses a broad field and a wide variation of practice and theory.

- just as counselling overlaps with counselling psychology,[3] so the history, practice, theory and organisation of psychotherapy overlaps with psychoanalysis, with psychology, in both its clinical and counselling applications, and with counselling, although some argue that the disciplines and practice are distinct, even extremely so.[4] Over the years, fierce arguments have been made for and against the distinction between psychoanalysis and psychotherapy.[5] More recently, and especially since the advent of what has been referred to as the 'relational turn', there has been more rapprochement between psychoanalysis and psychotherapy, and between psychoanalytic and humanistic psychotherapy.

In their excellent book, *Psychotherapy for the People*, Lewis Aron and Karen Starr argue that psychoanalysis and psychotherapy should not be seen as binary oppositions; rather, 'they should be defined dialectically, as each always including the other'.[6] Moreover, within certain approaches, theoretical orientations or modalities (terms I tend to use interchangeably throughout this book), such as the person-centred approach, counselling and psychotherapy are seen as synonymous. Much of the literature in the field(s) use both or all terms more or less interchangeably, and many national and international organisations include both psychotherapy and counselling in their title. At the same time, organisations that do name the two activities or disciplines, such as the International Association for Relational Psychoanalysis and Psychotherapy (http://iarpp.net), do so precisely because they consider there to be a distinction between them and wish to encompass both.

- in a number of countries, the distinction between these activities and professions is less to do with practice or theory and more the result of the history of the development of the professions and their organisation(s), related politics (usually to do with the medical establishment determining who may train as a psychotherapist), or splits between the disciplines and/or professions, and subsequent legislation: ie. the governance of title ('psychotherapist'), and scope of practice (clinical, educational, research etc), implications of which I discuss in Chapters 7 and 8.

- in most countries, psychotherapy is viewed, if viewed at all, as psychology's poor relation. In the eyes of the public and the media, matters psychological are associated with and directed to psychologists, and sometimes counsellors, but rarely to psychotherapists. In a recent piece of research I conducted into the employment of psychotherapists in New Zealand District Health Boards (DHBs), one respondent assured me that their particular DHB employed 'psychiatrists, psychologists and other registered health professionals in mental health that provide counselling services'.[7] In numerous publications, both professional and academic, as well as policy documents, psychotherapy is equated with psychology, relegated under psychology,[8] counselling, or 'talking therapies',[9] or, worse, ignored altogether. The common conflation of psychotherapy with other disciplines predominantly disadvantages psychotherapy and psychotherapists.

Personally, I don't see an inherent difference between psychotherapy and psychoanalysis, or between psychotherapy and counselling, but, for the purposes of this book, I have tended to confine my examination to 'psychotherapy'.

As far as the critical is concerned:

- there is a range of definitions of 'critical' and what constitutes 'critique'.

- there are several traditions of critical theory and practice, to some of which psychotherapy has contributed. Here I'm thinking of the Frankfurt School of critical theory, which combined Marxist and Freudian ideas.[10]

- while there is a critical – and radical – tradition in psychotherapy, it is largely historical, and thus appears somewhat outdated, and is rarely taught and often hard to find. That said, a number of people have done a lot of work to provide critical perspectives and make critical perspectives more available. These include Andrew Samuels[11] and Nick Totton,[12] journals such as *Free Associations*,[13] *Psychotherapy and Politics International*,[14] and recent publications such as the *Handbook of Critical Psychology* (which encompasses psychotherapy).[15]

In response to this, I discuss the nature of being critical in Chapter 1, critical theory in Chapter 4, and, throughout the book, highlight where the practice and theory of psychotherapy may be seen and reclaimed as critical, and even subversive, activities.

Aims, structure and scope of the book

The aims, structure and scope of the book are:

1. to provide a critical examination of psychotherapy that may be read at all levels and has an accessible, dialogic and conversational style. In his book *The Grammar of Living*, David Cooper proposed a vision of books 'as dialogues in which what goes on in a book becomes a joint creation by all of us'.[16] In writing in this way, I also aim to use language that is psychologically descriptive rather than medical.[17] Indeed, the undue medicalisation of psychotherapy is a concern to which I respond throughout the book.

2. to write a book that will be read by practitioners (both beginner and experienced), educators and trainers, and by others interested in psychotherapy, whether as clients, potential clients, potential trainees, other professionals, or social commentators.

3. to reflect psychotherapy across its various traditions, forces, schools and modalities, *and across cultures* – an aim that not only represents pluralism and diversity but also internationalism.[18]

4. to encourage continued reflexivity – that is, critical reflection on psychotherapy as a practice, discipline and profession, and a reflexivity that offers social criticism.

With these aims in mind, I have taken an approach that is:

- philosophical, in that it deals with fundamental issues of being human, and the nature of things such as relationships and how people change. Thus, I talk in terms of (and explain what I mean by) ontology, epistemology and so on (especially in Chapters 4 and 6). Generally, and especially in the education and training of psychotherapists, I don't think enough is made of the philosophical underpinnings of psychotherapy and the different approaches to psychotherapy, a recent and excellent exception to which is Manu Bazzano and Julie Webb's edited book on *Therapy and the Counter-tradition*.[19]

- historical, with regard to some of the traditions, concepts and discussions in psychotherapy. Thus, when presenting ideas and references, I tend to do so in chronological order, so as to reflect the development of ideas and thinking.

- political, on the basis that it would be hard to examine psychotherapy from a critical perspective without being political. In this I am particularly indebted to the work of Andrew Samuels and Nick Totton, each of whom has offered a consistent focus on what Samuels refers to as the 'crucial interplay' between psychotherapy and politics,[20] which Totton has developed especially in his book *Psychotherapy and Politics*.[21]

- reflexive, in that it encourages and, I hope, demonstrates critical consciousness throughout, and especially advocates this in terms of practice (in Chapters 3, 5 and 7).

- practical, on the basis that, as Karl Marx puts it: 'The philosophers have only interpreted the world... the point is to change it.'[22] I address practice specifically in Chapters 3 and 5, but also make points about critical practice throughout the book.

- developmental, in terms of the journey of engaging with psychotherapy, both as an interested reader and in terms of becoming, being and belonging as a psychotherapist – that is, from practice (Chapter 3), through knowledge or theory (Chapter 4), by developing critical reflection through personal therapy, supervision and professional development (Chapter 5), through research (Chapter 6) and education and training (Chapter 7), and thence being, becoming and belonging as a professional (Chapter 8).

The philosophical influence on and in the book is explicit when I discuss in Chapter 1 the nature of being critical and, in Chapter 2, the nature of psychotherapy – that is, 'psyche' and 'therapy' – and its scope and purpose. On the basis that we usually experience or practise something before we study or theorise about it (at least, many of us used to), in Chapter 3 I address different elements of practice: qualities, attitudes, conditions, skills and competence – words and concepts that reflect how psychotherapy practice has been understood historically. I conclude this chapter with a discussion of praxis, a concept that emphasises the interrelationship between practice and theory. This discussion leads into the next chapter, where I examine theory from a critical perspective in the context of four intellectual traditions: the Enlightenment, Romanticism, modernism (and, specifically, critical theory) and postmodernism. In Chapter 5, I reflect critically on two elements that support critical practice: personal therapy and supervision (I consider a third, continuing professional development, later, in Chapter 7). In Chapter 6, I discuss the knowledge that underpins research: that is, both the methodology (the philosophy of practice and research) and the method (the practice). In Chapter 7, I consider various aspects of education and training in psychotherapy, including the implications of the fact that most of the founding fathers and mothers of psychoanalysis and psychotherapy were themselves not educators. I discuss the education of psychotherapists in the context of the apprenticeship model, alongside the influence of (predominantly private) training institutes, as well as the formal and informal acculturation to the profession of psychotherapy, and continuing – or sustaining – professional development. Two hundred years on from its academic beginnings, psychotherapy is widely regarded as a profession and is hugely organised, and in Chapter 8, and by way of concluding the book, I offer some critical reflections on psychotherapy as a discipline, as a profession, and as offering social criticism.

In offering a critical examination of psychotherapy as well as an argument for critical psychotherapy, these chapters offer a commentary on, respectively, being critical, critical being, critical practice, critical knowledge, critical reflection, critical research, critical education and critical organisation.

Inevitably, there are gaps in what the book covers. Some gaps are deliberate exclusions, such as different forms of therapy (child and adolescent psychotherapy, couple and family therapy etc), which merit volumes of their own in this series. Generally, I have made broad points of criticism that I think could be applied to these different forms, although colleagues trained and specialising in them would include more specific and, no doubt, other criticisms. Other gaps reflect the inevitable limitations in my reading and experience. So, my criticism of the Western intellectual tradition is informed by critical traditions that include post-colonialism and some indigenous perspectives, but is less informed by African and Eastern writers. A third kind of gap concerns emphasis and nuance – my critical analysis and examination is based on a critique of power (ultimately derived from Marxism, feminism and race and cultural studies), but this is generally more implicit than explicit throughout the book. Other gaps that are accidental and/or unconscious will, no doubt, be picked up by the reader and/or reviewers.

While this organisation of the book is intentional, it is nonetheless personal (autobiographical) and, inevitably, idiosyncratic. There are certain themes in this book that reflect my experience and values. Carl Rogers proposes: 'One cannot engage in psychotherapy without giving operational evidence of an underlying value orientation and view of human nature.' He continues: 'It is definitely preferable, in my estimation, that such underlying views be open and explicit, rather than covert and implicit.'[23] I agree, and for that reason have set out my stall throughout the book, including some of my autobiographical, philosophical and political influences. By doing so, I invite you, the reader, to consider how your 'underlying value orientation', as well as your views of human nature and society, influences your approach to or view of psychotherapy, whether as client, interested layperson, or social commentator, and, if you are practising psychotherapy, your work.

Endnotes

1. Shakespeare W (1984/1622). *Othello* (N Sanders ed). Cambridge: Cambridge University Press (Act II, Scene I, lines 907–908).
2. For details of which see: Tudor K (2016). *Conscience and Critic: the selected works of Keith Tudor*. London, UK: Routledge.
3. Indeed, in an earlier book in this series, they were combined (see: Feltham C (2013). *Counselling and Counselling Psychology: a critical examination*. Ross-on-Wye: PCCS Books), although I was– and, I am sure, many counsellors would have been – surprised to see these two disciplines combined, as counselling has a long tradition that is entirely separate to psychology, especially in its more medicalised form.
4. Eysenck writes that: 'Clinical psychology demands competence in the fields of diagnosis and/or research, but therapy is something essentially alien to clinical psychology.' Eysenck H (1949). Training in clinical psychology: an English point of view. *American Psychologist 4*(6): 173–176.
5. For an excellent discussion of which, see: Aron L, Starr K (2013). *Psychotherapy for the People: toward a progressive psychoanalysis*. New York, NY: Routledge.
6. Aron & Starr (2013), p357.
7. Tudor K (2018). *Public Sector Psychotherapy in Aotearoa New Zealand: alternative and other facts* (submitted for publication).
8. Three years ago, I was appointed as Professor of Psychotherapy; some time after I was introduced by a colleague (who is a psychologist) as Professor of *Psychology*. Talking about this later with another colleague, they commented that I should probably regard the unintended slip as a promotion.
9. Te Pou o Te Whakaaro Nui (2009). *A Guide to Talking Therapies in New Zealand*. Auckland, NZ: The National Centre of Mental Health Research, Information and Workforce Development.
10. Geuss R (1981). *The Idea of a Critical Theory*. Cambridge: Cambridge University Press.
11. Samuels A (1993). *The Political Psyche*. London: Routledge. Also: Samuels A (2001). *Politics on the Couch*. London: Profile Books.
12. Totton N (2000). *Psychotherapy and Politics*. London: Sage.
13. See http://human-nature.com/free-associations/index.html (accessed 28 October 2017)

14. http://onlinelibrary.wiley.com/journal/10.1002/(ISSN)1556-9195 (accessed 28 October 2017).
15. Parker I (2015). *Handbook of Critical Psychology*. London: Routledge.
16. Cooper D (1976). *The Grammar of Living: an examination of political acts*. Harmondsworth: Penguin (p9). I have partly done this by using voice-recognition software, a first for me in writing a book and which I think (and hope) has enhanced its conversational style. (I have, nevertheless, still edited the text, as there were some interesting and humorous misinterpretations, my favourite of which was 'homo ludens' (Chapter 1), which became 'I'm a loose end' and then 'Homo mood ends'.)
17. Newnes C (2014). *Clinical Psychology: a critical examination*. Ross-on-Wye: PCCS Books (chapter 2).
18. Of course, the book also reflects my own experience and proclivities. This is perhaps most evident in the examples I use, which, theoretically at least, derive more from transactional analysis and the person-centred approach. Nevertheless, I regard them as generalisable and applicable to other theoretical orientations and situations.
19. Bazzano M, Webb J (2016). *Therapy and the Counter-tradition: the edge of philosophy*. London: Routledge.
20. Samuels (1993) (p4).
21. Totton (2000). Andrew Samuels and Nick Totton also instigated the journal *Psychotherapy and Politics International*.
22. Marx K (1975/1888). Theses on Feuerbach. In: Colletti L (ed). *Karl Marx: early writings* (G Benton trans). Harmondsworth: Penguin (p423).
23. Rogers CR (1957). A note on 'The Nature of Man'. *Journal of Counseling Psychology* 4(3): 199–203 (p199).

CHAPTER 1

Being critical

> Modern European criticism was born of a struggle against the absolutist state. (Terry Eagleton)[1]

As this book is concerned with critical examination, this opening chapter examines being critical, beginning with some of my own history with regard to this. I go on to discuss critique and criticism, and present four aspects that define a critical approach, on which I draw throughout the book. I then discuss what I regard as two threats to critical thinking – dogmatism and fundamentalism, and conclude with a brief discussion of critical thinking, which informs this critical examination. This chapter serves as an introduction to the methodology and method of the book, and the next chapter as an introduction to the subject of the enquiry: namely, psychotherapy.

My own interest in critique

In terms of my background with regard to critique and criticism, my family was Unitarian, a non-conformist (Christian) faith[2] that represents and stands as a critique of Trinitarianism. My maternal grandfather was a Unitarian minister, and my father a lay preacher. Among other things, Unitarians talk about 'Faith, Freedom and Reason', and from this background I inherited an appreciation of faith and faiths, of freedom and liberty-based liberal values, and of rational argument. These perspectives were enhanced by my study of and first degree in philosophy and theology, in which I was introduced to philosophical criticism. My critical faculties and capacities were developed and enhanced by my first professional training as a social worker on a course informed by radical social work theory and practice;[3] by my contact with feminists and feminism, and by my membership of and activity in a revolutionary socialist organisation, which, among other things, introduced me to critical race politics.[4] My experiences during this time gave me a sensitivity to the fact and consequences of the asymmetry of relationships, which I understood – and still understand – primarily in terms of power. Indeed, my engagement with the struggle(s) against asymmetry of power has been a large part of my working life.

It was as a social work student that I first came across radical psychiatry and the writings of Claude Steiner, Hogie Wyckoff and others,[5] which influenced not only my understanding of psychiatry and radical therapy but also my choice of modality – transactional analysis – when I embarked on psychotherapy training. My father had been a conscientious objector during the Second World War, and from him I inherited a strong sense of values and conscience, and the ability, when necessary, to object. When, in 2009, I got a job in academia, I was delighted to discover that the *New Zealand Education Amendment Act 1990*, which outlines the characteristics of universities, includes that: 'They are primarily concerned with more advanced learning, the principal aim being to develop intellectual independence,'[6] and that: 'They accept a role as critic and conscience of society.'[7] My own critical writings have encompassed social work education;[8] the politics of disability;[9] the psychiatric system;[10] mental health promotion;[11] person-centred theory and practice;[12] culture;[13] psychotherapy and counselling;[14] professionalisation and, specifically, regulation, and registration;[15] transactional analysis practice and theory,[16] especially radical psychiatry,[17,18] and humanistic psychology.[18]

Being critical – being curious, enquiring, discriminating, discerning, reflective, and so on – is part of being human (see Chapter 2). Daniel Stern identifies this as the intersubjective sense of self[19] (see Chapter 4), which coincides with what Allan Schore refers to as the 'critical period' in the infant's development – that is, the development of a capacity for being critical.[20]

Arguably, psychotherapy encourages critique in that it provides the opportunity and space for the client to reflect (critically) on their life, what it is about their ways of thinking, feeling and acting that keeps them stuck, and what ways they could think, feel and act differently that could be liberating. Psychotherapy – or, rather, aspects of and certain approaches to psychotherapy – has contributed to the critical tradition. For instance, Michael Yellow Bird, Professor and Director of the Tribal Indigenous Studies programme at North Dakota State University, acknowledges that he used Augusto Boal's social justice theatre, based on Jacob Moreno's theatre of the oppressed, 'to help my students make the connection between critical thinking and critical consciousness'.[21] Furthermore, there is a more specific connection between psychotherapy and critique in that psychotherapy training is predominantly conducted at a postgraduate level, which implies that students/trainees have a first degree or equivalent. For instance, in terms of what's required of transactional analysts with regard to critique and being critical:

- in the certified transactional analyst (CTA) written examination, the candidate is asked to '[s]how your critical reflection throughout'[22]

- in the CTA oral examination, they are asked to demonstrate that they 'can critique both TA and other approaches'[23] and can demonstrate 'some ability to critique and to integrate with TA theory'[24]

- in the TSTA oral examination, the candidate must demonstrate that s/he '[k]nows theory and can critique it, compare, and contrast it with other models'.[25]

In universities, such training leads also to a master's degree; in the independent tertiary training sector, the qualification would be considered 'M' (ie. master's) level. It is widely and internationally accepted – and expected – that the criteria for a master's or M-level qualification include the capacity for critical awareness, critical reflection and critical argument.[26] This tradition goes back several centuries and across many different cultures, and is not, as Colin Feltham argues, particularly recent or simply 'fashionable'.[27]

Critique and criticism

Critique is a method of disciplined, systematic analysis of a specific text, body of work, or oral discourse. In philosophy, it refers to a methodical practice of doubt, as practised, for example, by the 17th century French philosopher René Descartes, who used doubt to ascertain knowledge.[28] The English word 'critique' derives from the Ancient Greek κριτική (kritik), meaning the faculty of judgment: that is, being able to discern, for example, an argument, a thesis, theory and practice. Unfortunately, both critic and criticism, words that derive from the same etymological root as critique, have, in popular use, tended to mean or to be associated with negative judgment and, despite attempts to discern between critique and criticism, have generally clouded the positive or dispassionate use of critique. In this book, both critique and critical are used positively. Richard Paul points out: 'The word [critical] has a long established tradition going back to the word *kritikos* in Greek that implies judiciousness, precision, and accuracy. It also has the meaning of "essential" and "crucial".'[29] It is in these former sense(s) that this book, alongside the others in the series, uses the term. Indeed, a number of books use critical to mean essential, crucial or central, including 'critical issues in psychotherapy',[30] but are hardly, if at all, critical in the sense in which I use the word. I think it is both interesting and significant to note that, in order to think and write critically, we need to reposition the word, concept and practice from a meaning that connotes being central to one that places it on and from the edge or the periphery.[31]

In an article written about coaching, John Mingers identified four important aspects to a critical approach,[32] which, subsequently,

Mark Saunders and Céline Rojon used to explain what is meant by a critical literature review,[33] and this is discussed further in Chapter 6.

The critique of rhetoric

This refers to the appraisal or evaluation of a problem with effective use of language, and the critique of language. Throughout the history of psychotherapy, there have been great debates about the meaning of words and, given that much of the original psychoanalytic writing was in German, about the significance of the translation of specific words and terms into English and other languages. As Ludwig Wittgenstein put it: 'Language is itself the vehicle of thought.'[34] Elsewhere, I and Mike Worrall discuss the power of language and the significance of metaphors, and especially the 'root metaphors' of different theoretical approaches in psychotherapy.[35] One example of a critique of the use of language in constructing theory is Graham Barnes' work on 'Homosexuality in the First Three Decades of Transactional Analysis', in which he critiques the psychopathology and pathologising of homosexuality.[36] In informing and developing my own critique here, I draw on discourse theory and, specifically, the work of Michel Foucault, the French philosopher and social theorist, and especially his emphasis on the importance of discourse and language in understanding power relationships.[37]

The critique of tradition

This refers to the use of evidence and ideas in the literature to help question (the) conventional wisdom. The history of psychotherapy is full of many examples of this; indeed, the development of psychotherapy over the last 200 years has been based on critique of what was then (previously) the tradition. Notable examples include Otto Gross's work;[38] Wilhelm Reich's Sexpol movement; Karen Horney's challenge of Freud's theory of penis envy; the challenge to heterosexism in psychotherapy practice and theory from gay therapists and queer theory, and similar challenges from black[39] and indigenous practitioners and theorists of racism in psychotherapy. A specific application of this critique in my own work is my systematic re-reading of Berne's *Transactional*

Analysis in Psychotherapy,[40] and my consequent elaboration of two sets of structural models of ego states, both of which derive from Berne.[41] To inform and sustain this critique in this book, I draw on critical theory, including Marxism,[42] feminism[43] and postcolonial studies,[44] as well as postmodernism and poststructuralism as reflected in the field of psychotherapy by colleagues such as Richard House,[45] Del Loewenthal[46] and Ian Parker.[47]

The critique of authority

This refers to the questioning of the dominant view(s), of which there are many examples in psychotherapy. Indeed, in a similar vein to the critique of tradition, most theoretical approaches or modalities in psychotherapy have developed as a result of their criticism of the then current authority – most particularly, humanistic psychology. In informing and developing this critique, in addition to the critical theories I have referred to above, I have also been particularly influenced by Raewyn Connell's development of 'Southern Theory',[48] a critique I present and apply in Chapter 4. This critique of authority also informs the cross-cultural and international perspective of this volume.

The critique of objectivity

This refers to the recognition that neither the knowledge nor the information under discussion is value free, and, more broadly, that it is not possible or desirable to be 'objective', especially in the human sciences, of which psychotherapy is a prime example. This critique has a significant impact on psychotherapy's view of the person and psychotherapeutic approaches to research (which I discuss in Chapter 6), as well as how psychotherapy is viewed as a discipline (Chapter 8). In informing and sustaining this critique, I draw on the philosophical tradition of phenomenology, and on writers such as Edmund Husserl, Martin Heidegger, Maurice Merleau-Ponty and Emmanuel Levinas.[49]

It is clear, then, that in this book I draw on a number of critical traditions to examine psychotherapy (see also Chapter 4), and I encourage you, the reader, to do so too. In this sense, this is not a 'how to' book, or a book that tells you 'how to examine', or even 'how to think about how to...', but a book that presents a number of ways in which we can think critically about a number of issues in the practice, field, profession, discipline and social criticism that is psychotherapy. Beyond this, it is my hope that the book reflects the tradition of criticism that is part of the public sphere. As Peter Hohendahl puts it:

> ... the concept of criticism cannot be separated from the institution of the public sphere. Every judgement is designed to be directed towards a public; communication with the reader is an integral part of the system. Through its relationship with the reading public, critical reflection loses its private character. Criticism opens itself to debate, it attempts to convince, it invites contradiction. It becomes part of the public exchange of opinions.[50]

Although much of the practice of psychotherapy is conducted behind closed doors, and mostly in the private sector, psychotherapy itself, its benefits, use and applicability, as well as its costs, contraindications, inaccessibility and abuse, is – or should be – a matter of informed public debate.[51] Although I don't discuss the abuse of clients by psychotherapists in any detail here, clearly this is a critical issue (in both senses of the word) for psychotherapy, its practitioners and its clients, and for society.[52] A number of the founding fathers of psychoanalysis and psychotherapy had sexual relationships with their patients or ex-patients (Carl Gustav Jung and Fritz Perls); others engaged in inappropriate sexual or sexualised contact with their patients or clients (Sándor Ferenczi) – and some even advocated this. One colleague I knew well told me quite openly that, when he was conducting international workshops (in the 1960s, 70s and 80s), he fully expected to sleep with at least one of the female participants. This was and is clearly an abuse of power, and is finally being discussed more openly and publicly. As far as psychotherapy is concerned, both the behaviour itself, and the condoning and/or minimising of such behaviour on the part of other colleagues, does leave the profession with a certain legacy that we need to understand, in terms both of the protection of patients and clients through the analysis of power and countertransference and of a certain reactive overprotectiveness that leads to more rigidity, rules and regulations – for instance, with regard to codes of ethics and professional practice (see Chapter 8).

The point here is that the more we discuss publicly the benefits and challenges of psychotherapy, including the difficult issues, the greater the likelihood that the public will engage with psychotherapy, both its practice and its theory, and at all levels, from individuals and groups through to organisations and government(s).

Threats to critical and free thinking

By now, it will be clear to the reader that I value freedom – and, specifically within psychotherapy, the freedom to practise (see Chapters 3 and 7),[53] the freedom to reflect on that practice (see Chapters 4 and 6), and the freedom to associate (see Chapter 8). At first glance, this may not seem very controversial; nevertheless, I think this freedom is under threat, intellectually, practically, professionally and politically. Here, I discuss specific threats from dogmatism and fundamentalism.

Dogmatism

The *Shorter Oxford English Dictionary* defines dogma as: '1. A philosophical tenet – That which is held as an opinion, or belief; [and] 2. A decree – The body of opinion formulated and authoritatively stated as in a doctrinal system.'[54]

There are four principal ways in which dogma (the thesis) and dogmatism (the attitude) are maintained: through purity, conformity, priesthood and certainty. Here I outline what I mean by these terms and illustrate them with examples, most of which relate to training, as that is where doctrine is taught and where dogmatic processes are established, which, in turn, influences the emerging psychotherapist's own thinking about psychotherapy and how they relate to and with clients. To those who might consider the use of the word 'doctrine' in this context somewhat contentious, I quote from an article by Saul Rosenzweig, who, some 80 years ago, used the word when referring to different forms of psychotherapy, and, specifically, the 'formal consistency with which the doctrine employed is adhered to'.[55]

Purity

Dogma is the tenet of a pure system. The greater the claim to psychological, political or theological purity, the more certain the dogma. If, as an early Christian, you believed that Jesus Christ was the son of God and that the Jews killed Jesus (who, of course, was a Jew), it was a short step, via references to certain verses of the Bible, to 'justifying' the persecution and killing of Jews. If, however, you look up the verses in the Bible that are said to justify the Christian persecution of the Jews,[56] you will discover that numerous people are identified as being responsible for the death of Jesus (the Pharisees, the scribes of the Pharisees, Herod and the Herodians, the Chief Priests, the religious leaders, Pilate, and the crowds) – but not the Jews or 'the Jewish Nation'.

It is an irony – and one with serious and sometimes deadly consequences – that 'purists' in all disciplines are often found wanting in historical or theoretical accuracy – a perspective that finds contemporary expression in the promotion of what are referred to as 'alternative facts'. I have found this in colleagues who identify as themselves as 'person-centred', sometimes with a religious, proselytising zeal, yet don't know the central tenets of Rogers' theory, and most notably those of the therapeutic conditions (see Chapter 3), let alone his theories of personality, behaviour, child development, psychopathology, education and so on. Another example are those who are fervently in favour of the state registration of psychotherapists and the statutory regulation of psychotherapy but who have not read the extensive literature on the subject, or the legislation by which they want psychotherapy regulated. Ignorance is generally more dangerous than blissful – at least for those on the receiving end of it.

Purity creates and depends on closed systems. The Nazi belief that only the Aryan race was capable of, or interested in, creating and maintaining culture and civilisations is one example of a closed system that justifies the oppression and, ultimately, extinction of anyone outside that system. Colonial conquests that confiscated land on the basis that it was unoccupied, or that the natives were uncivilised savages, were similarly based on a closed system that simply asserted the superiority of Western civilisation[57] – an assertion that finds current expression in the West with regard to Islamic culture. Closed systems depend on what Dix Morris and Frank Morris refer to as 'system-supporting rhetoric',[58] and Linda Riebel as 'self-sealing doctrines [which consist of] arming one's belief system with one or more tenets that explain away inconvenient evidence'.[59]

Examples of 'purity'

Within psychoanalysis, the concern to distinguish it from psychotherapy is perhaps the prime example of an attempt to create and maintain purity – one that was maintained originally through supervision or 'control analysis' (as it was originally named).[60] In transactional analysis (TA), the concern in some quarters to define 'core concepts' is an example of an attempt to define a 'purity' and, thereby, create a closed system that, by definition, excludes those concepts not considered to be 'core'.[61] This has its antecedents in Berne's own definition of the foundation of TA: 'Parent, Adult, and Child ego states were first systematically studied by transactional analysis, and they're its foundation stones and its mark. Whatever deals with ego states is transactional analysis, and whatever overlooks them is not.'[62] This is a clear example of an attempt to define TA in terms of what is (allowed) in and, therefore, what is (kept) out.

With regard to the maintenance and transmission of purity, it is particularly interesting to look at education and training (see Chapter 7). There is a danger, especially with 'training' (as distinct from education), that theories and methods are taught uncritically, and passed down through successive generations of students without much, if any, critical or contemporary reflection. For instance, when I was training in TA in 1988, our training year was taught traditional script theory. Sometime later I discovered that, while we were being taught this, Bill Cornell had just published his excellent article that deconstructed much of traditional script theory,[63] and I realised that, while our trainer(s) had presumably read this, they had not shared it with us. Some trainers argue that we should teach the original, traditional theory before presenting more recent theory. This, however, is a modernist and conservative view of the development of ideas, and, moreover, one that is often based on an implicit child development model of adult learning. Elsewhere, I have criticised the infantilisation of adult learners; I have always thought that these 'developmental' arguments were – and are – fallacious.[64] I felt somewhat on my own in this critique of authority until I came across Alan Jacobs' article on science and morality, in which he talks about 'older concepts' and 'outdated paradigms' in TA and makes the point: 'These original theories should be taught as history, not as final answers.'[65] The conservative (conserving) view comes about partly through the idealisation both of theory and of the original founding fathers and mothers of psychotherapy, and partly through the ignorance and/or (to be frank) laziness of some trainers: 'We can idealise... concepts so that the [original] inspiration becomes introjected rather than integrated, this can then lead to a sterilised application and deadening of a vibrant theory.'[66] Personally, I teach a contemporary approach on TA '101' introductory courses,[67] and introduce students to the two sets of structural models of ego states that have been identified in TA.[68] I do this simply and relatively quickly, and the adult learners get it. As an educator, I hold that adults can and do deal with difference and complexity in their everyday lives, and can do so in training.

Conformity

Conformity is when we change our behaviour, views or attitudes, due to the real or imagined influence of others, which we may think about in terms of introjection, projection, over-adaptation, or doing nothing. Conformity has been the subject of a number of psychological experiments, one of the most famous of which was the Asch conformity experiment (published in 1955 and 1956). Subjects were asked to match up different lengths of line, and the results demonstrated that a subject would conform to group pressure to agree that a particular line was the same length as another, even when it demonstrably wasn't.[69]

A crucial point for testing conformity comes in any qualifying exam. Students or trainees are often anxiously concerned about who will mark their case study and/or be on their exam board or panel. While a certain amount of anxiety is understandable and normal, there is a danger that candidates become more concerned about what their examiners might think than about how they present their work, their own ideas and themselves. In his keynote speech at the Institute for Transactional Analysis conference in 2000, Cornell expressed his concern that TA candidates were being examined for conformity. In the published version of this speech, referring to the oral examinations conducted by the European Association for Transactional Analysis (EATA), he wrote: 'I finished those exams with the thought that our organization is now teaching doctrine rather than theory and thinking.'[70] (For further discussion of this with regard to the education and training of psychotherapists, see Chapter 7.)

Herbert Kelman (1958) identifies three subtypes of conformity: compliance (ie. when a person conforms publicly, but keeps their own views in private); identification (ie. when a person conforms while they are a group member, publicly and privately, but not after leaving the group), and internalisation (ie. when a person conforms publicly and privately, during and after group membership).[71] For many reasons and in many situations, many people, including psychotherapists and psychotherapy trainees, comply and identify. Hopefully, as we get older and wiser – the two, of course, don't necessarily go together – we have less need to do so. The third subtype, the type of conformity engendered by cults and closed groups,[72] is more worrying and has more lasting effects. Sadly, there are too many examples of this in psychotherapy.

Examples of conformity

Two of the most disturbing examples of conformity in the history of psychotherapy are the establishment of the Göring Institute in Germany during the Third Reich, which practised a form of 'cleansed' psychoanalysis, designed to eliminate all aspects of its Freudian (ie. Jewish) origins,[73] and the participation of psychoanalysts in the House Un-American Activities Committee in the US, from the late 1930s into the 50s, to which a number of therapists provided case studies of their communist patients, thereby not only breaching patient confidentiality but also acting as political informers.[74] A present example of this is the implicit exclusion, by non-inclusion, of black people, ethnic minorities and indigenous people from psychotherapy education/training programmes.

Not many courses positively encourage students to challenge the course: the course requirements, curriculum, assessments etc, the staff, in terms of how they teach, or the theory on which it is based, especially if it is based on only one theory. Gone are the days of essay strikes, 'sit ins' and free universities. When I was asked teach on what was presented as a person-centred course (but which turned out not to be the case), I was surprised that the titles of the assignments were set by the tutors. This seemed at odds with Rogers' advocacy of the freedom to learn. In one of its documents on course accreditation, published in 1996, the then British Association for Counselling had, as one of its criteria for student entry, 'willingness to challenge and to be challenged'.[75] Regarding theory, Jacobs makes the point that: 'Unchallenged theory can be transformed into an ideology, thus permitting the use of even coercive treatment techniques.' He continues: 'Theory itself can become a transference object, thus symbiotically binding followers.'[76]

In the training, practice and organisation of the profession of psychotherapy, non-conformity and dissent are often discouraged and too often pathologised. A prime example of this in the history of psychotherapy is the oppression of gay therapists, especially by the psychoanalytic establishment, through the pathologising of homosexuality.[77] Right up until 2014, the UK Association for Christian Counsellors embraced counsellors who sought to 'convert' their gay male and lesbian clients to heterosexuality.[78] Furthermore, this kind of pathologising is embedded in and supported by theory: for instance, in transactional analysis theory, in the concepts of the Critical Parent and Rebellious Child.[79] Of course, such theory supports a closed system: if I express difference of opinion or dissent, I am being rebellious, and rebellion is a form of adaptation and pathology. The oppression and repression of dissent is maintained through what Foucault refers to as 'disciplinary power': 'If the discipline involved finds us a threat to its considered formulae (its belief system and ethics), we will be attacked or dismissed.'[80]

Worse, many – I would even say most – students training in psychotherapy are encouraged to conform. I think this is often based on a concern to adapt to a perceived norm. In Alberto Moravia's novel *The Conformist*, the hero, Marcello, confuses normality with conformity and, in his quest to conform, subjugates his already-repressed emotions.[81] This reminds us, should we need it, of the importance of creating a climate in which psychological freedom can flourish, both in the clinic and in educational settings, and of the dangers of suppressing this climate of freedom. One of the ways in which conformity is maintained is through interpretation, as Donald Winnicott warns: 'Interpretation outside the ripeness of the material is indoctrination and produces compliance.'[82] Patrick Casement questions whether psychoanalysis (at least within a training context) releases people to develop their own minds, and identifies a number of ways in which interpretation can be used in an oppressive way – by calling that with which we don't agree reversal, projection, displacement, avoidance, transference, projective identification, denial and splitting.[83] Winnicott also argues that 'not all resistance that is seen by the analyst is necessarily pathological', and acknowledges the concept of 'healthy resistance'.[84] Of course, this critique needs to be contextualised and balanced with the idealisation and demonisation of trainers by students, who may be expected to accept and hold projections that have little or no reality for them. Holding this balance reminds me of Rowan's series of dialectical interpolations, including the point that we must both believe and disbelieve the client.[85]

Priesthood

Dogma and doctrine are developed by theologians and interpreted by priests, who, generally, mediate – or, worse, rule – people's relationship with God. Thomas Szasz makes a link between this kind of rule and that of medicine, and especially psychiatrists: 'Since theocracy is the rule of God or its priests, and democracy the rule of the people or of the majority, pharmacracy is therefore the rule of medicine or of doctors.'[86] One way in which priesthood and its lay equivalents are maintained is through implicit pedagogy. This describes the function of a priest, pedagogue or teacher, and refers to instruction, training and discipline, especially in relation to the teaching of children and young people. It carries the sense of expertise, communicated and delivered with the authority of a traditional teacher or instructor, of teaching from Parent to Child – a relationship that, I think, informs a lot of teaching, not only in transactional analysis but also in psychotherapy as a whole. The most worrying example of this I've come across are trainers referring to their trainees as their children, and even as 'my babies'. Writing from a critical psychoanalytic perspective, Lomas expresses caution about the use of the 'parental metaphor'.[87] In various writings over the years, I have suggested that the concept of andragogy, initially coined by the German educator Alexander Kapp[88] and developed by Malcolm Knowles and others,[89] is more appropriate when referring to the education and training of adult learners (a point I develop in Chapter 7).

Examples of priesthood in psychotherapy

In transactional analysis, the terms and conditions of training and the requirements of the various levels of examination for internationally recognised certification are clearly set out in a *Training and Examination Handbook* (the *Handbook*).[90] In my opinion, it is one of the better examples of open communication about such terms and conditions, and stands as an invitation to clear contracting between the trainer(s), the trainee(s), and the international accrediting organisation(s). However, like most documents, it is open to interpretation, especially on the part of trainers, some of whom take a somewhat priestly role in such interpretations. One result of this is that trainees may come to rely on their interpretation, rather than the original word(s).

This dynamic is reflective of a broader one in the field of psychotherapy whereby trainers and supervisors generally take too much responsibility for students and practitioners (for further discussion of which, see Chapter 5), do too much 'gate-keeping' of the profession, and too readily mediate the relationship between practitioners and their codes of ethics and practice, rather than encouraging practitioners to think for themselves (also see Chapter 5). Some years ago, in response to what I kept hearing as reinterpretations and misinterpretations of the TA *Handbook*, I wrote an article on the terms and conditions for the tapes required for the CTA oral exam, in which I offered an exegesis, or interpretation, of these requirements. Further, I argued that mine was 'a protestant exegesis in proposing – or protesting – a direct relationship with scripture, in this case, text and tapes, rather than one necessarily mediated by priests, ie. trainers or supervisors'.[91]

In mediating people's relationship with the divine, priests take the centre stage, usually in front of an altar. In a similar way, by drawing the focus of attention to themselves, trainers and supervisors can get in the way of students' learning process. The problem of narcissistic trainers is not simply one of personality, pathology and power; it's a theoretical one: in effect, it proposes a particular theory of education or training based on learning from a charismatic trainer/priest/guru. Compare this with Rogers' idea of facilitative leadership, summarised by a passage from the Chinese mystic Lao Tse (1973),[92] whom Rogers (1986) quotes approvingly:

> A leader is best
> When people barely know he exists,
> Not so good when people obey and acclaim him.
> Worst when they despise him.
> But of a great leader, who talks little,
> When his work is done, his aim fulfilled,
> They will say 'We did this ourselves.'[93]

Certainty

The fourth way in which dogma, dogmatism and the dogmatic are maintained is through certainty or absolute sureness. It's not that we shouldn't be certain or sure of ourselves and others;

the problem is when this subjective certainty becomes and is presented as a kind of transcendent assurance, certainty or truth.[94] This is made more strange when we think that so much of the practice of psychotherapy is dealing with, and, indeed, encouraging, uncertainty, ambiguity, ambivalence, complexity and contradiction. As Jacob Moreno observes, in order to enter new territory, the person must be able to tolerate uncertainty and ambiguity.[95] Both dogma and fundamentalism are based on certainty, and this certainty, as Richard Dawkins puts it with reference to fundamentalism, 'subverts science and saps the intellect'.[96] One of the ways that certainty is maintained is by its immunity to critique – which is another reason why critique is crucial to promoting uncertainty, free thinking and open systems.

Examples of certainty

It is the certainty of those who are 'right' – and the righteousness of those who are certain – and people's readiness to subscribe to such certainty that underpin conformity, as the examples of the Göring Institute and the House Un-American Activities Committee demonstrate. Many, if not all, psychotherapeutic modalities have their own certainties that, by definition, cannot be challenged. One example of this in transactional analysis was the Cathexis Institute, in Oakland, California, in the late 1960s and early 70s, where the therapists involved were so certain of the beneficial effects and positive therapeutic outcomes of radical reparenting that they proceeded with abusive techniques. This was, in part, maintained through the creation of a family system in which a number of patients changed their names to that of the lead therapists. As such, it stands as an example of a closed, self-sealing system in which, as Jacobs puts it, ideology becomes thought reform.[97]

Fundamentalism

As a citizen and a therapist in our increasingly complex and conflictual world, I am interested in and concerned about fundamentalism and the rise of fundamentalist thinking, as well as the actions that follow from that thinking.

Broadly, fundamentalism is a movement or attitude requiring strict and literal adherence to a set of basic principles. The origins of fundamentalism lie in a movement in American Protestantism that arose in the early part of the 20th century in reaction to modernism. This Protestant fundamentalism stressed the infallibility of the Bible not only in matters of faith and morals but also as a literal historical record. The term itself is borrowed from the title of a four-volume set of books, published in 1909, called *The Fundamentals*.[98] The devil (as it were) is in the detail – in this case, the definite article. When I and Tony Merry wrote our *Dictionary of Person-Centred Psychology*,[99] the publishers originally wanted us to call it '*The* Dictionary…'. As we didn't intend the dictionary to be *the* only or last word, we didn't acquiesce to this request.

One of the definitions of fundamentalism is 'a usually religious movement or point of view characterized by a return to fundamental principles, by rigid adherence to those principles, and often by intolerance of other views and opposition to secularism'.[100] Sadly, it is all too easy to draw the parallels between these four characteristics of fundamentalism and fundamentalist attitudes in psychotherapy.

A return to fundamental principles

The word and concept of 'return' suggests a sense of nostalgia for something past – in this context, the original theory. This sentiment often also extends to the person of the founding father or mother, especially among those who knew them – a sentiment and process that, consequently, affects the view that subsequent (third, and by now, fourth and fifth) generations hold of them. It is a commonplace to say that disciples are, by and large, much more fundamentalist than the founders, whether this be of a religion, a religious sect or a school of psychotherapy. An example of this is the move to enshrine (and I use that word advisedly) 'core principles' of a particular approach – a move that also aims to assure 'purity'.[101]

A rigid adherence to those principles

Once such fundamental principles have been agreed (or imposed), it is a short step to demanding adherence to them. One example of this is the requirement for psychotherapists seeking qualification and/or professional accreditation or registration to sign up to a 'core theoretical model'. The result is that practitioners can become quite rigid about their particular theoretical orientation, approach or model, and quite closed to others. In some countries, many therapists refer to themselves as 'person-centred', based on having undertaken a training course which was/is nominally 'person-centred'. However, many of these courses are, in effect, generic courses, with little or no genuine foundation in person-centred philosophy, practice or theory. Such courses are commonly taught by trainers who themselves do not identify with the approach, and even those who do often misunderstand and/or misrepresent it.[102] In either case, the approach is rarely embodied in the practice of teaching or facilitation, or the organisation and requirements of the training.[103] One of the effects of this lack of foundation in genuine person-centred principles is that many students, practitioners, trainers and supervisors become defensive and dogmatic about what is 'person-centred', and obsessed with policing the approach. They will assert, for instance, that 'it's not person-centred to ask questions', or 'person-centred practitioners don't use techniques', or 'the core conditions are necessary and sufficient', none of which have any foundation in what Rogers wrote.

In the first edition of their very popular book *Person-Centred Counselling in Action*, Dave Mearns and Brian Thorne presented what they referred to as 'the person-centred counsellor's creed'.[104] From a perspective that values the freedom to learn and to think, and that supports an internal valuing and integrating process, to present a person-centred creed as a confession of faith and an expression of belief or doctrine was a strange contradiction between the message and the medium. Interestingly, in the second edition of their book, published in 1999, the authors dropped the creed.

An intolerance of other views

We can define ourselves positively – in terms of a particular belief or philosophy that we hold, for example. Equally, we can define ourselves negatively, in terms of what we are not. While this has merit in the context of (anti-)racism or (anti-)sexism, for example, we can get stuck in and with the sense of being oppositional and intolerant, rather than progressive and inclusive. In the history of psychotherapy, this has manifested itself especially in 'modality wars' between the various theoretical views, orientations or 'schools'. At times, this has resulted in sectarianism between different theoretical orientations, with the result that practitioners become partisan and partial, although this is mostly based on ignorance. Reflecting on this in relation to the person-centred approach, Mearns and Thorne write: 'It would seem that our approach has the strange capacity to threaten practitioners from other orientations so that they seek refuge in wilful ignorance or in condemnatory dismissiveness.'[105] In my experience, this works both ways, with person-centred practitioners condemning psychodynamic concepts out of hand, often out of ignorance. Nor is such intolerance simply a theoretical issue. Over the years, I have seen this impact on jobs and opportunities, such as the exclusion of students on a particular training course from a placement, simply on the basis of the theoretical orientation in which they are training.

The opposition to secularism

While religious fundamentalism opposes secularism, I see this manifested in reverse in the field of psychotherapy, in that, historically, there has been suspicion of and opposition to the spiritual and the religious (for further discussion of this, see Chapter 2).

In order to counter dogma, we need to promote 'impurity' or diversity, non-conformity, the view that ideas can come from people (clients, supervisees, trainees) rather than having to be mediated or approved by the 'priests', and uncertainty. In order to counter fundamentalism, we need to question fundamental principles, rigidity, intolerance and both secularism and spirituality – and to do so through being sceptical and critical, and, when necessary, by objection and disobedience.

However, in order to promote this kind of non-dogmatism and non-fundamentalism, we need to be anti-dogmatic and anti-fundamentalist. In theological terms, this is represented by the difference between Erasmus of Rotterdam (1466–1536) and Martin Luther (1483–1546). When, in 1517, Luther nailed his 95 theses to the church door in Wittenburg, he challenged the doctrines of the Catholic Church and, in effect, began the European Reformation. However, in doing so, he established another dogma.[106] Erasmus, on the other hand, inspired a movement of religious humanists who consciously and consistently opposed attempts to nail down the content of faith in terms of dogma, and so represented an anti-dogmatic tradition. I suggest that we need to be anti-dogmatic in order to create the space in which to be undogmatic (see Chapter 7), and that we create this space by engaging in critical thinking.

Critical thinking

Broadly, thinking is viewed as the mental process whereby beings form psychological associations and models about the world. The act of thinking produces thoughts. For John Chaffee: 'Thinking is a very practical, holistic, integrated mental activity we engage in to make sense of the world... The thinking process is a global, meaning-seeking activity that is the essence of being human.'[107] Of course, our thinking develops over time, and is dependent on our development from cradle (actually, *in utero*) to grave, and, therefore, involves others. It also involves our emotions. In his book *Descartes' Error*, the neuroscientist Antonio Damasio wrote: 'We are not thinking machines. We are feeling machines that think.'[108]

Critical thinking requires an ability to, and the capacity for, doubt. This may be traced back to ancient Greece and the sceptics, and Descartes, who promoted knowing through scepticism and doubt (see Chapter 2). As the American lexicographer Bergen Evans puts it: 'Freedom of speech and freedom of action are meaningless without freedom to think. And there is no freedom of thought without doubt.'[109] Alfred Lord Tennyson's words, 'There lives more faith in honest doubt, believe me, than in half the creeds,' epitomise the necessity of doubt as a foundation for faith – or, in relation to this discussion, for theory and learning. Sharon Salzberg puts this well:

> In order to deepen our faith, we have to be able to try things out, to wonder, to doubt. In fact, faith is strengthened by doubt when doubt is sincere, critical questioning combined with deep trust in our own right and ability to discern the truth.[110]

Salzberg reflects that, in Buddhism, this kind of questioning is known as 'skilful doubt', for which 'we have to be close enough to an issue to care about it, yet open enough to let questioning come alive'. She goes on to compare this with unskilful doubt, which is a kind of easy cynicism: 'The cynic not only doubts, however, but also refuses to investigate the object of that doubt.'[111]

A training in philosophy is a training in an appreciation of language, logic, criticism and scepticism – foundations that, I suggest, are essential for psychotherapy. Of course, 'honest doubt' gives rise to uncertainty and anxiety. As the Chinese proverb puts it: 'To be uncertain is to be uncomfortable, but to be certain is to be ridiculous.' As therapists, educators and consultants, we should be training people for doubt, uncertainty, anxiety and for being tentative. Albeit from very different theoretical perspectives, both Rogers and Casement talk about being tentative. Casement expresses particular concern about the dogmatic expert who persecutes and threatens the patient into 'a given way of understanding'.[112]

In distinguishing critical thinking from lateral, divergent and creative thinking, Stephen Brookfield argues that 'those terms don't have the oppositional and political flavor I see... embedded in critical thinking',[113] and that 'critical thinking is a very political process'.[114] Following this, it is clear that critical thinking, and, indeed, critical examination, require an ability and willingness to be oppositional and political – a point that, of course, has implications for the education and training of psychotherapists (see Chapter 7).

As for what this looks like in practice, Carole Wade and Carol Tavris have developed eight guidelines for critical thinking:

1. Ask questions, be willing to wonder.
2. Define the problem.

3. Examine the evidence.
4. Analyse assumptions and biases.
5. Avoid emotional reasoning (such as 'If I feel this way, it must be true').
6. Don't oversimplify.
7. Consider other interpretations.
8. Tolerate uncertainty.[115]

When I first came across these guidelines, I was struck by how relevant they are to the practice of psychotherapy. I have also drawn on them in writing this book, and, in so doing, have been mindful of what this approach to thinking demands of the reader. For both client and therapist, writer and reader, critical thinking is both necessary – and unsettling.

Endnotes

1. Eagleton T (2005/1984). *The Function of Criticism.* London: Verso (p9).
2. I place Christian in parentheses as I think that the logic of the Unitarian belief in the humanity of Jesus means that it is not a Christian faith. This was one of the debates I used to enjoy with my father, who, while agreeing with my logic, still identified as a Christian.
3. On the course, at the University of Kent at Canterbury (1977–1979), I had the good fortune to learn particularly from Mike Brake (social work and sociology), Janet Sayers (psychology) and Vic George (social policy).
4. This was Big Flame (https://bigflameuk.wordpress.com), which, among other influences, drew on the work of the Italian communist Antonio Gramsci (1891–1937) and the West Indian Marxist CLR James (1901–1989).
5. Steiner C (1971). Radical psychiatry manifesto. In: Agel J (ed). The Radical Therapist Collective. *The Radical Therapist.* New York, NY: Ballantine Books (pp280–282). See also: Steiner C, Wyckoff H, Goldstine O, Lariviere P, Schwebel R, Marcus J and members of The Radical Psychiatry Center (eds) (1975). *Readings in Radical Psychiatry.* New York, NY: Grove Press; also: Wyckoff H (ed) (1976). *Love, Therapy and Politics.* New York, NY: Grove Press; and, later, Wyckoff H (1980). *Solving Problems Together.* New York, NY: Grove Press.
6. Section (s)4(i).

7. Section (s)4(v). See also Tudor K (2017). *Conscience and Critic: the selected works of Keith Tudor*. London: Routledge.
8. Brown K, Tudor K (1981). Social work education and practice: reform and revolution – a theory for change. *Contemporary Social Work Education 4*(2): 101–112.
9. Tudor K (1989). The politics of disability in Italy [La lega per il diritto al lavoro degli handicappati]. *Critical Social Policy 25 9*(1): 37–55.
10. Sanders P, Tudor K (2001). This is therapy: a person-centred critique of the contemporary psychiatric system. In: Newnes C, Holmes G, Dunn C (eds). *This is Madness Too: critical perspectives on mental health services*. Ross-on-Wye: PCCS Books (pp147–160).
11. Tudor K (1996). *Mental Health Promotion: paradigms and practice*. London: Routledge.
12. See, for example, Tudor K (2011). Rogers' therapeutic conditions: a relational conceptualization. *Person-Centered & Experiential Psychotherapies 10*(3): 165–180.
13. From Singh J, Tudor K (1997). Cultural conditions of therapy. *The Person-Centered Journal 4*(2): 32–46, to Komiya N, Tudor K (2016). 'Reading the air', finding common ground: reconsidering Rogers' therapeutic conditions as a framework for understanding therapy in Japan. *Asia Pacific Journal of Counselling & Psychotherapy 17*(1&2): 26–38; and Ioane J, Tudor K (2017). The Fa'ásamoa, person-centred theory, and cross-cultural practice. *Person-Centered and Experiential Psychotherapies 16*(4): 287–302.
14. From Tudor K (1997). The personal is political – and political is personal: a person-centred approach to the political sphere. [Special issue.] *Person Centred Practice 5*(2): 4–10, to my current editorship of *Psychotherapy and Politics International* (ISSN 1556-9195).
15. See, for example, Tudor K (ed) (2011). *The Turning Tide: pluralism and partnership in psychotherapy in Aotearoa New Zealand*. Auckland: LC Publications. A revised, second edition was published in 2017 (see note 42, p262).
16. See, for example, Summers G, Tudor K (2000). Cocreative transactional analysis. *Transactional Analysis Journal 30*(1): 23–40.
17. See, for example, Minikin K, Tudor K (2016). Gender psychopolitics: men being, becoming, and belonging. In: Erskine R (ed). *Transactional Analysis in Contemporary Psychotherapy*. London: Karnac (pp255–273).
18. See, for example, Tudor K (2015). Humanistic psychology: a critical counter culture. In: Parker I (ed). *Handbook of Critical Psychology*. London: Routledge (pp127–136).
19. Stern D (1985). *The Intersubjective World of the Infant*. New York, NY: Basic Books.
20. Schore A (2000). Attachment and the regulation of the right brain.

Attachment & Human Development 2(1): 23–47.
21. Yellow Bird M (2005). Tribal critical thinking centers. In: Wilson WA, Yellow Bird M (eds). *For Indigenous Eyes Only: a decolonization handbook*. Santa Fe, NM: School of American Research Handbook (pp9–30) (p13).
22. See European Association for Transactional Analysis [EATA] Professional Training Standards Committee (2017). *EATA Training and Examination Handbook*. Section 8, p9. www.eatanews.org/training-manuals-and-supplements (accessed 9 July 2017).
23. EATA (2017). Oral examination TA educational scoring sheet, criterion 9, score 5.
24. EATA (2017). Oral examination TA educational scoring sheet, criterion 9, score 3.
25. EATA (2017). TSTA Oral examination theory, organisation and ethics segment, criterion 2, score 5.
26. Brown S (2013). What are the perceived differences between assessing at master's level and undergraduate level assessment? *Innovations in Education and Teaching International Journal 51*(3): 265–276.
27. Feltham C (2013). *Counselling and Counselling Psychology: a critical examination*. Ross-on-Wye: PCCS Books (p16).
28. Descartes suffers from a bad press as being responsible for Cartesian dualism, or what is more commonly referred to as the mind/body split, on the basis of his famous phrase 'Cogito ergo sum' ('I think, therefore I am'). The point he was making, however, was one about scepticism: he was testing what could be known through the process of doubting, and concluded that the only certainty was that he was thinking. Hence, the better translation would be 'I am thinking (or processing), therefore I am.' While I am defending Descartes, the other observation I would make is that his (1637) *Discourse on Method* was written in French, and he actually wrote 'Je pense, donc je suis', using the French in the spirit of anti-scholasticism to reach a wider audience. It was only in a later work, *Principles of Philosophy* (1644), that he used the Latin phrase.
29. Paul R (1993). Conversation. In: Esterle J, Cluman D (eds). *Conversations with Critical Thinkers*. San Francisco, CA: The Whitman Institute (pp91–101).
30. See, for example, Slife BD, Williams RN, Barlow SH (eds) (2001). *Critical Issues in Psychotherapy: translating new ideas into practice*. Thousand Oaks, CA: Sage.
31. In this, I have been very influenced by Raewyn Connell's work on 'Southern Theory'. Connell R (2008). *Southern Theory: the global dynamics of knowledge*. Crow's Nest: Allen & Unwin – for further discussion of which see Chapters 4 and 8.

32. Mingers J (2000). What it is to be critical? Teaching a critical approach to management undergraduates. *Management Learning 31*(2): 219–237.
33. Saunders MK, Rojon C (2011). On the attributes of a critical literature review. *Coaching: An International Journal of Theory, Research and Practice 4*(2): 156–162.
34. Wittgenstein L (1953). *Philosophical Investigations*. Oxford, UK: Basil Blackwell (p107).
35. Tudor K, Worrall M (2006). *Person-Centred Therapy: a clinical philosophy*. London: Routledge (chapter 1).
36. Barnes G (2004). Homosexuality in the first three decades of transactional analysis. *Transactional Analysis Journal 33*(2): 126–155.
37. Foucault M (2002/1969). *The Architecture of Knowledge* (AM Sheridan Smith trans). London: Routledge.
38. I am grateful to Gottfried Heuer for introducing me to the work of Otto Gross.
39. In my writing and in this book, I use 'black' – and, in Aotearoa New Zealand, 'brown' – in the political sense of the words. As Brah noted: 'The term "black" was adopted by the emerging coalitions amongst African-Caribbean and South Asian organisations and activists in the late 1960s and 1970s. They were influenced by the way the Black Power movement in the USA, which had turned the concept of Black on its head, divested it of its pejorative connotations in radicalised discourses, and transformed it into a confident expression of an assertive group identity' (p127). Brah A (1992). Difference, diversity and differentiation. In: Donald J, Rattansi A (eds). *Race, Culture and Difference*. London: Sage Publications (pp126–145).
40. Berne E (1975/1961). *Transactional Analysis in Psychotherapy*. London: Souvenir Press.
41. Tudor K (2010). The state of the ego: then and now. *Transactional Analysis Journal 40*(3&4): 261–277.
42. Sève L (1978). *Man in Marxist Theory and the Psychology of Personality* (J McGreal ed). Hassocks: Harvester Press.
43. Mitchell J (1975). *Psychoanalysis and Feminism*. Harmondsworth: Penguin.
44. Stewart-Harawira S (2005). *The New Imperial Order: indigenous responses to globalization*. Chicago, IL: Zed Books. See also: Akhtar S (2005). *Freud Along the Ganges: psychoanalytic reflections on the people and culture of India*. New York, NY: Other Press.
45. House R (2003). *Therapy Beyond Modernity: deconstructing and transcending profession-centred therapy*. London: Karnac. Also: House R (2010). *In, Against and Beyond Therapy: critical essays towards a 'post-professional' era*. Ross-on-Wye: PCCS Books.

46. Loewenthal D, Snell R (2003). *Postmodernism for Psychotherapists: a critical reader*. London: Brunner-Routledge. See also: Loewenthal D (2011). *Post-Existentialism and the Psychological Therapies: towards a therapy without foundations*. London: Karnac.

47. Parker I, Georgaca E, Harper D, Stowell-Smith M (eds) (1996). *Deconstructing Psychopathology*. London: Sage. Also: Parker I (ed) (1999). *Deconstructing Psychotherapy*. London: Sage.

48. Connell R (2008). *Southern Theory: the global dynamics of knowledge*. Crow's Nest: Allen & Unwin.

49. For an articulation of which, see Owen IR (2006). *Psychotherapy and Phenomenology*. Lincoln, NE: iUniverse.

50. Hohendahl PU (1982). *The Institution of Criticism*. Ithaca, NY: Cornell University Press (p52).

51. In his book, Peter Morrall accuses therapy of being 'dysfunctional; arrogant; selfish; abusive; infectious; insane; and deceitful'. Morrall P (2008). *The Trouble with Therapy: sociology and psychotherapy*. Maidenhead: Open University Press (p8).

52. Abuse in therapy has been discussed by a number of authors (see p68), including Newnes C (2016). *Inscription, Diagnosis, Deception and the Mental Health Industry: how psy governs us all*. Maidenhead: Palgrave Macmillan. Increasingly, the websites of professional associations are publishing notices of procedures and the findings of hearings and sanctions when their members have been found to have transgressed codes of ethical and professional conduct.

53. See Tudor K, Worrall M (eds) (2004). *Freedom to Practise: person-centred approaches to supervision*. Ross-on-Wye: PCCS Books. Also: Tudor K, Worrall M (eds) (2007). *Freedom to Practise II: developing person-centred approaches to supervision*. Ross-on-Wye: PCCS Books.

54. Onions CT (1983). *The Shorter Oxford English Dictionary*. Oxford: Oxford University Press (p591).

55. Rosenzweig S (1936). Some implicit common factors in diverse methods of psychotherapy. *American Journal of Orthopsychiatry* 6(3): 412–415 (p413).

56. Matthew 27:25; Mark 2:6, 2:16, 3:6, 15:10; Luke 23:4, 23:14, 23:20, 23:22, 23:25; John 8:44, and 1 Thessalonians 2:15ff.

57. Mahatma Ghandi is credited with offering a subversive critique of this, when he is said to have responded to the question, 'What do you think of Western civilization?' by saying, 'I think it would be a very good idea.'

58. Morris DG, Morris FR (1996). The anatomy of belief. *Transactional Analysis Journal* 26(3): 254–261 (p254).

59. Riebel L (1996). Self-sealing doctrines, the misuse of power and recovered memory. *Transactional Analysis Journal* 26(1): 40–45 (p40).

60. Moncayo R (2006). Lacanian perspectives on psychoanalytic supervision. *Psychoanalytic Psychology 23*: 527–541.
61. Steiner C (ed) (2003). Core concepts. [Special issue.] *Transactional Analysis Journal 33*(2).
62. Berne E (1973/1970). *Sex in Human Loving*. Harmondsworth: Penguin (p223).
63. Cornell WF (1988). Life script theory: a critical review from a developmental perspective. *Transactional Analysis Journal 18*(4): 270–282.
64. Tudor K (2003). The neopsyche: the integrating adult ego state. In: Sills C, Hargaden H (eds). *Ego States*. London: Worth Reading (pp201–231).
65. Jacobs A (1997). Berne's life positions: science and morality. *Transactional Analysis Journal 27*(1): 197–206 (p203).
66. Institute for Transactional Analysis (2007). *Conference Abstract*. Colchester: Institute for Transactional Analysis.
67. Tudor K (2014). Appendix 2. A co-creative 'TA 101': notes on the syllabus. In: Tudor K, Summers G. *Co-Creative Transactional Analysis: papers, responses and developments*. London: Karnac Books (pp251–262). See also: Summers G, Tudor K (2000). Cocreative transactional analysis. *Transactional Analysis Journal 30*(1): 23–40.
68. Tudor K (2010). The state of the ego: then and now. *Transactional Analysis Journal 40*(3&4): 261–277. See also: Summers G, Tudor K (2000). Co-creative transactional analysis. *Transactional Analysis Journal 30*(1): 23–40.
69. Asch SE (1955). Opinions and social pressure. *Scientific American* 31–35. Also: Asch SE (1956). Studies of independence and conformity: a minority of one against a unanimous majority. *Psychological Monographs 70*(416).
70. Cornell WF (2000). If Berne met Winnicott: transactional analysis and relational analysis. *Transactional Analysis Journal 30*(4): 270–275 (p270).
71. Kelman HC (1958). Compliance, identification, and internalization: three processes of attitude change. *Journal of Conflict Resolution 2*: 51–60.
72. Singer MT (1996). Therapy, thought reform, and cults. *Transactional Analysis Journal 26*(1): 15–22.
73. Cocks G (1997). *Psychotherapy in the Third Reich: the Göring Institute* (2nd ed). New Brunswick, NJ: Transaction Publishers. Goggin JE, Goggin West EB (2001). *Death of a 'Jewish Science': psychoanalysis in the Third Reich*. Lafayette, IN: Purdue University Press.
74. See Schwartz J (1999). *Cassandra's Daughter: a history of psychoanalysis*. London: Penguin.
75. British Association for Counselling (1996). *Courses Recognition Handbook*. Rugby: BAC.
76. Jacobs A (1997). Berne's life positions: science and morality. *Transactional Analysis Journal 27*(1): 197–206 (p203).

77. O'Connor N, Ryan J (1993). *Wild Desires and Mistaken Identities: lesbianism and psychoanalysis.* New York, NY: Columbia University Press.
78. This changed in 2014 – see Strudwick P (2014). Christian counsellors ban therapy aiming a 'converting' gay patients. *The Guardian*, 13 January. www.theguardian.com/world/2014/jan/13/christian-therapists-stop-conversion-therapy-turn-gay-patients-straight (accessed 28 April 2017).
79. For a critique of which see Tudor K (2010). The state of the ego: then and now. *Transactional Analysis Journal 40*(3&4): 261–277.
80. Foucault M (1980). *Power/Knowledge: selected interviews and other writings 1972–1977* (C Gordon ed). New York, NY: Pantheon Books.
81. Moravia A (1999/1951). *Il conformista* [The conformist]. South Royalton, VT: Steerforth Italia.
82. Winnicott DW (1971). *Playing and Reality.* London: Tavistock (p51).
83. Casement P (2002). *Learning From Our Mistakes: beyond dogma in psychoanalysis and psychotherapy.* New York, NY: The Guilford Press.
84. Winnicott DW (1971). *Playing and Reality.* London: Tavistock (p19).
85. Rowan J (2005) *The Future of Training in Psychotherapy and Counselling.* London: Routledge.
86. Szasz TS (1974). *Ceremonial Chemistry: the ritual persecution of drugs, addicts and pushers.* Garden City, NY: Anchor Press.
87. Lomas P (2001/1987). *The Limits of Interpretation.* Harmondsworth: Penguin.
88. Kapp A (1833). *Platon's Erziehungslehre, als Paedagogik für die Einzelnen und als Staatspaedagogik [Plato's educational theory as a pedagogy for the individual and as state pedagogy, or its practical philosophy].* Minden und Leipzig: Ferdinand Essmann.
89. Knowles MS, Holton EF, Swanson RA (1998). *The Adult Learner* (5th ed). Houston, TX: Gulf.
90. There are two very similar handbooks published by the EATA: EATA Professional Training Standards Committee (2017). *Training and Examination Handbook.* Geneva: EATA, and ITAA Professional Standards Commission (2014). *Training and Examination Handbook.* San Francisco, CA: EATA.
91. See also Tudor K (2007). Training in the person-centred approach. In: Cooper M, O'Hara M, Schmid P, Wyatt G (eds). *The Handbook of Person-Centered Therapy.* Basingstoke: Palgrave (pp379–389). Also Tudor K (2017). Section D: questions on theory and literature. In: Jovanoska K (2016). *From Script to CTA: tips and encouragement for successfully completing the written examination in transactional analysis.* Ljubljana: CTA-ebook-skupno (pp78–89).
92. Lao Tse (1973) *Tao Te Ching* (G-F Feng & J English trans). London: Wildwood House.

93. Rogers CR (1986). The dilemmas of a South African white. *Person-Centered Review 1*: 15–35.

94. See Wittgenstein L (1975). *On Certainty* (GEM Anscombe, GH von Wright eds; D Paul, GEM Anscombe trans). Oxford: Basil Blackwell.

95. Moreno JL (1964/1946). *Psychodrama. Vol 1* (rev ed). Beacon, NY: Beacon House.

96. Dawkins R (2006). *The God Delusion*. Boston, MA: Houghton Mifflin (p284). When I first presented some of this material in a workshop at a conference on the theme of dogma in 2007, my son Saul, who played a particular trading card game at the time, showed me a Yu-Gi-Oh card called 'Destiny Hero – Dogma', which, in the game, halves the opponent's life points. I thought and still think this is a good metaphor for the effect of dogma.

97. Jacobs A (1994). Ideology as thought reform. *Transactional Analysis Journal 24*(3): 39–55. See also Singer MT (1996). Therapy, thought reform, and cults. *Transactional Analysis Journal 26*(1): 15–22. Although I broadly agree with Jacobs' critique of the Cathexis Institute, I also acknowledge the ways in which some British colleagues have transformed this particular ideology – see Robinson J (1998). Reparenting in a therapeutic community. *Transactional Analysis Journal 28*(1): 88–94.

98. Torrey RA (1909). *The Fundamentals* (4 vols). Los Angeles, CA: Bible Institute.

99. Tudor K, Merry T (2002). *Dictionary of Person-Centred Psychology*. London: Whurr. (Republished by PCCS Books, 2006).

100. www.thefreedictionary.com/fundamentalist (accessed 28 October 2017).

101. An example of this in TA is Steiner C, Campos L, Drego P, Joines V, Ligabue S, Noriega G, Roberts D, Said E (2003). A compilation of core concepts. *Transactional Analysis Journal 33*(2): 182–191.

102. Over the years, a number of authors have identified misconceptions and misrepresentations of the person-centred approach. See, for example, Barrett-Lennard GT (1983). Understanding the person-centered approach to therapy: a reply to questions and misconceptions. In: McIlduff E, Coghlan D (eds). *The Person-Centered Approach and Cross-Cultural Communication: an international review, volume I*. Dublin, Ireland: Center for Cross-Cultural Communication (pp99–113); Tudor & Merry (2002); Wilkins P (2003). *Person-Centred Therapy in Focus*. London: Sage.

103. For further development of this critique, see Tudor K (2007). Training in the person-centred approach. In: Cooper M, O'Hara M, Schmid P, Wyatt G (eds). *The Handbook of Person-Centred Psychotherapy and Counselling*. Basingstoke: Palgrave (pp379–389).

104. Mearns D, Thorne B (1988). *Person-Centred Counselling in Action*. London: Sage.

105. Mearns D, Thorne B (2000). *Person-Centred Therapy Today: new frontiers in theory and practice.* London: Sage.
106. In TA terms, this would be referred to as an antiscript. In an interesting article on religious scripts, Isaacson (1974) identifies the counterinjunctions, injunctions and programme messages for different religious sects. For Lutherans, these are, respectively, 'Keep the doctrine pure, know what you believe', 'Don't learn anything else', and 'Stay away from non-Lutherans.' Isaacson CE (1974). Religious scripts. *Transactional Analysis Journal* 4(2): 38–40.
107. Chaffee J (1993). Conversation. In: Esterle J, Cluman D (eds). *Conversations with Critical Thinkers.* San Francisco, CA: The Whitman Institute (pp129–141).
108. Damasio A (1996). *Descartes' Error: emotion, reason, and the human brain.* London: Putnam.
109. Evans B (1946). *The Natural History of Nonsense.* New York, NY: Alfred A Knopf (p275).
110. Salzberg S (2002). *Faith: trusting your own deepest experience.* New York, NY: Riverhead Hardcover (pp56–57).
111. Salzberg (2002) (p58).
112. Casement P (2002). *Learning from our Mistakes: beyond dogma in psychoanalysis and psychotherapy.* New York, NY: The Guilford Press (p21).
113. Brookfield S (1993). Conversation. In: Esterle J, Cluman D (eds). *Conversations with Critical Thinkers.* San Francisco, CA: The Whitman Institute (pp7–27).
114. Brookfield (1993) (p19).
115. Tavris C, Wade C (1997). *Psychology in Perspective* (2nd ed). New York, NY: Longman. Also Wade C, Tavris C (1998). *Psychology* (5th ed). New York, NY: Longman.

CHAPTER 2

Psyche and therapy

> The wanderer has far to go
> Humble must he constant be
> Where the paths of wisdom lead
> Distant is the shadow of the setting sun.
> (Dave Cousins)[1]

Given that this book is concerned with psychotherapy, and given my stated interest in the critique of rhetoric and language, it seems important to begin this examination with the word 'psychotherapy'. Thus, in this chapter, I consider, first, the nature of therapy; second, the nature of psyche, and, third, the purpose of psychotherapy.[2] Following this, I offer a brief overview of psychotherapy, including its critical – and radical – traditions, and a summary of its critics and critiques. As such, this chapter stands as an introduction to the subject of the book and lays the ground for specific discussions about practice (in Chapter 3), theory (in Chapter 4), and the examination of the field in subsequent chapters.

The nature of therapy

The English word therapy comes from the Greek θεραπεία (*therapeia*), meaning curing, healing, service done to the sick, and waiting on. This is echoed in Jessie Taft's comment: 'The word "therapy" has no verb in English.'[3] She further reflects that the Greek noun from which the word 'therapy' is derived means 'a servant' and its associated verb is 'to wait', concluding that:

> I wish to use the English word 'therapy' with the full force of its derivation, to cover a process which we recognize as somehow and somewhat curative but which, if we are honest enough and brave enough, we must admit to be beyond our control.

This etymology of therapy is significant for a number of reasons.

A wider healing tradition

First, it links therapy to and places it in the context of other healing traditions, most of which pre-date the 19th century when, in 1811, Johann Heinroth was appointed to the Chair of *Psychische Therapie* at Leipzig University in Germany, and, in 1853, Walter Cooper Dendy introduced the term 'psycho therapeia'.[4] Such traditions are found all over the world and encompass a wide range of healing practices, from acupressure to Zang-fu – traditions and practices that, especially in the West, are often referred to as alternative or complementary medicine. While these terms have their exponents and their own implications, both place healing in some relationship with medicine, which, by implication, privileges medicine and the predominant Western alleopathic model (see below).

Most, if not all, of the founding fathers and mothers of psychotherapy favoured lay analysis,[5] and Freud himself also wrote in favour of 'peasant healers'. Unfortunately, the Western intellectual tradition, including its medical branch, has contributed to the suppression of many indigenous healing traditions. In Aotearoa New Zealand, for instance, the *Tohunga Suppression Act 1907*, which outlawed traditional Māori health practices, was only repealed less than 60 years ago (in 1962).[6] An example of an acknowledgement of such healing traditions occurred in 2011, when the Sigmund Freud Award for Psychotherapy, given by the City of Vienna in recognition of contributions to psychotherapy, was made to a group of Ngangkari indigenous healers comprising Toby (Ginger) Baker, Mr Peter and Andy Tjilari, and to Professor Helen Milroy and Lorraine Peeters.[7]

Humility

Second, the sense of service keeps psychotherapy – and psychotherapists – humble. Over the years, a number of writers have echoed Taft's sentiment that healing is (often) beyond our control. One of Berne's therapeutic sayings was, '*Je le pensay, Dieu le guarit*' (I treat them, God cures them),[8] and another was, '*Vis medicatrix naturae*', the curative power of nature. This humility is not simply or necessarily a moral or spiritual stance; it is also a response to the research into therapeutic outcome, suggesting that 'extra therapeutic factors' are more significant than therapist techniques, or even the therapeutic relationship[9] (see Chapter 5). This is not to discount the impact of the traditional 50-minute psychotherapeutic hour; it is simply to account for the signifance of the other 167 hours in the client's week.

Health, holism, and holiness

Third, the concept of healing leads us to health, making whole and holiness. The word 'health' has its roots in the old English *hǽlp*, *hǽl* (meaning whole), and *hǽlen* (heal). Graham links these origins to the old English *halig* and German *heilig* (meaning holy): 'Etymologically speaking, therefore, to be healthy is to be whole or holy, which clearly embraces both spiritual and physical features rather than merely the latter.'[10]

It is easy to link psychotherapy to illness and pathology. I was recently asked, in a non-psychotherapeutic work context, why someone would go to see a psychotherapist, and I answered by referring to what psychotherapy does for people with certain conditions, problems or concerns. The questioner seemed satisfied, but I added: 'Of course, you don't have to have a problem in order to see a psychotherapist. You might go because you're curious about yourself and some of the patterns you have that affect how you think about yourself and how you interact with others.' (Interestingly, this addition elicited some slightly embarrassed laughter among the other colleagues present.) Nonetheless, I was wanting to represent something about the role of psychotherapy in enhancing and promoting health.[11]

While most people think of themselves as whole, much of how we understand ourselves, at least in Western thinking, is based on breaking down and compartmentalising ourselves – for instance, into 'the self' and 'selves'. Although this is, to some extent, inevitable, it is worth remembering the organismic wholeness of our experience:

> The pattern of the excitation that occurs in the system as the result of a stimulus cannot be sufficiently characterized by noting merely the state of excitation in the 'near part'. The rest of the system, the 'distant part'... is also in a very definite state of excitation. Each movement of one part of the body is accompanied by a definite change in the posture of the rest of the body.[12]

Of all the forms of psychotherapy, gestalt therapy is the one most directly associated with the concept of holism, although I and others have also claimed and explored it as a principle and philosophical basis of the person-centred approach,[13] and it is most integrated in biodynamic and other forms of body psychotherapy. Writing about existentialist psychoanalysis, Jean-Paul Sartre asserts that: 'The principle of this psychoanalysis is that man is a totality and not a collection.'[14] More recent research in neuroscience supports the holistic nature of the organism – as Damasio puts it: 'The human brain and the rest of the body constitute an indisociable organism, integrated by means of mutually interactive biochemical and neural regulatory circuits.'[15]

The etymological link between healing and holiness is particularly significant as, traditionally, psychotherapy has had a somewhat ambivalent relationship with spirituality and especially religion, which, historically, derives from Freud's own view of religious belief being 'a lost cause' and representing a 'childhood neurosis'.[16] Much has been written about Freud's own relationship to religion in general, and Judaism in particular, and the legacy of this, especially for and in psychoanalysis and psychodynamic psychotherapy.[17] While some early psychoanalysts worked on including spirituality in the anlaytic process,[18] it is true to say that people who are religious or have faith and are interested in psychotherapy, whether as a client or a trainee, have generally found more of a home within Jungian (analytic) psychology – at one point Jung himself said that he was less interested in analysis and more concerned with the numinous – and within the humanistic tradition, a number of practitioners of which have written about the interface between religion, spirituality and psychotherapy.[19]

Independence from medicine

Fourth, as healing is distinct from medicine, so is psychotherapy; indeed, Freud himself was at pains to support such a distinction: 'For we do not consider it at all desirable for psycho-analysts to be swallowed up by medicine and to find its last resting-place in a text book of psychiatry under the heading "Methods of Treatment".'[20] Elsewhere, he makes it very clear that psychoanalysis is not a specialised branch of medicine:

> Psycho-analysis is a part of psychology; not of medical psychology in the old sense, not of the psychology of morbid processes, but simply of psychology. It is certainly not the whole of psychology, but its sub-structure and perhaps even its entire foundation. The possibility of its application to medical purposes must not lead us astray. Electricity and radiology also have their medical application, but the science to which they both belong is none the less physics.[21]

One manifestation of such independence, at least as far as Freud was concerned, was that psychoanalysis could be practised by lay people as well as doctors,[22] the professional implications of which I discuss in Chapter 8.

In this context, it is concerning that so many psychotherapists are uncritical of the authority of medicine – ie. the medical model itself, its bias and its dominance – and, worse, that they turn to medical rather than psychotherapeutic models for explanations. A common – and, from a critical perspective, somewhat worrying – example of this is with regard to the American Psychiatric

Association's *Diagnostic and Statistical Manual of Mental Disorders (DSM)* (now in its fifth edition).[23] Despite the extensive criticisms of the *DSM* system,[24] and the fact that psychotherapy, in all its variations (see below), has a number of theories of the origins of distress and dysfunction, often and broadly referred to as psychopathology, psychotherapists (clinicians and educators) too often turn first to the *DSM*. As Richard Mowbray puts it:

> ... a perspective that envisages psychotherapy as a treatment and cure business focusing on the illness or problem to be alleviated (ie. a 'medical model' activity) conflicts with a view of it as something primarily concerned with individual authenticity and uniqueness.[25]

Of course, psychotherapists working in the public sector alongside doctors, psychiatrists, psychologists and psychiatric nurses, who themselves may be informed by the *DSM*, may find it useful to have a working knowledge of its use – as well as its abuse. In this sense and for this purpose, being familiar with the dominant language or discourse is important, not only in order to be able to communicate with colleagues but also, as Paula Collens comments, 'to be able to challenge the dominant discourse and to create the space for the marginal persective'.[26] My argument is that fluency in this language is not required, as psychotherapists are not training as psychiatrists or to diagnose psychiatrically, and nor is it desirable, as it distracts from psychotherapists becoming fluent in the language(s) of psychotherapy and its (their) understanding of disease and disorder. Beyond the argument about having knowledge in order to understand and communicate, it's as if psychotherapists, or at least a significant number of us, aren't sufficiently confident in the language of psychotherapy and our capacity to speak it to help our clients to know themselves better.

Service

Finally, the etymology of therapy associates it with service, a stance and an attitude – a discussion I pick up in Chapter 3.

The nature of psyche

Having considered the nature of therapy, I now turn to discuss what it is that we are seeking to make whole, ie. the psyche.

Psyche, from the Greek ψυχή (*psūkhē*), refers to soul or spirit; the Latin equivalent of which is *anima*. The concept of the psyche is central to the work of the Greek philosopher Plato (c427–c348 BCE), who made a number of arguments for the immortality of the soul. Aristotle (c384–c322 BCE) wrote an influential treatise on the psyche, Περί Ψυχῆς (*De Anima* or *The Soul*),[27] and his theory of three souls (vegetal, animal and rational) dominated psychology until the 19th century. As a character, Psyche first appears in the novel *The Metamorphoses*, written by Lucius Apuleius Madaurensis (c170–c124 BCE), which concerns the overcoming of obstacles of love between Psyche (soul, the breath of life), and Eros, and their ultimate union in a sacred marriage – a story that stands as an interesting metaphor for psychotherapy.

In psychotherapy, psychoanalysis and other forms of what is generally referred to as 'depth psychology', the psyche refers to those forces in an individual that influence thought, behaviour and personality. Freud proposed that the psyche (the German word *Seele* stands for both psyche and soul) comprises three structural systems: the id (the instinctual drives), the superego (the person's conscience, influenced by internalisation of norms and morality), and the ego (which is conscious, and serves to mediate between and integrate the drives of the id and the prohibitions of the superego). Jung was careful to distinguish between psyche and soul, stating that: 'By psyche, I understand the totality of all psychic processes, conscious as well as unconscious. By soul, on the other hand, I understand the clearly demarcated functional complex that can best be described as "personality",'[28] and it is true to say that, of all the theoretical approaches in psychotherapy, Jungian therapy (also known as analytic psychology) is the one that most uses and explores the term.

Although psyche is the root word and defining concept of the discipline of psychotherapy, it is only one of many terms and concepts that we use in our efforts to know, understand and communicate about ourselves. Other significant words, or phrases and concepts, include human nature and human being(s), mind, body and spirit, and personality, discussion of which provides the philosophical background to specific theoretical concepts that I consider in Chapter 4.

Human nature and human being(s)

What it is to be human, what a human being is, and how that humanness and *being* is expressed are questions that have been exercising women and men since time – or we – began. Here, I discuss three aspects of homo sapiens, which, in his interesting and eponymous book on the subject, Yuval Harari dates as evolving 200,000 years ago from the genus *homo*, which itself dates back 2.5 million years.[29]

Homo sapiens

For some, the term *homo sapiens* represents a view of a mankind that is knowledgeable, if not wise, and one that emphasises 'man' as philosopher and scientist – a representation that, of course, is found in psychology and psychotherapy. Sartre describes the human being as 'a perpetual, searching historization';[30] George Kelly, the founder of personal construct psychology, writes about 'inquiring man', a phrase that encapsulates his view of the person as a scientist testing their experience and construction of that experience, hence personal constructs[31] – and, whence, the concept of the scientist-practitioner.[32] In many ways, this conception is linked to the view of human beings promoted in and by the various traditions encompassed by the Enlightenment, a tradition whose influence on psychotherapy I discuss in Chapter 4.

Everyone has a view of about human nature, and especially the degree to which we can change or not. Phrases like 'You can't step in the same river twice',[33] 'The only certainty is change', 'You can't teach an old dog new tricks', 'It's just how I am – it's my nature' all represent particular views about human nature and an underlying philosophy about life – and different philosophies have different implications for psychotherapy. Thus, for instance, existentialism identifies four basic dimensions to human existence, within each and all of which we struggle with the givens of the past and the possibilities for the present and future, and with the meaning of our lives. As Emmy van Deurzen-Smith, an existential therapist, explains:

> ... the existential approach considers human nature to be open-minded, flexible and capable of an enormous range of experience. The person is in a constant state of becoming... this impermanence and uncertainty give rise to a deep sense of anxiety (Angst), in response to the realization of one's insignificance, and simultaneous responsibility to have to create something in the place of that emptiness. Everything passes and nothing lasts.[34]

Views about human nature tend to reflect three different approaches, the first two of which have their intellectual origins in the Platonic notion of the mind as an entity that pre-exists a particular human existence.

Based on this, the first view is that we are born 'good', with certain positive, pro-social tendencies, and that bad behaviour, and even 'evil', represent ways in which we turn away from our natural, inherent goodness. This view underpins the work of a number of humanistic therapists, including Rogers, who wrote that he regarded mankind as 'positive, forward moving, constructive, realistic, trustworthy... and not basically hostile, antisocial, destructive, evil'.[35]

Also based on some concept of pre-existence, the second view is that we are born with something we must make good, whether this is a result of being sinful, alienated, or in some way problematic or pathological. Freud once said: 'I have found little that is "good" about human beings. In my experience, most of them are trash, no matter whether they publicly subscribe to this or that ethical doctrine or to none at all.'[36] In a similar vein, Paul holds 'that the best definition of the human species is "the self deceiving animal"'.[37]

The third view, which dates back to the writings of Aristotle, is based on the concept of the *tabula rasa*, an unscribed tablet or blank slate, and represents the concept that we are born neutral, with nothing inscribed on us, our psyche or personalities. This view was developed by the Stoic school of philosophy, which emphasised that the mind starts blank but acquires knowledge as the outside world is impressed or inscribed upon it; it influenced, some centuries later, empiricists such as the British 17th century philosopher John Locke. In his *Essay Concerning Human Understanding*, Locke argues that the human mind is a blank slate and that data and rules for processing data are formed solely by one's sensory experiences. This perspective favours nurture over nature, and, for Locke, means that individuals are free to author their own souls. Commenting on the differences and similarities between empirical and existential psychoanalysis, Sartre writes:

> Both consider that there are no primary givens such as hereditary dispositions, character, etc. Existential psychoanalysis recognizes nothing *before* the original upsurge of human freedom; empirical psychoanalysis holds that the original affectivity of individual is virgin wax *before* its history.[38]

Homo politicus

Aristotle's view that man is a social/political animal reflects what we might term *homo politicus* and a broad sense that the person cannot be understood separately from their environment. This is not simply a moral and/or political perspective; it is one that is supported by the research that acknowledges that 'extra therapeutic factors' are the single most important factor in determining the efficacy of therapeutic outcome (see also Chapter 6).[39] Psychotherapy has always considered the impact of the political on the personal, if not so much the personal on the political. As early as 1910, Ferenczi wrote to Freud about 'the sociological significance of our analyses in the sense that in our analyses we investigate the real conditions in the various levels of society… just as they are mirrored in the individual'.[40] However, it is also true to say that psychoanalysis and psychotherapy, and probably most of its practitioners, have been ambivalent about and even antagonist towards politics and to those who link the two:

As early as 1908, Freud admonished Otto Gross, who had a significant influence in this respect on Ferenczi, *not* to link psychoanalysis with radical politics. Gross did not obey, and was excluded from the psychoanalytic establishment. Ferenczi only continued to publish his radical political ideas in Hungarian, a language Freud did not speak.[41]

Marx also had a concept of human nature that was essentially *social*: 'The real nature of man is the totality of social relations.'[42] However, on the basis of his materialist conception of history, he goes further, arguing that there is no such thing as *individual* human nature, but, rather, the 'nature' of the human depends on the social relations and conditions of the time. Thus, human nature is determined by social and economic relations and is therefore different in different historical eras and different economic and cultural contexts.[43] Another analysis, on the basis of indigenous perspectives about culture, cultural identity and cultural responsibilities, leads to a similar conclusion: in effect, that 'I am because we are'. Although this view is central, explicit and lived in many, if not most, indigenous cultures and contexts, aspects of a 'we' psychology have also been articulated by a number of Western thinkers. Martin Buber wrote: 'A soul is never sick alone';[44] Sartre commented that psychoanalysis considers 'man' in the world, in all his 'situations';[45] Andras Angyal developed the concept of homonomy as an inherent trend alongside that of autonomy;[46] Winnicott famously said, 'There is no such thing as a baby... A baby cannot exist alone but is essentially part of a relationship';[47] George Klein coined the term 'wego' in contrast to ego;[48] and, elsewhere, I have suggested that 'we are' is the fundamental life position in transactional analysis.[49] All of these represent different, and sometimes differing, theories about human nature, informed by different intellectual traditions (see Chapter 4).

This social/political perspective is also reflected in ideas and discussion about identity in terms of race and culture (both in Western and indigenous traditions), sexuality, disability etc, and how integral these are to who a person *is*. Finally, this social/political perspective on human nature also provides the basis for viewing humans as part of nature, and, thus, a link to the environment, to ecopsychology and ecotherapy and to personal and ecological health and sustainability.

Homo ludens

All mammals play, but none pursue play or spend so much time playing or seeking entertainment as humans; indeed, the German writer Friedrich Schiller wrote that we're only human when we're at play. I include the concept here[50] partly because it links with psychotherapeutic ideas about the centrality of play,[51] and with therapeutic approaches that encourage creative and artistic expression (see Chapter 3). This perspective has certainly influenced me, both as a practitioner and as a theorist, and especially in my development, with Graeme Summers, of co-creative transactional analysis.[52]

Mind, body, spirit

Different philosophical traditions have also influenced what we understand by the terms mind, body and spirit. Plato held a dualistic view of man, whereby the soul, or mind, is a non-material entity that exists apart from the body, and has three parts: Appetite, Reason and Spirit. Depending on which of these three elements is dominant in a person, they will be focused on gain (from desire), knowledge, or success (from self-interest and self-assertion). While Plato favoured Reason and the intellect, the ideal was for these three elements of the soul to be in harmony, a condition he described as justice or wellbeing.[53]

Unfortunately, many people separate mind, body and spirit. In the Western intellectual tradition, this is often attributed to Descartes' work and method, epitomised in his famous saying, 'I think, therefore I am', as if he were prioritising thinking and cognition over other human activities. In fact, as noted in Chapter 1, Descartes was advocating thinking as a way of doubting and being sceptical; he was not privileging thinking over feeling.

Nevertheless, thinking, intellectual processing and the mind have often been privileged over other forms of knowing, such as feelings and emotions, bodily sensations, aesthetics, connection with the environment and so on – and in Chapter 3, I examine the significance of the separation of these aspects of what it is to be human for different methods of psychotherapy. In response to the dualistic split between mind and body, many have looked to other traditions – Eastern, indigenous, and Southern – which, it is argued, represent more holistic, integrated and connected thinking/feeling/being. While I think this is broadly true, I also think there has always been a perspective within the Western tradition that views mind, soul and spirit as aspects of the whole person, and, as such, of concern to psychotherapy, or at least to some psychotherapists.[54]

In the past 25 years, informed by research conducted predominately by developmental psychologists and neuroscientists, more psychotherapists have become interested in the working of the brain, and, given our increasing understanding of the plasticity of the brain, the impact of psychotherapy in enhancing change in our neural circuits.[55] As a result, some psychotherapists are refining their practice, and a prime example of this is John Arden's work on brain-based therapy.[56] While this is an exciting and significant development, we should not confuse the brain with the mind: 'Our brains are not in a vat, but in our bodies. Our minds are not in our bodies, but in the world,' as Clifford Geertz reminds us.[57]

Personality

The concept of personality is central to psychotherapy; indeed, arguably, one of the defining features of psychotherapy is that it has a general theory of personality.[58] As with most terms in philosophy, psychology and psychotherapy, what Jung referred to as the 'demarcated functional complex' – that is, the personality – is defined and understood differently. Freud viewed it as synonymous with the mind, within which, as mentioned, he distinguished the id (the instinctual drives seeking immediate satisfaction), the superego (social norms and conscience), and the ego (which deals with the real world outside the person and mediates between the id and the superego). This was developed by some of his followers, including Anna Freud, Heinz Hartmann and David Rapaport, who became associated with ego psychology, a development of psychoanalysis that influenced and was further developed by René Spitz, Margaret Mahler, Erik Erikson and Eric Berne.

Essentially, the term 'personality' refers to individual differences in characteristic patterns of thinking, feeling and behaving. Thus, most, if not all, modalities in psychotherapy have their particular models of personality, based on their understanding of the person, which inform how they can help their clients change. For instance, I and Worrall, influenced by organismic psychology and personology, suggest a 'fluid and individual understanding of personality',[59] and, reflecting Marxist and feminist analysis, argue for the importance of social relations and context in understanding the development and manifestation of personality.

Whatever our understanding of personality, the point is that psychotherapists have one – which is why it is strange that, instead of basing our understanding, work and argument on what we know, and with which, presumably, we agree, many psychotherapists, as noted, turn to the *DSM* for its working definition of personality and of personality disorder. For example:

> A personality disorder is an enduring pattern of inner experience and behavior that deviates markedly from the expectations of the individual's culture, is pervasive and inflexible, has an onset in adolescence or early adulthood, is stable over time, and leads to distress or impairment.[60]

This dependence on the American Psychiatric Association's definition of personality is strange for three reasons: first, this is a psychiatric and not a psychotherapeutic understanding of personality; second, it represents a more fixed and rigid review of personality than most psychotherapeutic theories (see Chapter 4), and third, it is based in Western thinking, and far from universal.

The purpose of psychotherapy

From the discussion at the beginning of the chapter, it follows that the purpose of psychotherapy is to heal the psyche, or to make or to restore it to a (or its) whole – and even to its holiness. Beyond this, or perhaps before, different theoreticians and practitioners have emphasised different purposes of psychotherapy, which follow from different views of the person, group, society, change etc, and which have implications for different perspectives on the role of the psychotherapist. Here, I identify seven concepts that represent different and differing thinking about the purpose of psychotherapy: thinking that informs the views of both therapist and client.[61] While they were developed predominantly in the context of individual psychotherapy, these concepts also apply to group therapy, couple therapy etc.

Insight

Insight, the principal focus of classical psychoanalysis, is based on the view that a person's difficulties arise from their lack of understanding of, for instance, their motivation(s), the impact of unresolved conflict, or confusion. The patient gains insight through a conversation, initially conducted as a psychoanalysis, with the analyst offering interpretations of the patient's defences. Historically, this was *the* goal of psychoanalysis, which did not focus on or promote cure or change. Indeed, this is the main criticism of this purpose of therapy/analysis – that, while the patient may gain insight, they don't necessarily change. In a critique of psychoanalysis, Owen Renik, a former editor of *Psychoanalytic Quarterly* and programme chair of the American Psychoanalytic Association, suggests that psychoanalysis is the author of its own diminution, in that it moved away from its original focus on symptom relief to favour endless analysis with no or little reference to measuring progress against symptoms.[62] I have some sympathy with Renik's criticism and his emphasis on the practical; nevertheless, insight, gained through dreaming, free association and reverie, as well as interpretation, can be the basis of and precursor of action, and, as a concept, is close to the 'awareness' promoted in humanistic psychology.[63]

Individuation

Originally developed by Jung and related to his theory of self (as distinct from ego),[64] individuation describes a process of self-realisation: 'the discovery and experience of meaning and purpose in life; the means by which one finds oneself and becomes who one really is.'[65] This process requires the integration of both conscious and unconscious material, and both collective and individual elements. It is also, as a process of realisation, close to awareness, which is generally regarded as a humanistic purpose and value. While Jung himself viewed individuation as a development associated with the second half of life, neo-Jungians, notably Michael Fordham, describe this process as beginning in infancy and continuing through adolescence into adulthood.[66] Given the interest in integrative therapy (see p65 below), it is interesting to reflect on whether integration would be viewed as a purpose of psychotherapy.[67] I think it probably is, although more implicitly than explicitly; insofar as it refers to the integration of affect, behaviour and cognition, of mind, body and spirit, and of different aspects of personality, in terms of the present taxonomy, I consider it a core aspect of individuation.

Connection

The view that human beings are interconnected and seek connection means that therapy is, or should be, concerned with the healing of disconnection and the restoration of connection. While this view is informed especially by cultural, indigenous and feminist perspectives on therapy, the importance of connection may also be found in what might be seen as mainstream (Western) thinking, such as homonomy (Andras Angyal),[68] belonging (Abraham Maslow),[69] universality (Irvin Yalom),[70] mutual recognition (Jessica Benjamin),[71] and social actualisation (Corey Keyes).[72] This view of the purpose of therapy challenges more individualistic views of the individual and of the main purpose of therapy being self-awareness and/or self-actualisation.

Adaptation

The idea that therapy can help people to change their thinking or behaviour so that they survive and function more successfully is a central concept in behavioural psychology, and was also a feature of mainstream American ego psychology.[73] In Jean Piaget's developmental theory, adaptation is an important process that is critical to cognitive development, principally through accommodation and assimiliation.[74] The main critique of this purpose of therapy is based on a concern about where the pressure to adapt comes from: in other words, whether the client is accommodating and adapting to others and/or society, rather than following what they genuinely want to do, think and feel. As noted, a still topical example of this concern are those 'reparative therapies' that aim to convert gay people to heterosexuality.[75] If we consider that a certain amount of adaptation is important, such as the necessary socialisation required in order to live with others, then it might be more precise to clarify that the critique is of 'over-adaptation' (which, in transactional analysis, is one of a number of what are termed passive behaviours).

Cure

In some ways, cure is related to the previous purpose of adaptation. Whilst this word and concept is generally more often associated with the medical model of diagnosis → treatment → cure, it was also used by radical psychiatrists to emphasise the aspiration of and their commitment to facilitating change – 'therapy means change, not adjustment'[76] – in the context of their critique of interminable analysis that didn't necessarily result in any change. Nevertheless, the critique of adaptation is echoed in relation to cure, in terms of the power of the medical model and the medical or medicalised practitioner to decide what constitutes cure. Rogers put this well in an interview recorded in the last year of his life and published posthumously:

> Too many therapists think they can make something happen. Personally I like much better the approach of an agriculturalist or a farmer or a gardener: I can't make corn grow, but I can provide the right soil and plant it in the right area and see that it gets enough water; I can nurture it so that exciting things happen. I think that's the nature of therapy. It's so unfortunate that we've so long followed a medical model and not a growth model. A growth model is much more appropriate to most people, to most situations.[77]

Authenticity

Authenticity, and its related terms (congruence, genuineness, realness, fully functioning etc), is often described in terms of the process(es) of being, becoming and belonging.[78] It is one of the cornerstones of humanistic psychology, and stands in contrast to over-adaptation. The value of being authentic and 'true', of course, has a longer history. This is captured by Shakespeare's Polonius, when he advises his son, Laertes: 'This above all: to thine own self be true, | And it must follow, as the night of the day, | Thou canst not then be false to any man.'[79] As I and Worrall put it: 'Authenticity describes mankind in relationship and unity with itself and nature – and, if not united, being prepared and willing to do something about it.'[80] While, as a concept and process, it has certainly been more developed within humanistic psychology, it is is also found in other traditions. Ian Craib's work on *The Importance of Disappointment* and his exploration of 'the disappointed self' that experiences normal human misery, envy, fragmentation, helplessness, dependence, paradox and so on, describe an authenticity that challenges 'the false self but [which] late modernity encourages'.[81] Also, I would say that Thomas Ogden's vision of psychoanalysis as a 'therapeutic enterprise with the goal of enhancing the patient's capacity to be alive to as much as possible of the full spectrum of human experience'[82] is a good description of, at least, an important component of authenticity. The main critique of this way of being is that it can be self-indulgent and asocial; I have certainly come across people who justify their bad behaviour by saying 'I was (just) being honest'.

Liberation

Liberation also describes aliveness, but does so using a different language and, thereby, represents a different theoretical perspective. While a number of therapeutic traditions, in particular the radical ones (see p66 below),[83] would support the purpose of therapy being liberation, not all would necessarily use that language. One that did – and still does – is radical psychiatry, which views and conceptualises people's problems in terms of alienation, thus:

'Alienation = Oppression + Mystification + Isolation', and their (re)solution in terms of liberation: ie. 'Liberation = Awareness + Contact + Action.'[84]

Of course, there are many ways in which people are alienated, and, therefore, many ways in which we might express a praxis of liberation. Following Marx's original analysis, many Marxists have tended to focus on alienation from labour, although Marx himself also writes about being alienated from social relations and from species-being, and neo-Marxists, indigenous people and environmentalists talk variously about alienation from the land, the environment, including other species, and the planet – an analysis that resonates with post-humanist thinking (see also Chapter 4).

The nature and purpose of therapy are, of course, inextricably linked and inevitably personal: that is, they reflect the views and underlying values of the practitioner. While I was writing this book, I took a short break with my wife; we were on a car ferry and I got talking to one of the other passengers, who, at one point in the conversation, asked me, 'So, what *is* psychotherapy?'[85] I paused briefly, and then spoke for about five minutes, at the end of which I asked her if what I'd said made sense. She said: 'Oh, yes. It's a kind of free-thinking way to help troubled folk.' I thought this was a great summary – and one which, of course, reflects my own 'take' on psychotherapy.

Social purpose

Finally, I suggest that there is another purpose to therapy that is not so much for the individual, the couple, or even the group, but is more concerned with society. The social – and especially the sociological – criticism of psychotherapy is that it individualises private troubles that are, or, at least, are *also,* public issues. Thus, for example, in individual psychotherapy, a young mother who is not coping with her demanding child may learn that her inability, or reduced ability, to cope has its origins in her own childhood, but may not be encouraged to express her anger about her unsupportive partner and/or extended family, or the lack of free or low-cost nursery provision in her community.

By contrast, there are two senses in which psychotherapy has a social purpose: for the individual her/himself, and for psychotherapy itself.

The first sense is an expression of social actualisation (referred to on p57 above), and may take the form of clients, through their therapy, becoming (and being and belonging as) better people *in relationship*: as mothers, fathers, family members, neighbours, colleagues and citizens.[86] One of the theoretical implications of this is that we need to develop concepts, theories, models and meta-models in and of therapy that account for this, such as the extension of Martha Stark's taxonomy of one-person, one-and-a-half-person, and two-person psychologies[87] to 'two-person-plus psychology', in order to account for the impact, influence and importance of context, including the environment.[88]

The second sense is the impact of psychotherapy on society. Despite the fact that psychotherapy is commonly viewed as dealing individually with individuals, it has always had a wider and more social vision. In a letter written just before the end of the First World War, Sigmund Freud spoke of his hope that 'the conscience of society will awake and remind it that the poor man should have just as much right to assistance for his mind as he now has to the life-saving help offered by surgery'.[89] He went on to argue that neuroses threaten public health as much as diseases such as tuberculosis, and for the establishment of free clinics and the provision of a 'psychotherapy for the people' (for further discussion of this, see Chapter 8).

A brief overview of psychotherapy

As I noted in the Introduction, there is a wide variation of psychotherapy practice and theory. This is due, first, to the influences on psychotherapy of different disciplines, and, second, to the consequences of the first splits in the psychoanalytic movement,[90] as well as subsequent splits and developments in the various forces of psychology and modalities of psychotherapy.

Although it is commonplace to trace the lineage of psychotherapy back to Freud (who by now must be at least a great-grandfather), psychotherapy existed before him and was influenced by a number of different traditions, disciplines and professions, including:

- healing traditions – early Egyptian papyri (c1,550 BCE) mention dementia and depression, and Hippocrates of Kos (c460–c370 BCE) taught that melancholia has a biological cause.[91]

- medicine – in the Western tradition, from the mental healing practices of Paracelsus (1494–1541), a Swiss physician; of Franz Anton Mesmer (1734–1815), an Austrian physician who first developed a concept of what he came to call animal magnetism (later known as mesmerism, and later still as hypnotism, which links with Wilhelm Reich's later work on orgone energy), to others who first used the term 'psycho-therapy' (see p64 and p75, note 100).

- psychiatry – from the work of Philippe Pinel (1745–1826), who, as director of the Bicêtre and Salpêtrière asylums in Paris, initiated a non-violent and non-medical moral treatment, which Grob describes as 'a warm and trusting familial environment in which [patients] could feel that their mental condition did not in any way preclude participation in normal human activities'.[92]

- academia – from the appointment, in 1811, of Johann Heinroth as (the first) Professor of Psychic (Psycho) Therapy.

- lay practitioners and consumers – including, from the mid-19th century, spiritualists, the mind cure movement and the mental hygiene movement.[93]

- ministry – formally, from 1904, in the work of Elwood Worcester (1862–1940), who, as minister of the Emmanuel Church in Boston, Massachusetts, developed a programme that 'fused religious faith and scientific knowledge' in the treatment of functional nervous disorders.[94]

- psychology – from the work of William James (1842–1910), who, among other things, investigated different levels of consciousness; of Lightner Witmer (1867–1956), who, in 1896, established the first psychological clinic, at the University of Pennsylvania, to assist children with educational impairments, and was the first to use the term 'clinical psychology' to denote a distinct profession; and of John Watson (1878–1958), who claimed psychology as 'a purely objective experimental branch of natural science' and its theoretical goal as 'the prediction and control of behavior'.[95]

- social work – in this context, from the establishment in 1909 of the first child guidance clinic in Chicago (although the term 'child guidance clinic' was not coined until 1922).

In this context, psychoanalysis had to find and claim its place and, while Abraham Brill argued for this to be in medicine,[96] Freud was opposed to this, arguing that psychoanalysis was part of psychology.[97] The differences between the two regarding the question of lay analysis and analysts were to become key in the development not only of the profession but also of the disciplines of psychoanalysis and psychotherapy.

With regard to the history and development of psychotherapy itself, most commentators refer to three traditions, or 'forces': psychoanalysis (from the 1890s), behaviourism (from 1913 and Watson's first article on the subject), and humanistic psychology (from the early 1960s and, specifically, 28–30 November 1964, when an invitational conference was held at Old Saybrook, Connecticut, US). However, there are a number of problems with this division, not least the implication that they are all forces of psychology, rather than psychotherapy; that they do not compare like with like,[98] and that there are further developments in the field that are equally or better considered as forces or traditions, such as the transpersonal, transcultural and indigenous. Moreover, while it is acknowledged that Freud is the founding father (or great-grandfather) of psychoanalysis,[99] because of the initial and subsequent splits within psychoanalysis, many other modalities or schools of psychotherapy, especially in the humanistic tradition, can trace their ancestry back to 'the Viennese doctor'. Even those humanistic approaches that disagree with much psychoanalytic theory and practice would acknowledge that their founders were only one or two handshakes away from Freud: Jessie Taft and Carl Rogers via Otto Rank; Fritz Perls via Wilhelm Reich; Eric Berne via Paul Federn, and via Eric Erikson by way of Anna Freud and Helene Deutsch etc. However, it is worth remembering that, while Freud coined the term 'psychoanalysis', he himself had to shake the hand of someone else who was one of the first to use the word 'psychotherapy'.[100]

As a result of the establishment of a number of differing modalities/orientations/schools within these traditions, the number of different approaches to psychotherapy has multiplied. By 1980, there were more than 250 different approaches to psychotherapy;[101] by 1994, more than 400;[102] by 1996, more than 450,[103] and latest estimates suggest that there are now more than 1,000 separately named psychotherapies (albeit some are minor variations of previous approaches). While some are clearly distinguishable from their parent influences and other approaches, others appear based more on 'the narcissism of minor differences',[104] and subscribe more to market forces than psychological ones. The same narcissism manifests in sectarianism between and about the various approaches. For instance, in his article on the efficacy of psychodynamic psychotherapy, Jonathan Shedler argues – or, rather, simply asserts – that the evidence that non-psychodynamic therapies are in part effective is 'because the(ir) more skilled practitioners utilize interventions that have long been central to psychodynamic theory and practice'.[105]

At the same time, and more specifically in the early 1970s, an increasing number of practitioners were drawing ideas from different schools of therapy – a practice that was referred to as eclecticism, although few therapists identified or would identify as 'eclectic', mainly because it sounds too diffuse and/or casual. Some used other terms for their practical or technical eclecticism, such as 'multimodal therapy' (associated with the work of Arnold

Lazarus), or systematic treatment selection (associated with the work of Larry Beutler). Others, who were more interested in the integrity of theory, developed ideas about integrative psychotherapy,[106] which, generally, is distinguished from eclectic psychotherapy by the fact that it has some organising principle by which it integrates different theory and practice: for instance, the therapeutic relationship.[107] While we may still suffer from living in a professional culture in which the narcissism of small differences thrives, for some, we are 'beyond Schoolism' (Petrūska Clarkson),[108] in an era of pluralism (Andrew Samuels),[109] and, indeed, in an era of post-professionalism (House).[110] Perhaps even more challenging, and especially for those of us who identify, or who have identified, quite strongly with the humanistic tradition in psychology and psychotherapy, we are also in an intellectual era of post-humanism.[111]

Finally, all this is, of course, influenced by context, including geography and the varied history and development of psychology and psychotherapy in different countries and cultures. Thus, in smaller countries, such as Aotearoa New Zealand, there is a limited choice of theoretical orientations or modalities in which one can train in psychotherapy,[112] and many countries (possibly most) do not have a tradition of psychotherapy.

Critical – and radical – psychotherapy

With rare exceptions, most histories of psychotherapy tend to overlook the fact that it is based on progressive thinking and that it has always had critical and radical theorists and practitioners. Aron and Starr remind us that 'for a long time psychoanalysis was as much a social movement, a movement for reform in education, social policy, and culture as it was a treatment method'.[113] Here (see Table 2.1), by way of challenging mainstream history and of reclaiming the critical tradition, I list, in chronological order, some key theories and developments in this tradition, many of which inform the perspective put forward in this book.[114]

Table 2.1 – The traditions of radical therapy[115]

Year	Tradition
1908	Mutual analysis, as practised by Carl Jung and Otto Gross with each other, and, before that, by Gross and his anarchist friends; from the mid-1920s by Sándor Ferenczi; and in the 1960s, co-counselling
1910s	Psychodrama and sociometry, expressed in the form of the Theatre of Spontaneity (Jacob Moreno) and (in the 1970s) the Theatre of the Oppressed (Augusto Boal.) Feminist therapy, which may be traced back to the work of Sabina Spielrein (1910s–1930s), and later from the work of Karen Horney (1940s) onwards, and its variants, ie. psychoanalytic feminist therapy, radical feminist therapy, humanistic feminist therapy, and therapy informed by woman-of-colour feminism
1920s	Marxist psychoanalysis, represented by the work of Wilhelm Reich, and by Lacanian and Freudo-Marxist psychoanalysis
1960s	Anti-psychiatry, represented by the work of RD Laing and David Cooper
1964	Marxist humanism, influenced by writers such as Herbert Marcuse and Erich Fromm
1970	Indigenous therapy[116]
1971	Radical psychiatry, also referred to as 'radical therapy', represented in the work of Claude Steiner, Hogie Wyckoff and others
1970s	Process-oriented psychology, based on the work of Arnold Mindell
1975	Red therapy, developed by a leaderless group of socialists in London
Mid-1970s	Pink and queer therapy, inspired by the work of Josette Mondanaro and Richard Isay
1979	Social action psychotherapy, based on the work of Sue Holland
1979	Social therapy, based on the work of Fred Newman
Early 1980s	Ecotherapy, inspired by the work of Joanna Macy
Mid-1980s	Anti-oppressive therapeutic practice, the therapeutic version of practice developed in the field of social work
2012	Power-sensitised counselling, developed by Susan Sprong

Critics – and critiques – of psychotherapy

By way of concluding this chapter, I offer a brief overview of the principal critics and critiques of psychotherapy. These fall into a number of categories:

- critiques from within psychotherapy, as evidenced by the traditions noted above. There have also been, and are, colleagues who criticise other approaches (than their own) within psychotherapy in debates that have been referred to as 'modality wars', and others who criticise others within a specific modality, which at times has led to the development of new approaches.

- critiques from outside psychotherapy, by various writers, including:

  - Hans Eysenck, who questioned what he viewed as the lack of scientific evidence for psychotherapy, and, in one now famous study, showed that, in a two-year follow-up of two groups of patients receiving and not receiving psychotherapy, 66% in *both* groups felt better, while 33% felt unchanged or worse. Moreover, Eysenck suggested that the improvement reported could be accounted for by 'spontaneous remission'.[117]

  - Thomas Szasz, who argued that there should be a separation between psychiatry and the state[118] and that mental illness was a myth,[119] and critiqued the gatekeeping role that mental health professionals play.[120]

  - George Albee, who questioned the unbridgeable gap between the percentage of the population who have a diagnosable psychiatric condition, and the small number of therapists offering relatively long-term therapy.[121]

  - Jeffrey Masson, who, as a qualified psychoanalyst and director of the Sigmund Freud Archives,[122] exposed what he saw to be Freud's abandonment of the seduction theory for personal rather than scientific reasons, and, having been on the inside of psychotherapy, is now implacably 'against therapy'.[123]

  - David Smail, who argued against pretentious models of therapy and for the recognition of the political roots of distress.[124]

- Donald Eisner, who criticised psychotherapy for its lack of definition and distinctions, its self-referential justifications, and for a number of its theories, including the unconscious and transference, and its techniques.[125]

- critiques from sociologists – a tradition that includes Jerome Frank, Paul Halmos, Philip Rieff, Nikolas Rose, Philip Cushman, Frank Furedi and Katie Wright, whose criticisms are well-summarised by Colin Feltham in his volume in this series.[126] To them, I would only add Peter Morrall, who has built a detailed critique of therapy as dysfunctional, arrogant, selfish, abusive, infectious, insane and deceitful.[127]

- critiques from clients or ex-clients, consumers and/or survivors, including, notably, Anne France,[128] Carter Heyward,[129] Rosie Alexander,[130] Anna Sands,[131] and Yvonne Bates[132] – and it is not insignificant that all these authors are women.

Having examined the background to psyche and its therapy, I turn in the next chapter to discuss its practice.

Endnotes

1. Cousins D (1972). Benedictus. *Grave New World*. [Album.] London: A&M.
2. I am especially grateful to Gottfried Heuer for his generous reading and comments on an earlier draft of this chapter.
3. Taft J (1933). *The Dynamics of Therapy in a Controlled Relationship*. New York, NY: Macmillan (p3).
4. Jackson SW (1999). *Care of the Psyche: a history of psychological healing*. Yale, CT: Yale University Press. Subsequent references to 'psycho-therapeutics' were made in 1872 by Daniel Hack Tuck; to psychotherapy by Charles Lloyd Tuckey in 1889, the year in which the word was also used by Frederik van Eerden and Albert Willem to describe their clinic in Amsterdam, and in 1896, when a German journal changed its name to include the word 'Psychotherapie'– see Shamdasani S (2005). 'Psychotherapy': the invention of a word. *History of the Human Sciences* 18(1): 1–22.
5. Freud S (1959/1926). The question of lay analysis: conversations with an impartial person. In: Strachey J (ed & trans). *The Standard Edition of the*

Complete Psychological Works of Sigmund Freud, vol 20. London: Hogarth Press (pp183–250).

6. Woodard W (2014). Politics, psychotherapy, and the 1907 Tohunga Suppression Act. *Psychotherapy and Politics International 12*(1): 39–48.

7. This was made at the Sixth Congress of the World Council for Psychotherapy in Sydney, Australia, the significance of which is discussed in San Roque C (2012). Aranke, or in the long line: reflections on the 2011 Sigmund Freud Award for psychotherapy and the lineage of traditional indigenous therapy in Australia. *Psychotherapy and Politics International 10*(2): 93–104.

8. Berne E (1966). *Principles of Group Treatment.* New York, NY: Grove Press (p63). Berne attributes this 'slogan' to Ambroise Paré, the 16th century French barber surgeon, one of the fathers of surgery and modern forensic pathology.

9. Asay TP, Lambert MJ (1999). The empirical case for the common factors in therapy: qualitative findings. In: Hubble MA, Duncan BL, Miller SD (eds). *The Heart and Soul of Change: what works in therapy*. Washington, DC: American Psychological Association (pp33–36).

10. Graham H (1992). Imaginative assessment of personal health needs. In: Trent DR (ed). *Promotion of Mental Health.* Aldershot: Avebury (pp53–62) (p53).

11. See Tudor K (1996). *Mental Health Promotion: paradigms and practice.* London: Routledge. Also: Tudor K, Worrall M (2006). *Person-Centred Therapy: a clinical philosophy.* London: Routledge; and Tudor K, Summers G (2014). *Co-creative Transactional Analysis: papers, dialogues, responses, and developments.* London: Karnac.

12. Goldstein K (1995/1934). *The Organism.* New York, NY: Zone Books (p99).

13. See Tudor & Worrall (2006).

14. Sartre J-P (1958/1943). *Being and Nothingness: an essay on phenomenological ontology* (HE Barnes trans). London: Methuen & Co (p568).

15. Damasio A (1996). *Descartes' Error: emotion, reason and the human brain.* London: Penguin (pxvii).

16. Freud S (1968/1927). The future of an illusion. In: Strachey J (ed & trans). *The Standard Edition of the Complete Psychological Works of Sigmund, vol 20.* London: Hogarth Press (pp1–56) (p53).

17. For recent volumes on which, see Aron L, Starr K (2013). *Psychotherapy for the People: toward a progressive psychoanalysis.* New York, NY: Routledge; and Berke J (2015). *The Hidden Freud: his Hassidic roots.* London: Karnac.

18. Here, I acknowledge the work of Otto Gross, Erich Mühsam and Johannes Nohl – see Heuer G (2009). The sacral revolution.

International Journal of Jungian Studies 1(1): 68–80; and Heuer G (2017a). *Freud's 'Outstanding' Colleague/Jung's 'Twin Brother'*. London: Routledge.

19. Here I am thinking of the work within the person-centred tradition of Brian Thorne. In 2009, the Society for the Psychology of Religion and Spirituality, a Division of the American Psychological Association, launched a journal titled *Psychology of Religion and Spirituality* (www.apa.org/pubs/journals/rel/).

20. Freud S (1959/1926). The question of lay analysis: conversations with an impartial person. In: Strachey J (ed & trans). *The Standard Edition of the Complete Psychological Works of Sigmund Freud, vol 20.* London: Hogarth Press (pp183–250) (p248).

21. Freud S (1959/1926). The question of lay analysis: conversations with an impartial person. Postscript. In: Strachey J (ed & trans). *The Standard Edition of the Complete Psychological Works of Sigmund Freud, vol 20.* London: Hogarth Press (pp251–258) (p252).

22. Freud S (1959/1926).

23. American Psychiatric Association (2013). *Diagnostic and Statistical Manual of Mental Disorders* (5th ed). Washington, DC: APA.

24. See Kovacs AL (1996). We have met the enemy and he is us. *AAP Advance*, winter: 19. Also Eisner D (2000). *The Death of Psychotherapy: from Freud to alien abductions.* Westport, CT: Praeger; and Nursing Times (2013). Controversy over *DSM–5*: new mental health guide. *Nursing Times*; 24 August. www.nursingtimes.net/controversy-over-dsm-5-new-mental-health-guide/5062548.article (accessed April 2017); and van der Kolk B (2014). *The Body Keeps the Score: brain, mind, and body in the healing of trauma.* London: Viking.

25. Mowbray R (1995). *The Case Against Psychotherapy Registration: a conservation issue for the human potential movement.* London: Trans Marginal Press (p14).

26. Collens P (2017). Personal e-mail communication, 31 May.

27. Lewes GH (1864). *Aristotle: a chapter from the history of science, including analyses of Aristotle's scientific writings.* London: Smith & Elder.

28. Jung CG (1971/1921). Psychological types: definitions. In: Jung CG. *The Collected Works of C G Jung, vol 6* (RFC Hull trans). Princeton, NJ: Princeton University Press (pp408–486) (definition 48, para 797).

29. Harari YN (2011). *Sapiens: a brief history of humankind.* London: Vintage Books.

30. Sartre J-P (1958/1943) (p569).

31. Kelly G (1991/1955). *The Psychology of Personal Constructs.* London: Routledge. See also Bannister D, Fransella F (1986/1971). *Inquiring Man: the psychology of personal constructs* (3rd ed). London: Croom Helm.

32. Created by David Shakow – see Baker DB, Benjamin Jr LT (2000). The affirmation of the scientist-practitioner: a look back at Boulder. *American Psychologist* 55(2): 241–247.
33. Attributed to Heraclitus of Ephesus (c535–c475 BCE).
34. van Deurzen-Smith E (1996). Existential therapy. In: Dryden W (ed). *Handbook of Individual Therapy*. London: Sage (pp166–193) (p169).
35. Rogers CR (1957). A note on 'The Nature of Man'. *Journal of Counseling Psychology* 4(3): 199–202 (p200).
36. Freud S (1963). Letter to Oskar Pfister, 9 October 1918. In: Meng H, Freud EL (eds). *Psychoanalysis and Faith: the letters of Sigmund Freud and Oskar Pfister* (E Mosbacher trans). New York, NY: Basic Books (p61).
37. Paul R (1993). Conversation. In: Esterle J, Cluman D (eds). *Conversations with Critical Thinkers*. San Francisco, CA: The Whitman Institute (pp91–101) (p95).
38. Sartre J-P (1958/1943) (p569).
39. Asay TR, Lambert MJ (1999). The empirical case of the common factors in psychotherapy: quantitative findings. In: Hubble MA, Duncan BL, Miller SD (eds). *The Heart and Soul of Change: what works in therapy*. Washington DC: American Psychological Association (pp23–55).
40. Ferenczi S (1993). Letter from Sandor Ferenczi to Sigmund Freud, 22 March 1910. In: Brabant E, Falzeder E, Giampieri-Deutsch P (eds & trans). *The Correspondence of Sigmund Freud and Sandor Ferenczi, 1908–1914, vol 1*. Cambridge, MH: Harvard University Press.
41. Heuer G (2017b). Personal e-mail communication, 4 June. See also: Heuer G (2017a).
42. Marx K (1975/1888). Theses on Feuerbach. In: Benton G (trans). *Karl Marx: early writings*. Harmondsworth: Penguin (pp421–423).
43. See, for instance: Sahlins M (1972). *Stone Age Economics*. New York, NY: de Gruyter – a book that influenced my thinking on this point.
44. Buber M (1999/1951). Healing through meeting. In: Agassi JB (ed). *Martin Buber on Psychology and Psychotherapy: essays, letters and dialogue*. New York, NY: Syracuse University Press (pp17–21) (p21).
45. Sartre J-P (1958/1943) (p569).
46. Angyal A (1941). *Foundations for a Science of Personality*. New York, NY: Commonwealth Fund.
47. Winnicott DW (1957/1947). Further thoughts on babies as persons. In: Winnicott DE. *The Child and the Outside World: studies in developing relationships* (J Hardenburg ed). London: Tavistock Publications (pp134–140).

48. Klein GS (1976). *Psychoanalytic Theory: an exploration of essentials.* New York, NY: International Universities Press.
49. Tudor K (2016). 'We are': the fundamental life position. *Transactional Analysis Journal* 46(2): 164–176.
50. It is also the subject of a book written by the Dutch historian and cultural theorist Johan Huizinga: Huizinga J (1955/1938). *Homo Ludens; a study of the play-element in culture.* Boston, MA: Beacon Press.
51. See Winnicott DW (1971). *Playing and Reality.* London: Tavistock Publications.
52. Tudor K, Summers G (2014). *Co-creative Transactional Analysis: papers, responses and developments.* London: Karnac; and Summers G, Tudor K (2000). Cocreative transactional analysis. *Transactional Analysis Journal* 30(1): 23–40.
53. See Stevenson L (1987/1974). *Seven Theories of Human Nature* (2nd ed). Oxford: Oxford University Press.
54. For a collection of essays that explore the relationship between these concepts, see Bulkeley K (2005). *Soul, Psyche, Brain: new directions in the study of religion in brain-mind science.* New York, NY: Palgrave Macmillan.
55. See Cozollino L (2010). *The Neuroscience of Psychotherapy: healing the social brain* (2nd ed). New York, NY: Norton & Co; and Rossouw P (2014). *Neuropsychotherapy: theoretical underpinnings and clinical applications.* St Lucia: Mediros.
56. See, for example, Arden J (1997). *Brain2Brain: enacting client change through the persuasive power of neuroscience.* New York, NY: Wiley; and Arden J (2008). *Brain-based Therapy with Adults: evidence-based treatment for everyday practice.* New York, NY: Wiley.
57. Geertz C (2000). *Available Light: anthropological reflections on philosophical topics.* Princeton, NY: Princeton University Press (p210).
58. See Rosenzweig S (1936). Some implicit common factors in diverse methods of psychotherapy. *American Journal of Orthopsychiatry* 6(3): 412–415.
59. Tudor K, Worrall M (2006). *Person-Centred Therapy: a clinical philosophy.* London: Routledge (p148).
60. American Psychiatric Association (2013). *Diagnostic and Statistical Manual of Mental Disorders* (5th ed). Washington, DC: APA (p645).
61. One of the great strengths of Duncan and Miller's work on *The Heroic Client* is their acknowledgement that the client has a theory of change.
62. Renik O (2006). *Practical Psychoanalysis for Therapists and Patients.* New York, NY: Other Press.
63. Stevens JO (1971). *Awareness: exploring, experimenting, experiencing.* Boulder, CO: Real People Press.

64. Heuer points out that Jung's concept of individuation derives from Gross's elaboration of individuality and self, which, in turn, was influenced by Gross's reading of Pyotr Kropotkin's thinking about individualisation. Heuer (2017b). See also Heuer (2017a).
65. Schmidt M (2017). *Individuation and the Self*. [Online.] London: The Society of Analytical Psychology. www.thesap.org.uk/resources/articles-on-jungian-psychology-2/about-analysis-and-therapy/individuation (accessed 17 January 2018).
66. Fordham M (1985). *Explorations into the Self*. London: Academic Press.
67. I am grateful to Louise Embleton Tudor for raising this point.
68. Angyal A (1941). *Foundations for a Science of Personality*. New York, NY: Commonwealth Fund.
69. Maslow AH (1943). A theory of human motivation. *Psychological Review* 50(4): 370–396.
70. Yalom I (1967). *The Theory and Practice of Group Psychotherapy*. New York, NY: Basic Books.
71. Benjamin J (1995). Recognition and destruction: an outline of intersubjectivity. In: Benjamin J. *Like Subjects, Love Objects: essays on recognition and sexual difference*. New Haven, CT: Yale University Press (pp27–48).
72. Keyes CLM (1998). Social well-being. *Social Psychology Quarterly* 61(2): 121–140.
73. See Hartmann H (1958). *Ego Psychology and the Problem of Adaptation* (D Rapaport trans). Madison, CT: International Universities Press.
74. Piaget J (1977). *Knowledge and Development*. New York, NY: Springer.
75. For a response to which see UKCP (2017). *UK organisations unite against Conversion Therapy*. Press release, 16 January. [Online.] London: UKCP. www.psychotherapy.org.uk/news/uk-organisations-unite-against-conversion-therapy (accessed 12 December 2017).
76. A slogan on the cover of the book collated by The Radical Therapist Collective (1971). *The Radical Therapist*. (J Agel producer/ed). New York, NY: Ballantine Books.
77. Carl Rogers, in Rogers CR, Russell DE (2002). *Carl Rogers, the Quiet Revolutionary: an oral history*. Roseville, CA: Penmarin Books (p259).
78. See Tudor K, Worrall M (2006). *Person-Centred Therapy: a clinical philosophy*. London,: Routledge.
79. Shakespeare W (2003/1603). *Hamlet* (P Edwards ed). Cambridge: Cambridge University Press (Act 1, Scene 3, lines 78–81).
80. Tudor & Worrall (2006) (p157).

81. Craib I (1994). *The Importance of Disappointment.* London: Routledge (p168).
82. Ogden T (2005). *This Art of Psychoanalysis.* London: Routledge (p8).
83. Steiner C (1971). Radical psychiatry: principles. In: The Radical Therapist Collective (1971). *The Radical Therapist.* (Producer/ed J Agel.) New York, NY: Ballantine Books.
84. In their writings, the American radical therapists acknowledged the influence on their thinking and work of, among others, Marx, Engels, Reich, Erich Fromm, Simone de Beauvoir, Fritz Fanon, RD Laing and Adrienne Rich.
85. I should say that I always appreciate this question, as I think it's a good opportunity and good practice to be able to say what psychotherapy is in lay language. Indeed, I recommend to students that they practise answering this question.
86. See Tudor K, Hargaden H (2002). The couch and the ballot box: the contribution and potential of psychotherapy in enhancing citizenship. In: Feltham C (ed). *What's the Good of Counselling and Psychotherapy? The benefits explained.* London: Sage (pp156–178).
87. Stark M (1999). *Modes of Therapeutic Action: enhancement of knowledge, provision of experience, and engagement in relationship.* Northvale, NJ: Jason Aronson.
88. Tudor K (2011). Understanding empathy. *Transactional Analysis Journal* 41(1): 39–57.
89. Freud S (1955/1919). Lines of advance in psycho-analytic therapy. In: Strachey J (ed & trans). *The Standard Edition of the Complete Psychological Works of Sigmund Freud, vol 17.* London: Hogarth Press (pp157–168) (p167). For a collection that reclaims and advances the progressive and humanistic origins of psychoanalysis, see Aron L, Starr K (2013). *Psychotherapy for the People: toward a progressive psychoanalysis.* New York, NY: Routledge.
90. Between Freud and Adler (in 1911), Freud and Stekel (1912), Freud and Jung (1913/1914), Freud and Rank (1924), and Freud and Reich (1934).
91. For a discussion of Ancient Greek psychotherapy, see Kourkouta L (2002). Ancient Greek psychotherapy for contemporary nurses. *Journal of Psychosocial Nursing and Mental Health Services* 40(8): 36–39.
92. Grob GN (1966). *The State and the Mentally Ill: a history of Worcester State Hospital in Massachusetts, 1830–1920.* Durham, NC: University of North Carolina Press (p11).
93. For further details of which, see Cautin RL (2010). A century of psychotherapy, 1860–1960. In: Norcross JC, VandenBos GR, Freedheim DK (eds). *History of Psychotherapy: continuity and change.* Washington,

DC: American Psychological Association (pp3–38). Also Beer C (1908). *A Mind that Found Itself.* Pittsburgh, PA: University of Pittsburgh Press; and Tudor K (1996). *Mental Health Promotion: paradigms and practice.* London: Routledge.

94. Caplan E (1998). *Mind Games: American culture and the birth of psychotherapy.* Berkeley, CA: University of California Press.

95. Watson JB (1913). Psychology as the behaviorist views it. *Psychological Review 20*: 158–177 (p158).

96. See Jacoby R (1983). *The Repression of Psychoanalysis.* New York, NY: Basic Books.

97. Freud S (1961/1930). Civilization and its discontents. In: Strachey J (ed & trans). *The Standard Edition of the Complete Psychological Works of Sigmund Freud, vol 21.* London: Hogarth Press (pp57–146) (p72).

98. For a more detailed critique see Tudor K (2013). From humanism to humanistic psychology and back again. *Self & Society: an International Journal for Humanistic Psychology 40*(1): 35–41.

99. Although even psychoanalysis was also developed independently – for instance, in India by Girindrasekhar Bose, for discussion of which see Akhtar S (ed) (2005). *Freud Along the Ganges: psychoanalytic reflections on the people and culture of India.* New York, NY: Other Press.

100. When he visited Hippolyte Bernheim and his colleagues in the 'Nancy School' in France to discuss the use of hypnotism.

101. Herink R (ed) (1980). *The Psychotherapy Handbook: the A-Z handbook to more than 250 psychotherapies as used today.* New York, NY: New American Library.

102. Corsini RJ, Wedding D (eds) (1995). *Current Psychotherapies* (5th ed). Itasca, IL: Peacock Publishers.

103. MacLennan N (1996). *Counselling for Managers.* London: Gower.

104. Freud used this phrase in his essay on 'Civilization and its Discontents', commenting that such differences are frequently found in 'communities with adjoining territories, and related to each other in other ways as well, who are engaged in constant feuds and in ridiculing each other'. Freud S (1961/1930). Civilization and its discontents. In: Strachey J (ed & trans). *The Standard Edition of the Complete Psychological Works of Sigmund Freud, vol 21.* London: Hogarth Press (pp57–146) (p114).

105. Shedler J (2010). The efficacy of psychodynamic psychotherapy. *American Psychologist 65*(2): 98–109.

106. For a comprehensive view of which, see Norcross JC, Goldfried MR (eds) (1992). *Handbook of Psychotherapy Integration.* New York, NY: Basic Books.

107. See Clarkson P (1995). *The Therapeutic Relationship.* London: Whurr.

108. Clarkson P (1989). Beyond schoolism. *Changes* *16*(1): 1–11.

109. Samuels A (1989). Analysis and pluralism: the politics of psyche. *Journal of Analytical Psychology* *34*(1): 33–51.

110. House R (2010). *In, Against and Beyond Therapy: critical essays towards a 'post-professional' era.* Ross-on-Wye: PCCS Books.

111. According to the American philosopher Francesco Ferrando, the term 'post-humanism' has a number of meanings, including anti-humanism – ie. theory that is critical of traditional humanism and its ideas about humanity and the human condition; cultural post-humanism – a branch of cultural theory, one aspect of which is the deconstruction of the human condition; philosophical post-humanism, which focuses on the ethical implications of extending the focus of moral philosophy to beyond human species; transhumanism, which looks at technologies to eliminate ageing and enhance human capacities; the replacement of humans by artificial intelligence; and voluntary human extinction. See Ferrando F (2013). Posthumanism, transhumanism, antihumanism, metahumanism, and new materialisms: differences and relations. *Existenz* *8*(2): 26–32. www.existenz.us/volumes/Vol.8-2Ferrando.pdf (accessed 8 February 2017).

112. Currently these are bioenergetics (in Wellington); Hakomi (Napier); Jungian analysis (which training takes place in both New Zealand and Australia); psychodrama (Auckland); relational psychotherapy (Auckland), and transactional analysis (in Auckland, Christchurch, Dunedin, and Wellington). In recent years, training programmes in gestalt, psychoanalytic psychotherapy and self-psychology have all closed.

113. Aron L, Starr K (2013). *Psychotherapy for the People: toward a progressive psychoanalysis.* New York, NY: Routledge (p28). See also Danto EA (2005). *Freud's Free Clinics.* New York, NY: Columbia University Press.

114. This is based on a review of different forms of what I and others view as 'radical therapy'. See Tudor K, Begg K (2016). Radical therapies: a critical review. *The Journal of Critical Psychology, Counselling and Psychotherapy* *16*(2): 81–92.

115. In this table, I have tended to focus on particular forms of radical therapy. I am aware that there are other forms of therapy that are or may be radical, or that have some aspects of radicality – for example, relational psychoanalysis, which is, in part, informed by feminism and analyses of power and of social/cultural context.

116. While this is difficult to date, as, arguably, it has a long history, 'indigenous psychotherapy' has only relatively recently been referred to as such. See Torrey EF (1970). Indigenous psychotherapy: theories and techniques. *Current Psychiatric Therapies* *10*: 118–129.

117. Eysenck H (1952). The effects of psychotherapy: an evaluation. *Journal of Consulting Psychology* *16*: 319–324.

118. Szasz TS (1974a). *Ceremonial Chemistry: the ritual persecution of drugs, addicts and pushers.* Garden City, NY: Anchor Press.
119. Szasz T (1974b). *The Myth of Mental Illness: foundations of the theory of personal conduct.* New York, NY: Harper & Row.
120. Szasz T (1987). *Insanity: the idea and its consequences.* New York, NY: Wiley.
121. Albee G (1990). The futility of psychotherapy. *The Journal of Mind and Behaviour 11*(3&4): 369–384.
122. Housed in the US Library of Congress and Freud's former residence at 20 Maresfield Gardens, London.
123. Masson J (1990). *Against Therapy.* London: Fontana.
124. Smail D (1993). *The Origins of Unhappiness: a new understanding of personal distress.* London: HarperCollins. Also Smail D (2001). *The Nature of Unhappiness.* London: Robinson; and Smail D (2005). *Power, Interest and Psychology.* Ross-on-Wye: PCCS Books.
125. Eisner D (2000). *The Death of Psychotherapy: from Freud to alien abductions.* Westport, CT: Praeger. In one passage he summarises what he refers to as 'five fictions' that the past century of psychoanalysis has perpetuated: that psychoanalysis is superior to other forms of therapy; that analysing the transference relationships is necessary for a successful analysis and can be accurately measured; that dream interpretation and free association are valid investigatory tools that chip away at and reveal the unconscious; that at the root of neurosis is repressed sexual infantile conflicts, and that psychoanalysts have identified the active therapeutic ingredients that are responsible for producing change in behaviour (p37).
126. Feltham C (2013). *Counselling and Counselling Psychology: a critical examination.* Ross-on-Wye: PCCS Books.
127. Morrall P (2008). *The Trouble with Therapy: sociology and psychotherapy.* Maidenhead: Open University Press.
128. France A (1988). *Consuming Psychotherapy.* London: Free Association Books.
129. Heyward C (1993). *When Boundaries Betray Us: beyond illusions of what is ethical in therapy and life.* San Francisco, CA: Harper.
130. Alexander R (1995). *Folie à Deux: an experience of one-to-one therapy.* London: Free Association Books.
131. Sands A (2000). *Falling for Therapy: psychotherapy from a client's point of view.* Basingstoke: Palgrave.
132. Bates Y (ed) (2006). *Shouldn't I Be Feeling Better by Now?* Basingstoke: Palgrave Macmillan.

CHAPTER 3

Methods, practice and praxis

> First there is experiencing, then there is a theory.
> (Carl Rogers and John K Wood)[1]

From an experiential perspective, practice comes before theory. I experienced psychotherapy as a client before undertaking a training course (the implications of which I discuss further in Chapter 7). Although, as a practising social worker and counsellor, I had experience of working with clients, as a trainee psychotherapist, I practised my psychotherapy skills with my fellow trainees before beginning to see clients for psychotherapy. It is in this spirit that this chapter on critical practice precedes the next chapter on critical knowledge, although, as all practice is based on theory (and method on methodology), this chapter also refers to the theory of practice and the ethics of that practice.[2]

As the subject of this chapter is the practice of psychotherapy, it is focused more on what the psychotherapist or practitioner does. That said, I also discuss the implications of practice and method for what the client does or is expected to do. Most methods in psychotherapy began in the context of working with individuals, and have subsequently been applied to and in other forms of therapy (child and adolescent psychotherapy, couples therapy, group therapy etc). However, some forms of therapy – for instance, psychodrama and group analysis – have developed their practice and theory in the context of working with groups.

Given there is such a wide variation of psychotherapy practices and theories, and of psychotherapies, it is clearly impossible to do justice to them all, let alone offer a critical examination of them. Therefore, I focus here on the more widely known and used. In the first half of the chapter, I discuss a number of common practices or methods in psychotherapy across its different traditions, beginning, appropriately enough, with listening. In the second half, I take a broadly historical look at methods, qualities, attitudes, conditions, skills (including techniques), and competence, and reflect on the significance and implications of these different terms. I conclude with some thoughts about praxis, which, I suggest, should include a new or renewed focus on critical thinking.

Despite certain dogmatic attempts to keep things, including practice, pure, the practice of psychotherapy has developed and changed over the years. Moreover, some of the founding fathers appear to have been less dogmatic than their disciples, although this is perhaps less surprising than it appears: founders may be the innovators, but their disciples are often the ones who consolidate and instutionalise the innovation, and thus become dogmatic. As Adam Phillips observes: 'Disciples are the people who haven't got the joke.'[3] Just about 100 years ago, Freud himself was advocating an openness to adapting his technique. In the context of describing his vision for free clinics, he wrote:

> We shall then be faced by the task of adapting a technique to the new conditions... we shall need to look for the simplest and most easily intelligible ways of expressing theoretical doctrines... It is very probable, too, that the large-scale application of therapy will compel us to alloy the pure gold of analysis freely with the copper of direct suggestion.[4]

For his part, Rogers, whose person-centred therapy reputedly eschews techniques, believed: 'The techniques of the various therapies are relatively unimportant except to the extent that they serve as channels for fulfilling one of the conditions.'[5] He then went on to illustrate this by describing 'reflecting feelings' as a technique that communicates a sensitive empathy and an unconditional positive regard.

Methods

Here, as a way of encompassing psychotherapeutic practice across theoretical orientations or modalities, I identify seven methods: listening, analysing, directing, touching, empathising, confronting and minding, and under each heading I briefly discuss key aspects of the method. I should make it clear that these methods do not correlate with the seven concepts I describe in Chapter 2, although listening, analysing, directing, touching, empathising, confronting and minding do, in various ways, facilitate and further the purpose of insight, individuation, connection, adaptation, cure, authenticity and liberation. Writing about existential psychoanalysis, Sartre suggested that its method was comparative:

> Since each example of human conduct symbolises in its own manner the fundamental choice which must be brought to light, and since at the same time each one disguises this choice under its occasional character and its historical opportunity, only the comparison of these acts of conduct can affect the emergence of the unique revelation which they all express in a different way.[6]

Listening

Psychotherapy is commonly referred to as 'the talking cure', and certainly, from the client's perspective, this is true. It is, however, interesting to note that, while this phrase is attributed to 'Anna O', one of Freud's early patients, she was, in fact, commenting on the value of 'the *listening cure*' – that is, what the psychoanalyst or psychotherapist needed, and needs, to do[7] – and thereby provided perhaps the first-known piece of 'practice-based evidence' (a concept I discuss further in Chapter 6). In the circumstances, this appears a somewhat strange reinterpretation, but it is perhaps significant as it puts the emphasis (talking) and responsibility back on to the patient/client.

Clearly, psychotherapists need to listen, and, as Søren Kierkegaard argued, 'The ear is the most spiritually determined of the senses.'[8] Drawing on the philosophy of Heidegger, Peter Wilberg regards listening as the missing dimension of counselling and psychotherapy, as, in his view, the listening that is taught and practised in therapy is more about 'doing to' rather than 'being with'.[9] The first training in therapy I did (in the early 1980s) was with Peter Fleming at the Pellin Institute in London, and in Montecorice in Italy. Early on in the training, Peter gave us a paper on what he identified as seven levels of listening – categories that I found, and still find, useful, and use here to frame some thoughts on listening.[10]

1. Passive listening

This combination of meditation and listening 'aims to blank the mind and let in the other person whole and complete without the interference of the listener's thoughts, assessments, diagnosis, programmes and ideas'.[11] In order to listen, the listener needs to be able to be quiet, and to quieten their own inner world, including any distractions that might interfere with their ability to listen. This leads psychotherapists to be able to be silent and to hold a silence, but herein lies a problem, in that silence can become oppressive and lead to what Ann France refers to as 'the cult of silence'.[12] Another consumer, Anna Sands, refers to the 'stony silence' of a psychoanalyst who then spent time asking her patient about why she (the patient) found this discomforting.[13]

2. Listening to content

This is based on the conventional notion of listening but enhanced by practice and discipline. My social work training in the 1980s included the practice of conducting an interview with a client and, afterwards, making extensive notes (process recordings) on what they had said. These notes, in those days hand-written, ran to between half a dozen and a dozen pages. With this discipline, in a short time, my listening and recall improved considerably. Of course, this listening will be affected by conscious and unconscious editing, such as forgetting or mis-remembering.

3. Listening to the obvious

In his original notes on this level of listening, Fleming writes about having a verbal (aural) and visual 'bird's eye view of what is being presented'[14] and acknowledges the phenomenological basis of this. The 'obvious' includes the first thing the client says, slips of the tongue, repetition, themes, 'door-handle confessions', and so on. Being open to this level of listening requires what Freud refers to as 'evenly hovering' or 'evenly suspended attention',[15] or the even treatment of what is said, which phenomenologists refer to as horizontalisation.[16]

4. Listening to the message in the voice

This level of listening focuses on 'the character and the quality of a person's voice without regard to the content of the words'.[17] Here the listener is attuning to the rhythm, pitch, volume and emotional content of the client's voice. My own experience of practising this involved passive listening (preferably with my eyes closed), in order to distinguish the voice from the content (although, in his notes on this level of listening, Fleming cautions against being too quick to diagnose on the basis of this message alone).

5. The emotional response of listening

This is listening with our gut, to our intuition, and to our countertransferential, and transferential, responses to the client, in response to the above ways of listening.

6. Listening for goodwill

This level is concerned with listening and assessing the client's willingness to consider the possibility of change. It may involve listening for inconsistencies, incongruence (person-centred psychology), or ulterior transactions or psychological games (transactional analysis). Interestingly, Robin Shohet has argued that, since observing confidentiality relies on a person's goodwill, we would be better contracting with the client for goodwill than for confidentiality.[18]

7. Listening for internal logic

This level is 'the coming together of all the parts into a whole. It is the combining of the material being presented now with material presented in [or from] the past'.[19]

Any model of listening raises some questions as to the purpose of listening: for instance, whether it is enough that the psychotherapist listens in order that the client can be introspective; whether the fact that the psychotherapist is listening is in itself therapeutic or curative; whether the psychotherapist is listening in order to know something about the client for later use (as Kohut proposes), and/or whether the psychotherapist needs to communicate that they have heard what the client is saying. On the second point, Rogers was very clear:

> To my mind, empathy is in itself a healing agent. It is one of the most potent aspects of therapy, because it releases, it confirms, it brings even the most frightened client into the human race. If a person can be understood, he or she belongs.[21]

On the last point, Rogers was also very clear. The sixth of his conditions for therapy is: 'That the client perceives, at least to a minimal degree, conditions four and five, [ie.] the unconditional positive regard of the therapist for him and the empathic understanding of therapist.'[21] Elsewhere, Rogers described this as 'the assumed condition',[22] and it is certainly the most important condition, as it is the one by which the client experiences and, in effect, assesses the therapy. Rogers adds: 'It is also well to point out that it is the client's experience of this condition which makes it optimal, not merely the fact of its existence in the therapist.'[23]

This point makes it clear that the client not only needs to talk but also needs to listen to whether the therapist is listening. In effect, this method requires the client to be open to relating their experience(s), to engage with their therapist, and to be able to be active in doing so in order to impact on this talking/listening relationship. In this sense, we should perhaps be reclaiming the concept of *homo audiens*.[24]

Analysing

Arguably, the most famous method of psychotherapy is contained in the word 'psychoanalysis' – that is, the analysis of the psyche, and, specifically, the analysis of the unconscious through dreams, transference and resistance. The most common form of analysis is individual, whereby the analyst analyses the analysand (patient or client), who, traditionally, lies on a couch and talks and associates freely. There are, however, other forms, including mutual analysis, with which Gross and Jung originally experimented[25] and that Ferenczi later developed, especially in work with difficult patients.[26] There are also other forms of therapy that use analysis: for instance, transactional analysis, in which transactions between and within people are analysed, usually on the basis of a diagnosis of their ego states.

While most therapists formulate some hypotheses about what the patient or client tells them, ideally the analyst or therapist should only communicate their conclusions *after* the patient or client arrives at their own understanding of what is going on for them. In this sense, a useful interpretation is akin to accurate empathy.

From a critical perspective, the main problem with analysis lies in the power dynamic between analyst and analysand, which is represented in the term itself that is traditionally used to describe the patient or client. This power finds particular expression in the concept of analysability: the notion that some patients are unanalysable, according to the analyst.

Directing

I include this as a method for a number of reasons: first, to acknowledge the history of psychotherapy, which originally included hypnosis, suggestion, persuasion and re-education; second, to include methods associated with the behaviourial tradition, which are now used by many psychotherapists, and third, to include psychodrama and other creative-expressive therapies in which the therapist directs the client in some way.

Although psychoanalysis and behaviourism would generally be viewed as not having a lot in common, it is perhaps useful to note that some of its techniques (as above) used by early psychotherapists and psychoanalysts were quite behavioural, although they dropped them relatively quickly. Nowadays, it is practitioners of cognitive behavioural therapy who are, perhaps, the most directive of clients, specifically in relation to thought distortions and maladaptive behaviour. Their techniques commonly include, for instance, teaching new information-processing skills, self-instructions (motivational self-talk, distraction etc), relaxation exercises etc, identifying adaptive coping strategies with the client (eg. minimising negative or self-defeating thoughts), and setting goals. There are also forms of family therapy, such as strategic therapy, that use directives – that is, telling a client or family what to do.

In psychodrama, the director is one of five instruments,[27] and has the three functions of producer, counsellor and analyst. As A Paul Hare and June Hare put it: 'As director, attacking and shocking the subject is at times just as permissible as laughing and joking with him; [although] at times he may become indirect and passive and for all practical purposes the session seems to be run by the subject.'[28] Similarly, creative expression therapists will direct clients to dance, draw, move, paint, posture, push, shout, sing, and so on. Some years ago, I had the good fortune to work as part of a small group with Natalie Rogers. During the day, she encouraged us to create a drawing or painting, first singly then collectively. As I went to take a paintbrush, she suggested that I choose crayons. When I asked why, she said that she thought I might find it more immediate if I used a medium with which I had direct physical contact through my fingers (rather than the paint at the end of a paintbrush) – and, therapeutically, she was absolutely right. Discussing this with her afterwards, she explained that, as a creative expressive therapist, she was not afraid to direct someone, and, in that sense, she differed from her father's more non-directive therapeutic approach. It is not insignificant that, to the two conditions that Carl Rogers' identified as fostering creativity – that is, psychological safety and psychological freedom and permissiveness[29] – Natalie Rogers added a third, that of offering stimulating and challenging experiences.[30]

The problem with directing and, more broadly, with directivity in psychotherapy is twofold: power, and methodology. Telling – even suggesting to – someone what to do brings with it an enormous responsibility, especially for the consequences of the client's actions, should they do what they are directed to do. Moreover, philosophically, depending on their views of human nature and the nature of change etc (for discussion of which, see Chapter 4), most psychotherapists would perhaps object to directing the end (such as a particular action), as distinct from directing the therapeutic means (ie. the process).[31]

Some therapists base their work very clearly on a contract, and thus justify their directing of the client on that basis. However, some forms of direction, such as the paradoxical injunction (whereby the therapist says something directive in order to provoke the client *not* to do what therapist has said) is based on deliberate manipulation and surprise and, therefore, is not amenable to a predetermined contract.

Touching

Although Freud himself applied the use of the 'pressure technique' (to the head),[32] by 1904 he had abandoned this as a technique, explicitly remarking that he avoided touching his patients.[33] Since then, psychoanalysis has predominantly excluded physical contact between analysts and their patients. However, while there has always been something of a taboo in psychotherapy about touching clients, psychotherapists have always done so, although they have not always admitted it or articulated a rationale for it. Berne would shake hands with his patients, but only after they had established a therapeutic alliance. Such abstinence may be highly professional, but it may also be highly defensive:[34] notwithstanding the appropriate prohibition on inappropriate touch, not touching at all may be experienced by the client as somewhat inhuman, for, as Jules Older suggests:

Touching	Not-touching
is not a	is a
technique:	technique.[35]

While any contact that is sexual or sexualised is not appropriate, and is unprofessional, unethical and, in some circumstances, illegal, most physical contact and touch between therapist and client or supervisor/trainer and supervisee/trainee, such as a handshake or other form of greeting, or even a hug, may be considered and experienced as appropriate. Of course, touch is highly contextual, in the sense that its meaning is affected and mediated, especially and specifically, by culture and gender.

Moreover, there is a tradition of body psychotherapy, much of which does involve the use of therapeutic touch, often in the form of massage. This derives from Reich, especially his work on character analysis,[36] and has been taken forward by Alexander Lowen, who developed bioenergetic analysis,[37] and by others, including more recent neo-Reichians.[38] It is arguably the most sensitive method or practice, as it both requires the client to be more vulnerable and, to some extent, makes them so, precisely in order to break or move through their character structure or somatic defences. This tradition has also been influential outside its own modality, as evidenced in more recent years by the fact that other theoretical orientations/modalities are discussing their own understanding of the body and the somatic.

From a critical perspective, touch and/or physical contact with clients is a profoundly delicate matter, however positively it is used, as the impact of its misuse, and the implications of re-traumatising previously traumatised clients, are equally significant. For this reason, the therapeutic use of touch is perhaps best undertaken judiciously and in the context of group work, where it can be witnessed by others.

Touching is also used in a more metaphorical sense, as in 'I'm touched by that', or 'What you said was very touching' (which is similar to the way that the word 'holding' is used). While, in some ways, both reflect common usage, it is also significant that the word used is 'touch', as it suggests a certain desire not only for the feeling but also for the physicality – and, perhaps, for physical contact (ie. to be held and/or touched), alongside the feeling.

Empathising

Empathy has a long history. It is the basis of connecting, or having what Adler referred to as *Gemeinschaftsgefühl* or 'fellow feeling', and of understanding, and is a method or practice in most, if not all, theoretical orientations.[39] Here I distinguish between *empathising* as a method or practice and *being empathic* as a quality (for further discussion of which, see pp95–96 below).

Rogers' concept of empathic understanding stands in a tradition of psychology that contrasts understanding (*Verstehen*) with explanation (*Erklaren*)[40] – a distinction that underpins the concept of empathic understanding in person-centred therapy and distinguishes it from other therapies that seek to analyse, interpret or explain.[41] Another key distinction with regard to empathy is the difference between Rogers' view of empathy as in itself curative and Kohut's view that empathy is an 'information-gathering activity', used in order to make accurate interpretations. This distinction not only informs the therapist's motivation for empathising; it also represents different theoretical viewpoints about empathy, methodology and method.

While Rogers tends to refer to empathic *understanding*, neither the experience of empathy nor the object of the therapist's empathy or empathising is confined to the mind, the intellect or the cognitive aspect of the person. From a holistic perspective, our empathising is affective, behavioural, cognitive, political, somatic, spiritual and much more. In this sense, it may be more accurate to think and talk about 'resonating' than empathising – a word that echoes our human capacity for limbic resonance and links this method to the theory of limbic regulation.[42]

Usually, the direction of such empathising or resonating is from the therapist to the client, although in couple therapy the emphasis is generally on helping the partners to empathise or resonate with each other, and in group work the empathy of other group members can be a powerful and curative factor. Finally on this, empathy is not something that a person receives passively: there is a view that the client needs to empathise with the therapist's empathy in order to receive or resonate with it.

Confronting

This method encompasses a range of practice, from the relatively gentle posing of an alternative view to more brutal forms of 'attack therapies', such as those promoted by Synanon.[43] Berne defines confrontation as the use of information previously elicited 'in order to disconcert the patient's Parent, Child or contaminated Adult by pointing out an inconsistency'.[44] Peter Schmid explores the concept and practice of encounter in person-centred psychology (where it is most commonly used in the context of the 'encounter group'), and points out: 'The word meaning [of encounter] points to the "against", indicating vis-à-vis as well as resistance.'[45] He reconceptualises the meaning of 'en-counter' in terms of philosophy, dialogical anthropology, theology and personality development, and argues that 'each encounter involves meeting reality and being touched by the essence of the opposite'.[46]

More broadly, John Heron suggests: 'Confronting interventions directly challenge the rigid and maladaptive attitudes/beliefs/actions that limit the client or unnecessarily disturb or limit others, and of which the individual is defensively unaware – to a greater or lesser degree.'[47] He continues: 'In personal development work, confronting interventions seek to raise consciousness about conventional and compulsive states of the person.'

Confronting interventions can – and, indeed, should – be powerful, but they can also be experienced as humiliating, and, therefore, the method needs to be used judiciously. Significantly, in his theory of therapeutic operations, Berne placed confrontation after interrogation (or, better, asking questions), specification and explanation, suggesting that it should only be done if the therapist has significant information about the client and has developed a therapeutic alliance with them.

Minding

This method refers both to the practice of mindfulness and, I suggest, to the therapist's practice of paying attention to and caring about the broader context of the client's (as well as their own) life. Generally, mindfulness refers to the quality or state of being conscious or aware of something; more specifically, with regard both to spiritual and psychotherapeutic practice, it refers to focusing one's awareness on the present moment and acknowledging and accepting all of one's feelings, bodily sensations and thoughts. As Jon Kabat-Zinn puts it: 'Mindfulness means paying attention in a particular way: on purpose, in the present moment, and non-judgementally.'[48] This is consistent with practice across a number of therapeutic modalities, and with Stern's work on the present moment.[49] There is an increasing interest in mindfulness across different therapeutic approaches, and it has been influential in the development of the third wave of cognitive behavioural therapy.[50] Commenting on meditation and meaning, Jeff Harrison acknowledges that the term 'mindfulness' is perhaps misleading, 'for it does not extrapolate a substantial separate self (mind) from ever-changing, emergent phenomena, nor does it sustain self-defensive epistemologies as forms of mastery over the world/self'.[51]

I agree with Harrison and suggest an extension – or, perhaps, an extended application – of the practice of mindfulness to *minding*, which includes the world outside the individual. This would involve a consciousness not only of the immediate environment (such as the consulting room), but also of the environment outside – a perspective that is central in therapeutic approaches informed by ecopsychology. Such minding would or should extend further to include those extra-psychotherapeutic factors that influence the client's therapeutic outcome (see Chapter 6), and the social/political world.

Four reflections on method(s)

No doubt, by now, the reader will have noticed the use of the gerund (the 'ing' form of the verb) to describe (these) psychotherapeutic method(s). This is intentional in that, when talking about practice and relationship (as in the therapeutic relationship), I generally do so by using verbs or verb forms, thus therapeutic *relating*.[52] This usage encourages thinking about practice as an action (or acting), as distinct from a thing (a noun). Also, arguably, this form opens up the method or activity as involving two parties and engaging both – a point that emphasises the co-constructive nature of therapy. Therapy is about people listening to and perhaps mutually analysing each other; co-directing; touching appropriately and with mutual consent; co-empathising; confronting, and/or minding about each other. This also represents what Webb refers to as 'description therapy', as distinct from 'prescription therapy'.[53]

Related to the first point is a second on the theme of power. From a critical perspective, all method(s), including the ones discussed here, are – or should be – subject to an analysis of power.

As Glen Larner puts it:

> A deconstructing psychotherapy is obliged to be both powerful *and* non-powerful. It is the presence of this ambiguity of power in therapy which is conducive to change. That therapists can be powerful, but sacrifice themselves for the sake of the other, allows the power of the other to emerge.[54]

Thus, when listening, analysing, directing, (perhaps especially) touching, empathising, confronting, and/or minding, the deconstructive therapist needs to address issues and questions of power, justice and ethics, *in practice*. Examples of such questions are:

- Do I listen more attentively to my female clients than to my male clients?
- Am I impatient to share what I think is a particularly important interpretation?
- Do I talk differently to clients of different social status?
- If I touch my clients, am I touching them appropriately, and do I differentiate between different clients with regard to touch?
- How do I express empathy to clients of different age, class, ethnicity, gender, race and sexuality?
- Which clients do I confront more, and why?
- Which clients do I think about when I'm not at work, and why?

Third, these and other methods are both personal and contextual in that they are mediated by the person of the practitioner – and, of course, by how they are received and experienced by the client: one person's mild confrontation is another's devastating rebuke. Moreover, methods and practice in general are difficult to monitor, in that it is difficult to assess what psychotherapists actually *do* in their practice. As Craig Newnes points out in his volume in this series,[55] a clinical psychologist can qualify (at least in the UK) having had, at most, about 70 hours of supervised practice and only a few hours of 'live' supervision – ie. where the supervisor sits in on the session, which, of course, makes the session somewhat artificial. In psychotherapy education/training, both requirements are greater, although it is still difficult to see and assess practice.

Finally, while I think this is a useful summary of psychotherapeutic method(s), I am not claiming it is comprehensive. All approaches to therapy have their method(s), and, over the years, a number of practitioners have developed their own frameworks for practice, some of whom have proposed a meta-theoretical framework. One example of this is Heron's six categories of intervention, in which he describes two styles of intervention, the authoritative and the facilitative, each of which comprise three categories: respectively, the prescriptive, informative and confronting, and the cathartic, catalytic and supportive.[56] In Table 3.1, I suggest where the seven methods I identify exemplify Heron's categories.

Table 3.1 – The seven methods in terms of Heron's category analysis

Methods/practice	... in terms of Heron's six-category analysis
Listening	Facilitative – catalytic and supportive
Analysing	Authoritative – prescriptive and informative Facilitative – catalytic
Directing	Authoritative – prescriptive, informative and confronting Facilitative – cathartic
Touching	Authoritative – prescriptive Facilitative – cathartic and catalytic
Empathising	Facilitative – catalytic and supportive
Confronting	Authoritative – confronting
Minding	Facilitative – catalytic and supportive

From methods to competencies

The psychotherapeutic practice(s) described in the first part of this chapter reflect a variety of method(s) that have been variously developed as a result of practice, experimentation and speculation, supported by theory and research. Alongside the development of these methods, a number of practitioners and theoreticians have commented on other aspects of practice that I would categorise as comprising qualities, attitudes, conditions, skills and competencies.

I also view these as terms that reflect a broadly chronological scope of the development of psychotherapy practice, and an increasing concern to measure, assess and standardise its practice.

Qualities

The practice of psychotherapy has never been simply a question of techniques, skills or competencies. Freud himself said that the psychoanalyst should possess the personal qualities of discretion, character and trustworthiness,[57] arguing that:

> For the patient, then, it is a matter of indifference whether the analyst is a doctor or not... For him it is incomparably more important that the analyst should possess personal qualities that make him trustworthy, and that he should have acquired the knowledge and understanding as well as the experience which alone can make it possible for him to fulfil his task.[58]

Most of the pioneers of psychotherapy, at some point, talked and/or wrote about the qualities of the psychoanalyst/psychotherapist, including having a liking for and interest in the patient (Sandor Ferenzci),[59] and being contactful, authentic, acceptant and empathic (Rogers).[60] Others since have written about having creativity and a capacity for growth (Barry Proner),[61] and having firm mothering and unlimited warmth (Fernando Arroyave).[62]

The personal qualities of the therapist are clearly important, and, precisely because they are personal, their centrality raises two important questions: 1) are they absolutely necessary, or simply desirable, and 2) are they innate, or can they be developed through training?

Attitudes

From the Latin *aptus* and the French *attitude*, the English word attitude carries the sense of both disposition and posture and fitness and aptness, and both elements are to be found in the literature about the desirable and necessary attitudes of the psychotherapist. For many, there is considerable overlap between qualities and attitudes; for others, qualities are more innate and perhaps silent, whereas attitudes are communicated.

The idea that therapy is or involves service, which derives from Taft (see Chapter 1), suggests that the therapist's stance or attitude is one of service, of waiting, and of attending. This challenges the notion of the psychotherapist as expert, of being ahead of the client, or even of being 'alongside the client', which is a phrase commonly used, especially in humanistic therapy. The metaphor of service suggests, perhaps, that the psychotherapist is more *behind* the client – which, interestingly, conjures up an image of the psychoanalyst sitting behind the patient, or welcoming the client as a clinical host.[63]

Arguably, the most famous therapeutic attitudes derive from Rogers' theory of therapeutic conditions.[64] These were derived from Rogers' research into what appeared to work in therapy. Listening to recordings of therapy sessions, he and his colleagues conducted what was, in effect, a coding of the efficacy of the sessions, from which he identified six 'conditions' that, he proposed, were both necessary and sufficient for therapeutic, and, indeed, personality change to take place. For the therapist, there are four:[65] contactfulness; congruence or genuineness; unconditional positive regard, acceptance, or love, and empathic understanding, or empathy, all of which describe the therapist's attitudes as much as explain the conditions of therapy. (The numbering of these points reflects the numbering of the original six conditions (see also p98 below).)

1. Psychological contact

For Rogers, this specifies 'a minimal relationship' in which both therapist and client each 'makes some perceived difference in the experiential field of the other'.[66] In terms of the manifestation of this condition, the attitude is one of engagement, interest and, when necessary, generosity in reaching out to the other.

3. Therapist authenticity

The therapist's ability to be real, genuine, congruent or authentic only comes as a result of considerable personal and professional development, self-knowledge and self-acceptance, insight and self-discipline, and much more. It could – and, from a critical perspective, arguably should – include being critical, in that, as Ian Parker puts it, this 'does not mean finding the correct standpoint but it means understanding how we come to stand where we are'.[67] This is because, for Rogers, 'the therapist's symbolization of his own experience in the relationship must be accurate, if therapy is to be most effective'[68] – a statement that also provides a link between the person-centred concept of congruence and the psychodynamic concept of countertransference.[69] All this manifests in attitudes of humility, openness and, again, engagement.

4. Therapist acceptance

Taft, who influenced Rogers, describes a shift in her thinking, away from seeing therapy as 'a reform of the "other" through superior knowledge of life and psychology' to a therapy that is 'purely individual [ie. specific to the particular individual client], non-moral, non-scientific, non-intellectual, which can take place only when divorced from all hint of control, unless it be the therapist's control of himself in the therapeutic situation'.[70] This offers some background to Stanley Standal's[71] and Rogers' development of the concept and aspiration of what Rogers referred to as 'unconditional positive regard' – a concept that requires, among other things, an even-handed attention to all aspects of the client. This condition manifests in the therapist's attitude of prizing, acceptance, approval, warmth, appreciation and non-possessive love. Such qualities are not confined to humanistic psychologists or psychotherapists. Both Leo Stone, a graduate of the New York Psychoanalytic Institute, and Edith Jacobson, of the Berlin Psychoanalytic Institute, advocated that the analyst could convey warmth while preserving neutrality.[72]

5. Therapist empathy

The difference between a therapist having the quality of being empathic, as distinct from empathising as a method (see pp87–88 above), is one of attitude and posture, based, ultimately, on a hermeneutics of trust rather than mistrust. The therapist *is* empathic because s/he understands or wants to understand the client, because that understanding supports the inherent and positive direction of the organism. Interestingly, Heidegger is not convinced that, as a concept and a practice, empathy sits separately from *Dasein* (being or being-with); rather, he argues that empathy 'does not first constitute being-with; only on the basis of being-with does "empathy" become possible'.[73]

This emphasis on the qualities of the therapist or, more broadly, the helper or facilitator, and the application of Rogers' necessary and sufficient conditions to life outside therapy, has led to the identification and development of what is now referred to as the 'person-centred approach' being regarded as a way of being. This was first proposed and developed by Rogers in his book, *A Way of Being*,[74] and is well summarised by one of his colleagues, John K Wood:

> The person-centered approach... is neither a psychotherapy nor a psychology. It is not a school... itself, it is not a movement... it is not a philosophy. Nor is it any number of other things frequently imagined. It is merely, as its name implies, an approach, nothing more, nothing less. It is a psychological posture, if you like, from which thought or action may arise and experience be organized. It is a 'way of being'.[75]

While the Rogerian way of being emphasises the therapist's disposition and (psychological) posture, Berne's description of therapeutic attitudes reflects more the aspect of fitness and aptness. He advocates that the therapist has 'a fresh frame of mind', which comprises being in good health, both physically and psychologically, and being well prepared, clear and open.[76]

The psychotherapist's attitude, of course, derives from their thinking about the purpose of therapy (see Chapter 2), how they understand this theoretically (see Chapter 4), and the sociopolitical and cultural context of this practice and understanding. For example, Salman Akhtar views what he describes as the 'West–East psychoanalytic discord' as arising from 'the powerful individual and collective orientations of the two societies, respectively. In the West, autonomy and separateness are upheld as ideal to strive for, while in the East, premium is placed upon attachment and interdependence'.⁷⁷ He goes on to link matters of sociological theoretical concern, of optimal distance and optimal closeness, with technical implications of whether patients/clients view their analyst/therapist as a relative or not.

More recently, drawing on ideas from the French philosophers Levinas, Jacques Derrida and Paul Ricoeur, and from both psychoanalytic and humanistic traditions, Donna Orange has developed the theory and practice of 'clinical hospitality'.⁷⁸ She considers the work of these philosophers as offering:

> ... ethical challenges within and around the clinician's daily work... [and] reminders of the vocational aspects of a profession too often mired in the pressures to diagnose and prescribe, to evade and to murder, to totalize and to finalize.⁷⁹

Finally, following Stephen Brookfield, who talks about critical thinking as 'an ongoing mental disposition – a way of examining ourselves and our place in the world that is lifelong',⁸⁰ I propose that psychotherapists should develop more of a critical – and, indeed, argumentative – attitude.⁸¹

Conditions

The idea that there are certain conditions under and by which psychotherapy is effective is predominantly associated with Rogers' research and work. Indeed, his research in the 1950s predated and prefigured much of the more recent interest in 'common factors' research: that is, research that identifies factors common to and across different therapeutic modalities and approaches that account for the effectiveness of psychotherapy and, more broadly, of psychological treatments (see Chapter 6).⁸² In this context, there are a number of points to make about Rogers' approach.

First, given the association of Rogers with client-centred therapy and, subsequently, the person-centred approach, it is worth noting that, in his first formulation of the necessary and sufficient conditions for therapy, published in 1957, he presented his research and this theory as, in effect, an integrative theory, applicable to all therapeutic reationships/approaches.⁸³

Second, echoing philosophical logic, Rogers specifically framed the conditions as 'if..., then...' propositions – in other words, if such and such a condition is present, then change will occur. This construction sets the bar high for the impact of these therapeutic relationship variables.

Third, and perhaps most radically, the theory identifies conditions required of the client, which are (also with reference to the original numbering):

1. Psychological contact (see p94 above)

As this condition applies also to the client, it means that they, too, have to be willing to be in psychological contact and engaged in their therapy.[84]

2. Client incongruence

This refers specifically to an incongruence or inconsistency between the client's experience and their sense of self: ie. 'a discrepancy between the actual experience of the organism and the self picture of the individual insofar as it represents that experience'.[85] This requires the client not only to be vulnerable but also, to a greater or lesser extent, to be open about their vulnerability. While Rogers acknowledged this anxiety at the personal level, Bernie Neville argues for the extension of this to collective anxiety (involving family, workplace, nation, culture etc), species anxiety and planetary anxiety.[86]

6. Client experience and/or perception

Being empathic is a close cousin to being acceptant; indeed, in person-centred psychology, these are often paired as the two therapeutic conditions that need to be communicated to, or at least experienced by, the client in order for therapy and, indeed, personality change, to be successful.

Finally, although originally presented and framed as six 'conditions', over the years these have come to represent therapeutic attitudes, especially, but not exclusively, on the part of the therapist (see 'Attitudes' above),[87] which is another reason why it is a misrepresentation to refer to this theory as one about 'the core conditions'.

Skills

Although the original meaning of 'skill' comes from Old English and Old Norse words for discernment and knowledge, in many fields, including psychotherapy, it generally refers to practice and practical abilities, such as listening skills, assessment skills, ability to make a contract, ability to challenge etc. A significant part of training in psychotherapy is dedicated to skills development, although this varies quite widely between different theoretical orientations, and, arguably, skills training is more associated with counselling than with psychotherapy.[88]

Clearly, most people, both inside and outside the profession, would consider it desirable that psychotherapists are skilful practitioners, and that they have done some kind of apprenticeship to develop such skill. However, I see four factors that impact on this, as follows.

1. The lack of a clear distinction between psychotherapy and counselling, especially and specifically with regard to their respective set of skills

While some are not so concerned about this distinction, the fact that it is difficult to distinguish the two, and, at the same time, that psychotherapy is seen as having a higher status than counselling, means that some psychotherapists – and some psychotherapy education/training programmes – can appear a little light on developing skills or techniques, to the point that they appear to have few basic counselling skills, including listening skills (or, indeed, communication or certain social skills). It may be that there is too great a reliance in such programmes on students learning theory and developing personally, principally through personal therapy (for discussion of which, see Chapter 5), at the expense of practising psychotherapeutic skills (on each other) *before* working with clients.

2. The separation of skills from theory

One of the consequences of eclecticism in therapy was the separation of skills from theory. A prime mover in this was Robert Carkhuff, who was one of the first people to use the term 'core conditions',[89] and who used it in the context of distinguishing 'core, facilitative and action-oriented conditions' from other orientations to therapy by which the helper facilitates change in the client. In addition to genuineness, respect and empathic understanding, these included specific emphasis on emotional experiencing; concreteness in problem-solving; the ability to confront, and the ability to interpret the helping relationship.

However, the problem with developing skills without theory is that the practitioner doesn't have a base on or in which to ground or understand their skills or techniques, and thus the skill becomes more of an unthinking and unthoughtful technique. One of the classic books on such skills, *The Skilled Helper*, was written by Gerard Egan (originally published in 1975 and now in its 10th edition).[90] While Egan originally claimed his approach to be based on – and it is still viewed by some as representing – the client-centred or person-centred approach, his instructive and directive approach is clearly antithetical to person-centred theory and practice. His SOLER model – which instructs the helper to sit Square on, with an Open stance, Leaning slightly forward, maintaining good Eye contact, while being Relaxed – is a classic example of generalised and untheorised practice that, for that reason, suffers from a lack of any critical reflection – for instance, about its embedded cultural assumptions. Another aspect of the separation of skills from theory is a certain antagonism to theory from an anti-intellectual perspective.[91] Carkhuff, Charles Truax and, most notably, Egan, all of whom refer to 'core conditions' (and all of whom are often referred to as 'person-centred'), laid the ground for a human relations technology enterprise that, while popularising these particular conditions and attitudes, has moved a long way from the spirit and substance of Rogers' thought and person-centred practice. As Neville points out:

> He [Carkhuff] focused on the impact which the behaviour of one individual (the helper) has on the behaviour of another individual (the helpee) and

on finding a measurable relationship between cause and effect... the technique-centred, skills-based practice typified by Carkhuff and Egan still represents a certain type of orthodoxy and field.[92]

In the Introduction, I quoted Rogers' point – and preference – that practitioners should acknowledge their values and the 'operational' impact of these – ie. on their practice. I suggest that, in order to do this, practitioners can benefit from a greater understanding of philosophy and, as Bazzano and Webb put it, 'the informed confluence of the two disciplines – psychotherapy and philosophy'.[93] They suggest – and hope – that a grounding of psychotherapeutic practice in critical philosophy will halt the current slide of psychotherapy into what they refer to as 'psychotechnics'.

3. The development of counselling skills training

The past 25 years have seen the development of counselling skills training for people who are not psychotherapists or counsellors but who are in some helping profession or role, such as community workers, nurses, social workers, teachers and so on. While this has undoubtedly helped these professionals, it may have made it harder for counsellors, and particularly psychotherapists, to consider that training in these skills should be part of their education/training and development.

4. The move away from the apprenticeship model

Traditionally, training in psychotherapy took a long time and was viewed, by both trainer and trainee, broadly in terms of the apprenticeship model, whereby an apprentice was taken under the wing of a master for some – usually an indeterminate number of – years, during which the apprentice would learn 'on the job'. Crucially, this model and the training was absolutely dependent on the relationship between the apprentice and their master (see Chapter 7). With the establishment of training institutes, and in a cultural zeitgeist of consumerism and short-termism, the virtue of taking time over such training has been replaced by the more consumer-oriented practice of paying for a time-limited training in order to achieve a required qualification.

Competence

In itself, the ability to do something successfully or efficiently, which is the standard and basic definition and hallmark of competence, sounds reasonable, especially when framed in terms of developing ability or abilities, which usually involves the attainment of knowledge and skills. One well-known model of comptence is W Lewis Robinson's developmental model, in which the learner moves from unconscious incompetence, through conscious incompetence and conscious competence, to unconscious competence.[94] Influenced by Piagetian learning theory, Clarkson and Maria Gilbert added to this three intermediate processes: accommodation, assimilation and integration.[95] Putting these together, I represent it thus:

unconscious incompetence
    through *accommodation* leads
        to conscious incompetence and
        through *assimilation* leads
            to conscious competence and
            through *integration* leads
                to unconscious competence.

The addition of the three processes shifts the original stage theory to one that is much more about the process of developing competence. It also reflects the view that the development of competence is more about the personal integration of theory and practice than meeting external criteria. The more recent interest in cultural competence, which, broadly, involves being able to move between alternative cultural frameworks, shifts this model even further. As Steven López puts it: 'The alternative cultural lenses were those that reflected [both] *culture-specific* (emic) belief systems and *culture-general* (etic) belief systems.'[96] This statement reflects a competence that includes movement, questioning, being willing to be challenged, being able to let go, and openness.

However, all too often, competence and professional competence are framed simply as lists of abilities and/or knowledge that a) tend to remain at a basic level, rather than at a meta level; b) rarely refer to abilities regarding criticality or reflexivity, and c) when revised, tend to expand (rather than contract or be streamlined). In its statement of core clinical competences for generic psychotherapists (that is, in the generic scope of practice), under the headings of 'therapeutic relationship', 'human development', 'theory', 'assessment', 'intervention', 'other areas', 'cultural competence', 'ethical and legal practice' and 'reflective practice and continuing professional development', the Psychotherapists Board of Aotearoa New Zealand (PBANZ) identifies 44 competences. Of these, 26 are framed as abilities ('able to...'), 12 as knowledge ('knowledgeable of [or in]...'), and six as awareness ('aware of...'). The only reference to criticality appears under ethical legal practice, and states that all psychotherapists will be 'critically aware of...' certain legislation, codes and regulations. In each case, this is followed by the phrase 'and able to comply with'. While seven per cent of the Board's competences require New Zealand psychotherapists to be critically aware, their criticality is clearly and immediately constrained by the requirement to comply.

The concern, even obsession, with competence is part of a wider cultural zeitgeist that seeks to ensure therapeutic efficacy through manualised treatments, professional standards through increasing regulation, and skilled practitioners through training, as distinct from education.

Praxis

Having discussed psychotherapeutic method and practice, I propose that, from a critical perspective, praxis is a more accurate and integrated concept to describe what psychotherapists do.

Derived from the ancient Greek πρᾶξις, praxis is the process by which a theory, lesson or skill is enacted, embodied or realised in some way. For Aristotle, praxis (doing) was one of the three basic activities of mankind, the end goal of which was action. The other two activities were *theoria* (thinking), leading to truth, and *poiesis* (making), leading to production. Marxist philosophers have used the concept to emphasise action oriented towards changing society;[97] Hannah Arendt (1906–1975) argued that Western philosophy has focused too much on the contemplative life rather than the active life, with the result that we often miss the relevance of the philosophical ideas to everyday life. Similarly, a psychotherapy that focuses too much on contemplation, introspection, analysis and insight becomes, in Aristotle's terms, more theoretical than practical. While the unexamined life may not be worth living,[98] it is praxis that translates personal self-examination into action for the personal, interpersonal and social good.

There are certain advantages in using praxis to describe the activity of psychotherapy: it offers an integration of reflection with action; it links the practice of psychotherapy with a critical tradition, and one that accounts for the impact of the social world and, therefore, represents what I see as a 'social turn' in psychotherapy, and, finally, it connects the practice of psychotherapy to critical thinking.

Broadly, thinking is viewed as the mental process in which beings form psychological associations and models about the world. The act of thinking produces thoughts. For Chaffee, 'thinking is a very practical, holistic, integrated mental activity we engage in to make sense of the world... The thinking process is a global, meaning-seeking activity that is the essence of being human'.[99] Of course, our thinking develops over time, and is dependent on our development, from cradle (actually, from conception) to grave, and, therefore, involves others – hence, the importance of groups and of group psychotherapy.

In distinguishing critical thinking from lateral, divergent and creative thinking, Brookfield argues that 'those terms don't have the oppositional and political flavor I see as embedded in critical thinking'.[100] This suggests that, if we're educating or training psychotherapists in critical thinking, then we also need to train them to be, or at least be willing to be, oppositional, political, and even subversive – a point that echoes Steiner's point about the importance of disobedience.[101]

Endnotes

1. Rogers CR, Wood JK (1974). Client-centered theory: Carl Rogers. In: Burton A (ed). *Operational Theories of Personality*. New York: Brunner/Mazel (pp211–258) (p214).
2. It will be clear from this that I am critical of attempts to separate skills from theory, as is implied by some courses in counselling skills, and by documents that propose 'practice guidelines' without any reference to underlying theory, philosophy or values.
3. Phillips A (1996). *On Flirtation: psychoanalytic essays on the uncommitted life*. London: Faber & Faber (p62).
4. Freud S (1955/1919). Lines of advance in psycho-analytic therapy. In: Strachey J (ed & trans). *The Standard Edition of the Complete Psychological Works of Sigmund Freud, vol 17*. London: Hogarth Press (pp157–168) (pp167–168).
5. Rogers CR (1957). The necessary and sufficient conditions of therapeutic personality change. *Journal of Consulting Psychology 21*: 95–103 (p102).
6. Sartre J-P (1958/1943). *Being and Nothingness: an essay on phenomenological ontology* (HE Barnes trans). London: Methuen & Co (p569).
7. See Seeley K (2005). The listening cure: listening for culture in intercultural psychological treatments. *Psychoanalytic Review 92*(3): 431–452. Also Lloyd J (2009). The listening cure. *Continuum: Journal of Media & Cultural Studies 23*(4): 477–487.
8. Kierkegaard S (1956). *Either/Or*, vol 1. Princeton, NY: Princeton University Press (p66).
9. I am grateful to Margot Solomon for introducing me to Wilberg's work. Wilberg P (2004). *The Therapist as Listener: Martin Heidegger and the missing dimension of counselling and psychotherapy training*. Eastbourne: New Gnosis Publications.
10. Fleming P (1984). The seven levels of listening and contribution training. In: Pellin Centre. *Pellin Diploma Course Notes*. Kings Lynn: Pellin Centre (pp8–10). Available from The Pellin Centre, Avenue House, Tennyson Road, Kings Lynn PE30 5PA, UK.
11. Fleming (1984) (p8).
12. France A (1988). *Consuming Psychotherapy*. London: Free Association Books.
13. Sands A (2000). *Falling for Therapy: psychotherapy from a client's point of view*. Basingstoke: Palgrave (p12).
14. Fleming (1984) (p8). (See also note 3.)
15. Freud S (1958/1912). Recommendations to physicians practising psycho-analysis. In: Strachey J (ed & trans). *The Standard Edition of the Complete Psychological Works of Sigmund Freud, vol 12*. London: Hogarth Press (pp109–119) (p110).

16. Spinelli E (1989). *The Interpreted World: an introduction to phenomenological psychology*. London: Sage.
17. Fleming (1984) (p8).
18. This was at a workshop on supervision that Shohet led at Temenos, in 1997.
19. Fleming (1984) (p9).
20. Rogers CR (1986). Rogers, Kohut, and Erickson: a personal perspective on some similarities and differences. *Person-Centered Review 1*(2): 125–140 (p129).
21. Rogers CR (1959). A theory of therapy, personality, and interpersonal relationships as developed in the client-centered framework. In: Koch S (ed). *Psychology: the study of a science. Vol 3: formulations of the person and the social context*. New York, NY: McGraw-Hill (pp184–256) (p213).
22. Rogers CR (1967/1958). A process conception of psychotherapy. In: Rogers CR. *On Becoming a Person*. London: Constable (pp125–159) (p130).
23. Rogers (1967/1958) (p130).
24. Solomon M, Tudor K (2013). Listening: a way of being and thinking [synopsis]. In: Scherman R, Krägeloh C (eds). *Walking the Talk: the 2012 collection of oral presentations from the AUT School of Public Health and Psychosocial Studies*. Auckland: AUT University (pp84–88).
25. See Heuer G (2017). *Freud's 'Outstanding' Colleague/Jung's 'Twin Brother'*. London: Routledge.
26. Ferenczi S (1988/1932). *The Clinical Diary of Sándor Ferenczi* (M Balint ed, NZ Jackson trans). Cambridge, MA: Harvard University Press.
27. The others being: stage; the subject, actor or protagonist; therapeutic aides or auxilary egos, and the audience.
28. Hare AP, Hare JR (1996). *JL Moreno*. London: Sage (p46).
29. Rogers C (1967/1954). Toward a theory of creativity. In: Rogers CR. *On Becoming a Person*. London: Constable (pp347–359).
30. Rogers N (2000/1993). *The Creative Connection*. Ross-on-Wye: PCCS Books.
31. I say 'perhaps' as some therapists, especially those within the person-centred tradition, have qualms about this level or aspect of directivity. For an excellent and comprehensive discussion of this issue, see Levitt B (ed) (2008). *Embracing Non-Directivity: reassessing person-centred theory and practice in the 21st century*. Ross on Wye: PCCS Books.
32. See Freud **S** (1930/1893). Miss Lucy R. Case histories from studies on hysteria. In: Strachey J (ed & trans). *The Standard Edition of the Complete Psychological Works of Sigmund Freud, vol 2*. London: Hogarth Press (pp106–112).

33. Freud S (1953/1904). Freud's psycho-analytic procedure. In: Strachey J (ed & trans). *The Standard Edition of the Complete Psychological Works of Sigmund Freud, vol 7 (1901–1905): a case of hysteria, three essays on sexuality and other works.* London: Hogarth Press (pp247–254).

34. A classic example of this is Roger Casemore, who wrote about the importance of managing boundaries and not touching clients (Casemore, 2001), but was subsequently removed from membership by the British Association for Counselling & Psychotherapy, on grounds of serious professional misconduct, having engaged in a sexual relationship with a student while he was both her course director and supervisor. Casemore R (2001) Managing boundaries – it's the little things that count. In: Casemore R (ed). *Surviving Complaints against Counsellors and Psychotherapists.* Ross-on-Wye: PCCS Books (pp111–120).

35. Older J (1982). *Touching is Healing: a revolutionary breakthrough in medicine.* New York, NY: Stein & Day.

36. Reich W (1972/1933). *Character Analysis* (VR Carfagno trans) (3rd ed). New York, NY: Farrar, Strauss & Giroux.

37. Lowen A (1971). *The Language of the Body.* New York: Collier. (Originally published in 1958 as *Physical Dynamics of Character Structure.*)

38. Including Kellerman S (1985). *Emotional Anatomy.* Westlake Village, CA: Center Press; Staunton T (ed) (2002). *Body Psychotherapy.* London: Routledge, and Totton N (2003). *Body Psychotherapy: an introduction.* Milton Keynes: Open University Press.

39. A particularly comprehensive volume on the subject, and one that crosses theoretical orientations, is Bohart AC, Greenberg LS (eds) (1997). *Empathy Reconsidered: new directions in psychotherapy.* Washington DC: American Psychological Association.

40. A distinction first identified by the German historian and politician, Johann Droysen (1804–1884).

41. It also underpins the difference between Rogers' and Kohut's views on empathy, see Rogers CR (1986) and Tudor K, Worrall M (2006). *Person-Centred Therapy: a clinical philosophy.* London: Routledge.

42. See Lewis T, Amini F, Lannon R (2001). *A General Theory of Love.* New York, NY: Vintage Books.

43. Founded in 1958, Synanon was initially a drug rehabilitation programme that had a strong emphasis on high levels of confrontation of its clients. In the 1960s, it became an alternative community; later, a cult, and still later, a church. It was disbanded in 1991.

44. Berne E (1966). *Principles of Group Treatment.* New York, NY: Grove Press (p235).

45. Schmid P (1998). 'Face to face': the art of encounter. In: Thorne B, Lambers E (eds). *Person-Centred Therapy: a European perspective*. London: Sage (pp74–90) (p75).
46. Schmid (1998) (p81).
47. Heron J (2001/1975). *Helping the Client: a creative practical guide*. London: Sage (p59).
48. Kabat-Zinn J (1994). *Wherever You Go, There You Are: mindfulness meditation in everyday life*. New York, NY: Hyperion.
49. Stern DN (2004). *The Present Moment: in psychotherapy and everyday life*. New York, NY: WW Norton & Co.
50. See, for instance, Segal ZV, Williams JM, Teasdale JD (2000). *Mindfulness-Based Cognitive Therapy for Depression: a new approach to relapse prevention*. New York, NY: Guilford. Most cognitive behavioural therapists recognise three waves in the development of CBT: the first being the work of Aaron Beck and Albert Ellis; the second, the schema-focused approach of Jeffrey Young; and the third, a focus on altering the person's relationship to both thought and feeling, which includes the dialectical behaviour therapy of Marsha Linehan, the acceptance and commitment therapy of Steven Hayes and others, as well as mindfulness.
51. Harrison J (2014). Meditation and meaning. In: Bazzano M (ed). *After Mindfulness: new perspectives on psychology and meditation*. Basingstoke: Palgrave Macmillan (pp124–135).
52. See Tudor K, Summers G (2014). *Co-creative Transactional Analysis: papers, dialogues, responses, and developments*. London: Karnac.
53. Webb J (2016). Under arrest: Wittgenstein and perspicuity. In: Bazzano M, Webb J (eds). *Therapy and the Counter-Tradition: the edge of philosophy*. London: Routledge (pp147–155).
54. Larner G (1999). Derrida and the deconstruction of power as context and topic in psychotherapy. In: Parker I (ed). *Deconstructing Psychotherapy*. London: Sage (pp39–53) (p41).
55. Newnes C (2014). *Clinical Psychology: a critical examination*. Ross-on-Wye: PCCS Books (chapter 3).
56. Heron J (2001/1975). *Helping the Client: a creative practical guide*. London: Sage.
57. Freud S (1959/1926). The question of lay analysis: conversations with an impartial person. In: Strachey J (ed & trans). *The Standard Edition of the Complete Psychological Works of Sigmund Freud, vol 20*. London: Hogarth Press (pp177–250).
58. Freud (1959/1926) (p244).
59. See Thompson C (1944). Ferenczi's contribution to psychoanalysis. *Journal of Psychiatry, Interpersonal and Biological Processes* 7(3): 245–252.

60. Rogers CR (1942). *Counseling and Psychotherapy: newer concepts in practice*. Boston, MA: Houghton Mifflin.
61. Proner BD (1979). A review of *The Child Psychotherapist and Problems of Young People* by Daws & Boston. *Journal of Analytical Psychology* 24(4): 354–356.
62. Arroyave F (1986). Some implications of transference and countertransference in the treatment of dependence. *Journal of Analytical Psychology 31*: 199–206.
63. See Orange D (2012). Clinical hospitality: welcoming the face of the devastated other. *Ata: Journal of Psychotherapy Aotearoa New Zealand 16*(2): 165–178.
64. See Rogers CR (1957). The necessary and sufficient conditions of therapeutic personality change. *Journal of Consulting Psychology 21*(1): 95–103; and Rogers CR (1959). A theory of therapy, personality, and interpersonal relationships as developed in the client-centered framework. In: Koch S (ed). *Psychology: the study of a science. Vol 3: formulations of the person and the social context*. New York, NY: McGraw-Hill (pp184–256).
65. The remaining two are about the client: 2) client incongruence (the client is vulnerable and anxious), and 6) client perception (the client perceives the therapist's unconditional positive regard and empathc understanding).
66. See Rogers (1957) (p96).
67. Parker I (1999). Deconstruction and psychotherapy. In: Parker I (ed). *Deconstructing Psychotherapy*. London: Sage (pp1–18) (p4).
68. Rogers (1959) (p214).
69. See Wilkins P (2003). *Person-Centred Therapy in Focus*. London: Sage.
70. Taft J (1933). *The Dynamics of Therapy in a Controlled Relationship*. New York: Macmillan (pv).
71. Standal S (1954). *The Need for Positive Regard: a contribution to client-centered theory*. Unpublished PhD thesis. Chicago, IL: University of Chicago.
72. See Aron L, Starr K (2013). *Psychotherapy for the People: toward a progressive psychoanalysis*. New York, NY: Routledge.
73. Cited in Dreyfus H (1991). *Being-in-the-World: a commentary on Heidegger's 'Being and Time', Division I*. Cambridge, MA: Massachusetts Institute of Technology Press (p150).
74. Rogers C (1980). *A Way of Being*. Boston, MA: Houghton Mifflin.
75. Wood JK (1996). The person-centered approach: towards an understanding of its implications. In: Hutterer R, Pawlowsky G, Schmid PF, Stipsits R (eds). *Client-Centered and Experiential Psychotherapy: a paradigm in motion*. Frankfurt am Main, Germany: Peter Lang (pp163–181) (pp168–169).

76. Berne E (1966). *Principles of Group Treatment*. New York, NY: Grove Press.
77. Akhtar S (2005). *Freud Along the Ganges: psychoanalytic reflections on the people and culture of India*. New York, NY: Other Press (p16).
78. Orange (2012).
79. Orange (2012) (p165).
80. Brookfeld S (1993). Conversation. In: Esterle J, Cluman D (eds). *Conversations with Critical Thinkers*. San Francisco, CA: The Whitman Institute (pp7–27) (p8).
81. Tudor K (2016). *The Argumentative Therapist: philosophy, psychotherapy, and culture*. Public inaugural professorial lecture given at Auckland University of Technology, Auckland, Aotearoa New Zealand, 23 August. www.aut.ac.nz/__data/assets/pdf_file/0006/660282/Keith-Tudor_inaugural-professorial-address_23-August-2016_A4.pdf (accessed 17 January 2018).
82. The term 'common factors' was, in fact, first used by Saul Rosenzweig as long ago as 1936. See Rosenzweig S (1936). Some implicit common factors in diverse methods of psychotherapy. *American Journal of Orthopsychiatry, Mental Health & Social Justice 1936* 6(3): 412–415.
83. It wasn't until 1959, in the context of a much larger presentation of Rogers' theory of therapy, personality, and interpersonal relationships as developed in the *client-centred* framework, that these became associated specifically with client-centred therapy and the person-centred approach.
84. As some clients clearly are not in psychological contact and engaged in their therapy, this condition has led to a way of working with those who are 'pre-expressive', 'psychotic', or in some way 'contact-impaired' called 'pre-therapy'. See Prouty GF (1976). Pre-therapy, a method of treating pre-expressive, psychotic and retarded patients. *Psychotherapy: Theory, Research, Practice, Training 13*(3): 290–295; and Van Werde D (1994). An introduction to client-centred pre-therapy. In: Mearns D. *Developing Person-Centred Counselling*. London: Sage (pp121–125).
85. Rogers CR (1957). The necessary and sufficient conditions of therapeutic personality change. *Journal of Consulting Psychology 21*: 95–103 (p96).
86. Neville B (2012). *The Life of Things: therapy and the soul of the world*. Ross-on-Wye: PCCS Books.
87. Rogers' conditions have been the subject of much research debate over what is now 60 years. Unfortunately they have also been misrepresented and misinterpreted – see, for instance, Feltham C (2013). *Counselling and Counselling Psychology: a critical examination*. Ross-on-Wye: PCCS Books. For further elaboration, see Tudor K, Worrall M (2006). *Person-Centred Therapy: a clinical philosophy*. London: Routledge; and Tudor K (2011).

Rogers' therapeutic conditions: a relational conceptualization. *Person-Centered & Experiential Psychotherapies 10*(3): 165–180.

88. A Google search on books containing the phrase 'counselling skills' produced 48,100 citations, compared with just 3,980 for the phrase 'psychotherapy skills', and in most of the latter, psychotherapy was linked to counselling.
89. Carkhuff R (1969). *Helping and Human Relations. Vol I: selection and training*. New York, NY: Holt, Rinehart & Winston; and Carkhuff R (1969). *Helping and Human Relations. Vol II: practice and research*. New York, NY: Holt, Rinehart & Winston. However, the term was taken up by people much closer to Rogers than Carkhuff (Barrett-Lennard G, personal communication, 17 May 1999).
90. Egan G (1975). *The Skilled Helper*. Monterey, CA: Brooks/Cole-Thomson, now in its 10th edition (2013).
91. See Füredi F (2004). *Where Have All the Intellectuals Gone? Confronting 21st century philistinism*. London: Continuum. Explaining the rejection of a particular book proposal I had submitted, one major international publisher commented: 'It's too theoretical, but if you ever want to write a book about skills, we'll publish it.'
92. Neville (2012) (pp30–31).
93. Bazzano M, Webb J (2016). Introduction. In: Bazzano M, Webb J (eds). *Therapy and the Counter-Tradition: the edge of philosophy*. London: Routledge (pp1–5) (p3).
94. Robinson WL (1974). Conscious competency – the mark of a competent instructor. *Personnel Journal 53*: 538–539.
95. Clarkson P, Gilbert M (1991). The training of counsellor trainers and supervisors. In: Dryden W, Thorne B (eds). *Training and Supervision for Counselling in Action*. London: Sage (pp143–169).
96. López S (1997). Cultural competence in psychotherapy: a guide for clinicians and their supervisors. In: Watkins CE (ed). *Handbook of Psychotherapy Supervision*. New York, NY: Wiley & Sons (pp570–588).
97. These include August Cieszkowski (1814–1894), Antonio Labriola (1843–1904), and Antonio Gramsci (1860–1937).
98. A phrase attributed to the Greek philosopher Socrates (470?–399 BCE).
99. Chaffee J (1993) Conversation. In: Esterle J, Cluman D (eds). *Conversations with Critical Thinkers*. San Francisco, CA: The Whitman Institute (pp129–141).
100. Brookfield S (1993). Conversation. In: Esterle J, Cluman D (eds). *Conversations with Critical Thinkers*. San Francisco, CA: The Whitman Institute (pp7–27) (p25).

101. Steiner C (2004). *The Other Side of Power*. New York, NY: Grove Press. See also Ings W (2017). *Disobedient Teaching: surviving and creating change in education*. Dunedin: Otago University Press.

CHAPTER 4

Theory

> There's nothing so practical as good theory.
> (Kurt Lewin)[1]

Psychotherapy has been referred to as a science, an art and a philosophy, as well as a vocation, a profession and a discipline, and has been accused of being unscientific, mystical and a hoax. While Freud himself wanted to be seen as the neutral scientist, others have viewed him more as a moralist or philosopher. As Philip Reiff puts it: 'In psychoanalysis, Freud found a way of being the philosopher he desired to be, and of applying his philosophy to himself, humanity, the cosmos – to everything, visible and invisible, which as a scientist and physician he observed.'[2] Frank Lake, the neo-Reichian therapist, referred to his work as 'clinical theology'.[3] I and Worrall have advanced the view that person-centred therapy is, in effect, a clinical philosophy,[4] and others may well argue that this is also true of other theoretical orientations or modalities.

As I suggest in Chapter 3, all practice, skills and methods are based on theory, which in turn is a particular manifestation of an underlying philosophy that, of course, includes the practitioner's own 'value orientation' (see Introduction). In this sense, and as it would be impossible to review the breadth of psychotherapy theory in any depth here, I am more concerned to offer some critical perspectives about theory to help the reader make sense of the theories that inform their practice, that they espouse, and/or that they may be studying. Thus, in the first part of this chapter I consider the nature and purpose of theory, including identifying some criteria for theory and some problems with theory, and in the second part I outline four intellectual traditions – the Enlightenment, Romanticism, modernism and, specifically, critical theory, and postmodernism – and their impact on theories of and in psychotherapy.

Theory – its nature and purpose

Very few founding fathers or mothers of any school of psychotherapy justified their development of theory, let alone advanced any theory of theory (sometimes referred to as metaphysics or meta-theory). A search (in 2017) of the extensive Psychoanalytic Electronic Publishing database, comprising some 109,500 articles, produced only one article on the subject: 'On the theory of theory in psychoanalysis' by Leo Rangell.[5] In more than 1,500 articles published in the *Transactional Analysis Journal* between 1971 and 2017, there are only two mentions of a 'theory of theory'. The most relevant of these comes at the end of an article by Barnes, who reflects on a theory of theory that he views as, by definition, a critique, and which, in effect, offers a transactional analysis of TA.[6] Other schools of or approaches to psychotherapy are equally light on meta-theory. One notable exception to this is Rogers, who is explicit about his theory of theory and gives a rationale for the purpose and use of theory. Here, with reference to Rogers, Rangell, Barnes and some others, I offer some arguments as to the inevitability and necessity of theory.

The word 'theory' comes from words meaning contemplation, speculation and the basis of a mental view, conception or scheme of something that is held as an explanation. In this sense, theory is how we make sense of the world, and part of how we make sense of the world is to make sense of each other. Indeed, our progress as a species from non-human primates to homo sapiens is said to rest in our capacity to understand the subjective experience of others. Peter Fonagy and his colleagues refer to this as 'mentalisation',[7] which is defined as 'a preconscious or ego function that transforms basic somatic sensations and motor patterns through a linking activity'.[8]

Assuming that others have minds enables us to work together – an assumption that is consistent with two of Stern's senses of self: the sense of core self-with-another, and the sense of an intersubjective self. Building on the foundation of emergent and core relatedness, Stern considers that the infant is concerned with what is in her or his mind, what is in the mind of another person, and how that might be shared without words. In order to develop this sense of self-with-another, the infant needs to be able to share their affective states, and to attend to something jointly with another person. Stern suggests that 'the sharing of affective states is the most pervasive and clinically germane feature of intersubjective relatedness'.[9] The subsequent sense of an intersubjective self develops when the infant comes to realise that they have a mind of their own, and recognises that there may be differences in minds and that other people have minds as well – what Daniel Siegel refers to as 'mindsight'.[10] Stern argues that:

> This discovery amounts to an acquisition of a 'theory' of separate minds. Only when infants can sense that others distinct from themselves can hold or entertain a mental state that is similar to one they sense themselves to be holding is the sharing of subjective experience or intersubjectivity possible.[11]

In his later work, Stern developed the narrative sense of self and relatedness,[12] which supports the idea that theory is, necessarily, a narrative we develop about the world, and, indeed, is a necessary narrative in that it is how we construe and construct the world. Moreover, as this construction implies deconstruction, this suggests that theory changes, and should change, as it accounts for new information and different times and different contexts, a point to which I also refer below (p118).

Consistent with the concept of praxis discussed in the previous chapter, there is an important and interdependent relationship between theory and practice. Rangell argues that:

> Since psychoanalysis by definition is simultaneously a theory, a method of treatment, and a research procedure, each function and capacity in which psychoanalysis is used automatically applies to the other two. Theory applies to treatment as to neurosogenesis; psychoanalysis as a research method enhances theory and accomplishes treatment; and every psychoanalytic treatment is a research procedure which is guided by and often enlarges psychoanalytic theory.[13]

Finally, it is important to acknowledge that the client also has a theory – or, rather, a number of theories – not only about their problems or issues, but also about the world and the nature of change. In transactional analysis, this is acknowledged as part of its theory of life script, which identifies a person's beliefs about themselves, others and the world, as well as the conclusion(s) they draw from their experiences and construing of life.[14] In their book *The Heroic Client*,[15] Duncan, Miller and Sparks trace in the writings of a number of therapists over half a century what they refer to as 'the rich tradition' of the client's theory. This includes the point, made by Paul Hoch in 1955, that: 'There are some clients who would like to submit to a psychotherapeutic procedure whose theoretical foundations are in agreement with their own ideas about psychic functioning.'[16] This, of course, has important implications for the meeting between client and psychotherapist, and raises the intriguing prospect of matching clients and therapists on the basis of their theoretical and philosophical compatibility.

The purpose of theory

In the context of this critical examination of psychotherapy, theory primarily provides an understanding for practice. Indeed, Berne reportedly often said: 'There's only one paper to write, which is called "How to cure patients".'[17] In a comment about both practice and theory (which forms the epigram of the previous chapter), Rogers and John K Wood wrote: 'First there is experiencing, then there is a theory.'[18] Here, Rogers and Wood are clearly nailing their colours to an experiential mast. The implication is that theorists should develop their theory on the basis of and in response to experience and experiencing, and that the test for the usefulness of any theory is the extent to which it explains our experience of ourselves, others and our environment. In Rogers' case, the prime example of this was his formulation of the six necessary and sufficient conditions for personality change (see Chapter 3) – a theory that emerged from practice, and thus represents what Steve Morgan and David Juriansz refer to as 'practice-based evidence',[19] as distinct from evidence-based practice (see Chapter 6).

Theory also stimulates further thinking and research. Rogers defines theory as 'a fallible, changing attempt to construct a network of gossamer threads which will contain the solid facts', reflecting that, if it were viewed in this light, 'then a theory would serve, as it should, as a stimulus to further creative thinking'.[20] Theory often provides hypotheses that can then be tested through research, which, in turn, informs theory. While most theory is based on hypotheses and presented in a certain way, I have also detected an increasing number of references to theory as beliefs, as in, 'I *believe* in… [this or that theory].' Belief is also being used as a synonym for opinion. From a critical perspective, this is a problem, in that it positions theory as dogma, and the application of or adherence to the particular theory as a matter of faith. As Otto Kernberg observes: 'The religious assertion of faith in the existence of the deity and the essentially irrational nature of such a faith are not unlike the sense of conviction about the truth of psychoanalytic theory, particularly about the unconscious.'[21]

There are further views about the purpose of theory that are related to specific approaches. For Rangell: 'Psychoanalytic theory as a conceptual structure plays a dynamic part within the psychoanalytic process in the therapeutic alliance.'[22] In transactional analysis, the practitioner will tend to share TA theory and models with the client as a common language, not least so as to be able to analyse transactions visually. Indeed, it is a commonplace to say that you can tell a TA practitioner's consulting room by the presence of a whiteboard. For Mearns, in person-centred therapy:

> There is no attempt to use theory to predict the behaviour of an individual client. However, theory can be used by the person-centred counsellor to

begin to understand the client's experience as reported by the client. The theory will not give a detailed understanding – only empathy can do that.[23]

Criteria for theory

Following on from the identified purpose of theory, there are several criteria for or tests of any theory.

The first criterion is that theory is – or needs to be – practical. Kurt Lewin's famous assertion that 'There's nothing so practical as good theory'[24] informs this first criterion and suggests that theory needs to be clear, concise and accessible. Duncan Cramer proposes other criteria, such as testability, empirical support, clarity and logical consistency, simplicity, comprehensiveness, and fruitfulness, as well as practicality.[25] Unfortunately, a certain amount of theory is somewhat unclear, obtuse and inaccessible. Moreover, in some quarters, it appears that being obscure is valued – writing about transference to theory, Rangell observes that, 'Obscurantism does not detract but adds to a following.'[26]

Second, like good research, theory needs to be open: 'Theory does not ever prevent new observations: in its definition and meaning it is open and awaits more. In its essence theory is conjectural, not closed.'[27] This criterion suggests that theory is not only non-dogmatic, it is anti-dogmatic (see Chapter 1). Writing about transactional analysis theory, Jean Illsley Clarke expresses her deep concern that 'we do not turn any piece of theory into dogma so that it becomes what to think instead of how to think'.[28]

Drawing on what are considered to be standard criteria for research, theory also needs to be verifiable, falsifiable and generalisable (for further discussion of which see Chapter 6). Rogers (p117 above) refers to theory as being fallible; Linda Riebel observes that 'to be considered a science, a hypothesis must be capable of being proved false; if not, it is merely dogma'.[29] To these, I would add the criterion of changeability. Robert Kramer says of Rank that he 'improvised a new theory for each client'.[30] Rogers' use of the image of 'gossamer threads' (above) suggests both the strength and the fragility of theory, as well as the capacity of theory to change. Writing about his long experience of clinical practice, Jung wrote that there was 'no therapeutic technique or doctrine that is generally applicable',[31] and that he had to 'regard each case as a new experience, for which, first of all, I have to seek the individual approach'.[32]

Commenting on the role of theory with regard to psychotherapy research, McLeod[33] identifies three approaches: the first, whereby researchers are guided by a particular theoretical model; the second, in which researchers design studies to generate knowledge that is not linked to any specific theory, and the third, in which theory is generated from material gathered through research, hence grounded theory.[34] Interestingly, McLeod reports that there has been a decline in theory-informed psychotherapy research.

From a critical perspective, an important requirement of and for theory is that it is reflexive – that is, that it may and, indeed, should be able to be applied to itself – and thus that:

- psychoanalytic theory analyses the dynamics of its own theory
- behavioural theory considers the behaviour of theory (including how it adapts and is adapted etc)
- humanistic theory evaluates the basis of values (which are derived from humanism)
- person-centred theory centres on the person, as does its practice (and, therefore, is not theory-centred)
- transactional analysis offers a transactional analysis of its theory, eg. the 'life story' of script theory
- critical theory is able to critique itself.

Reflecting on the history of transactional analysis, and specifically three moments in which TA turned back on itself (at Berne's death, and with regard to the cathexis theory of schizophrenia and of alcoholism), and drawing on what he refers to as second-order transactional-cybernetics, Barnes offers just such a critical, reflexive reading of TA, and thus, as noted, a transactional analysis of transactional analysis.[35]

Finally, reflexive theory encourages both theoretician and practitioner to reflect on their own theory and/or the theories they espouse, and helps them to reflect on theory as an autobiographically-influenced construction. Citing Berne's view that the only paper worth writing is on how to cure patients (see above and Chapter 6), and following his own critique of the theoretical construction of psychopathology, Barnes concludes that such a case study, written by future transactional analysts, would not discuss psychopathologies or cure, but, rather, would show 'how they learned an individual's vocabulary and way of talking, how they used that individual's own theory to help her or him go on living and to move from the tragedy of human suffering to enjoy happy moments'.[36]

Most psychotherapy educators/trainers would probably agree that any theory of psychotherapy should encompass the following (see also Chapter 7):

- a theory of human nature, including a model of the person and the human mind and the social/political/cultural context of the person and mind
- a theory of human development and, similarly, of the context of that development
- a theory of health
- a theory of illness, including psychological disturbance/alienation/psychopathology/mental illness
- a theory of human change and ways in which change can be facilitated
- a theory of therapy, including the conditions, process, goals and/or outcomes, practice and methods of therapy, and the context of therapy (including relevant law and ethical frameworks)
- a theory of the role of both therapist and client.

Some problems with theory

Just as skills can be separated from and promoted over theory (as discussed in Chapter 3), so, too, can theory be(come) divorced from skills and reified, so setting it up to be idealised and/or demonised. Such transference to theory is – or, originally, was – often based on a transference to the theorist. For example, Freud tended to analyse theoretical differences and what he referred to as 'secessionist movements' as personal responses to and attacks on him, most of which came from colleagues who had also been patients, and justified this by referring to 'the intimate relations which exist in psychoanalysis between theoretical views and therapeutic treatment'.[37]

In his 1985 article on the relation of theory to psychotherapy practice, Rangell refers to the way in which psychoanalytic theory can be reacted to as a Persecutor, and balances his discussion of various rebellious activities against authority figures in psychoanalysis by acknowledging 'the role of authorities in provoking such protest behaviour'. He comments, specifically:

> I have seen many problems and institutes during the 1950s and 1960s where stagnation in advancement, linked to educational policies, laid the groundwork for the frustrations and disenchantments amongst younger members, which in the 1970s resulted in displacements of negative affect to theory.[38]

Although Rangell himself doesn't refer to Stephen Karpman's drama triangle,[39] I think that the other two roles that Karpman identifies, in addition to Persecutor – those of Rescuer and Victim – can equally be applied to the use and abuse of theory.

Theory may be used by the student or practitioner as a rescue to support unthoughtful or spontaneous practice, or to justify their choice of strategy, usually after the event – for example:

- 'I thought you were being really empathic,' says one student to another when, following a practice session, a tutor/facilitator is processing the student therapist's response (to a fellow student in the role of client).
- 'You're feeling bad because you're identifying with the client's projective material,' explains a supervisor to a therapist.

- 'I was (just) being congruent,' says a participant in response to being challenged about her behaviour in a workshop.

Each of these examples represents an over-identification with theory. This, of course, is perpetuated by the organisation of training, which is predominantly by theoretical orientation or modality and, consciously and/or unconsciously, encourages a 'brand loyalty' to theory.

An example of theory as victim is when practitioners turn against theory and, perhaps, also the theorist: 'You see, empathy doesn't work' (and so Rogers, Kohut and the others were wrong). Here, theory itself becomes the victim of the persecutory therapist who feels let down by, disappointed in, and/or even rejected by what they once found useful, explanatory and reassuring.

Four critical influences on psychotherapy theory

There are, of course, many influences on psychotherapy and its practice and theory. Here I refer briefly to four main (critical) strands of predominantly Western intellectual thought and, each in their own way, of criticism: the Enlightenment (from around 1640 to 1789); Romanticism (1774–1848); modernism (from the 1880s–1968), and specifically critical theory, and postmodernism (from 1969).[40] With each, I identify their influence on psychotherapy, especially with regard to the theories identified above (p120).

The Enlightenment

Also referred to as the Age of Enlightenment or the Age of Reason, this was an intellectual and philosophical movement that began in Europe in the mid-17th century, and was particularly dominant in the 18th century. Characterised by and centred on reason as the primary source of authority and legitimacy, this was a movement and an attitude whose spirit is captured in the phrase '*sapere aude*' (dare to know). The Enlightenment was forged in a critique of scholasticism[41] and dogma, particularly that of the Roman Catholic Church, and in opposition to absolute monarchy (based on the divine right of kingship). With its emphasis on ideals such as liberty, fraternity and equality, constitutional government, the separation of church and state and scientific method and progress, the Enlightenment influenced the English Revolutions (of 1640–1660 and 1688), the American Revolution (1765), the French Revolution (1789), and the Haitian Revolution (1791–1804), as well as other, subsequent revolutionary movements and moments.

Freud, a secular humanist, was very much a product of the Enlightenment, whence and hence came his views about science and religion (see Chapter 2). As Aron and Starr put it (with its original italics):

> *The distinction between the gold of psychoanalysis and the copper of suggestion is based on the ability to make a clear distinction between autonomous rational argument and irrational interpersonal influence... these distinctions are based on Enlightenment assumptions about rationality and positivist assumptions about the ability to distinguish truth and fantasy, rationality and irrationality.*[42]

Aspects of contemporary psychotherapy that may be traced back to the influence of the Enlightenment, include the following.

- With regard to a theory of human nature:

    – that we are self-determined and self-determining beings.

    – that we are driven from within – ie. that we have inherent drives, rather than being determined from without or above (ie. by God).

    – that, within the realm of the mental, every event has a preceding sufficient cause that may be understood by the postulation of preconscious and unconscious mental states

    – that the person and the human mind can best be understood as having a structure – for example, the Freudian tripartite model of id, superego and ego.[43]

    – that we are essentially conscious beings – as Sartre puts it: 'Existential psychoanalysis rejects the hypothesis of the unconscious: it makes the psychic act coextensive with consciousness.'[44]

- With regard to a theory of human development and of the context of that development:

    – that this proceeds through a series of stages, such as Erikson's psycho-social model of development.[45]

- With regard to a theory of health:

    – that there is an emphasis on autonomy and freedom, found, for example, in humanistic psychology and, specifically, Rogers' work.[46]

- With regard to a theory of illness:

    – that psychotherapy offers a critique of social conformity – in this sense, as E Ann Kaplan puts it, 'psychoanalysis itself is an Enlightenment project'.[47]

- With regard to a theory of human change and ways in which change can be facilitated:

    – that there is an emphasis on the rational and on thinking, most evident in cognitive behavioural approaches, although also apparent in others.

- With regard to a theory of therapy:

    – that, on a basis of a diagnostic formulation, therapy proceeds according to a set treatment plan – a perspective epitomised by the manualised treatments of cognitive behavioural therapies.

    – that therapy works on the basis of certain conditions, such as Rogers' necessary and sufficient conditions, which were formulated in terms of 'if…, then…' propositions (see Chapter 3).

- With regard to a theory of the role of both therapist and client:

    – that, however else it is conceptualised, it is based on a real relationship – as Anna Freud puts it:

> With due respect for the necessary strictest handling and interpretation of the transference, I feel still that we should leave room somewhere for the realization that analyst and patient are also two real people of equal adult status, in a real personal relationship to each other.[48]

She goes on to speculate 'whether our – at times complete – neglect of this side of the matter is not responsible for some of the hostile reactions which we get from our patients and which we are apt to describe to "true transference" only'.[49] It is also interesting to note that she referred to these as 'subversive thoughts', to be 'handled with care'.

– that it is based on 'a hermeneutics of suspicion'.[50]

- Also:

– that psychotherapy is a science.[51]

– that psychotherapy is orientated to the social world – a perspective that is found in the work of Freud himself, for, as Ernest Jones points out: 'His conclusions were, it is true, founded on the psychology of the individual, but it was Freud more than anyone else who taught us that every aspect of that individual is really a social one.'[52]

Romanticism

Romanticism was an artistic (literary, musical), and intellectual movement, originating in Europe at the end of the 18th century, characterised by an interest in and emphasis on emotion ('the artist's feeling is his law'[53]) and individualism, and a certain glorification and reification of nature and the past (more the medieval than classical era). The Romantic movement was in part a reaction to the age of Enlightenment, and to the scientific rationalisation of nature, and, in the UK, to the Industrial Revolution – all components of what was viewed as modernity. Isaiah Berlin[54] describes the core of Romanticism as an exploration of the inchoate, even violent, depths of the self in order to discover there the creative power to articulate and express one's most elusive and authentic self. In his discussion of the relevance and impact of Romanticism to and on psychotherapy, Jonathan Fay puts it clearly:

> Romanticism... developed the idea of individual interiority, a pre-conscious, affective experience of being that provides the existential foundation of personhood, of which rational mind is but one aspect or element. The Romantic movement identified and positively valued the uniqueness of each person's individual existence. Romantics were champions of outward differences, but only insofar as these outward differences were signifiers of a unique interiority. This is exactly what psychotherapy asserts in positing a preconscious emotional or feeling-based self, a unique identity that is the existential foundation of rational mind... [and] should not be allowed to be subsumed by rational mind.[55]

Aspects of contemporary psychotherapy that may be traced back to the influence of Romanticism include the following.

- With regard to a theory of human nature:
  – that we are interconnected with nature, and hence 'we psychology', 'wego' and 'we consciousness'.[56]
  – that we have instincts.
  – that we have an ego, the Freudian concept of which, for Neville, represents a 'heroic ego'.[57]
  – that human beings have a unitary theory of motivation, the actualising tendency, which reflects a broader, formative tendency in the universe.[58]

- With regard to a theory of human development:
  – that this is conceptualised with reference to certain myths, for example, the Oedipus complex. In Chapter 2, I reference Girindrasekhar Bose, an Indian psychoanalyst, who proposed a theory of primary feminity.[57] The correspondence between Bose and Freud, which took place over 16 years (1921–1937), included some disagreements, notably about Bose's theory of opposite wishes and his conceptualisation of the castration threat. In one letter, Freud commented that

Bose under-rated the efficiency of the fear of castration,[60] to which Bose responded by referring to 'the importance of the castration threat *in European cases*' (my emphasis), and went on to say: 'The desire to be female is more easily unearthed in Indian male patients than in Europe ones.'[61] More fundamental than the particular theoretical disagreement is the fact that these two men disagreed about what it is to be human – and, specifically, male and female. Commenting on this correspondence, Salman Akhtar writes of Freud: 'While he seemed to be intrigued by Bose's efforts, he was clearly unprepared to address the cultural specifics of Bose's ideas.'[62]

- With regard to a theory of health:
  – that the goal of life, which may be facilitated by psychotherapy, is to express one's unique individuality. While this is perhaps more associated with humanistic psychology, Strenger argues that, influenced by feminism, psychoanalysis also took up 'a Romantic expressivist view of the self'.[63]

- With regard to a theory of illness:
  – that we have been and are separated from our natural selves and environment.
  – that illness exacerbates consciousness.

- With regard to a theory of human change and ways in which change can be facilitated:
  – that we need to rediscover and restore connections within ourselves and between ourselves and others and nature.

- With regard to a theory of therapy:
  – that there is an emphasis on authenticity, the release or recovery of which is based on an essentialist view of the self.
  – that attention is paid to feeling(s), awareness and spontaneity. Berne's definition of autonomy is the release of three capacities: 'awareness, intimacy and spontaneity'.[64]

As William Whelton puts it: 'Freedom, spontaneity, and a subtle attention to feeling are all essential to this exploration. This is the artistry of the exploration and expression of the inner self,' and, 'Rogers is one distant stream of the democratization of that artistry.'[65]

- With regard to a theory of the role of both therapist and client:
  – that it is based on a 'hermeneutics of grace'[66] and a 'hermeneutics of trust'.[67]

- Also:
  – that psychotherapy is an art rather than science.[68]
  – that therapeutic action extends to 'two-person-plus psychology'.[69]
  – that psychotherapy can be part of and can contribute to transhumanism.

While it is easy to see Romanticism as in opposition to the Enlightenment, Fay views 'Romanticism as an extension of the Enlightenment and psychotherapy as the child of Romanticism'. He continues: 'I don't see Romanticism as ever having been opposed to the Enlightenment, although it did oppose the dictatorship of reason which Enlightenment ideals unwittingly let loose.'[70] The meeting of art and science is somewhat captured in the title of one of Schore's books on neurobiology, *The Science of the Art of Psychotherapy*.[72]

Modernism

Modernism was an artistic and intellectual movement that arose as a result of wide-scale transformations in Western society during the late 19th and early 20th centuries, including the consequences of and reactions to the First World War (1914–1918). Broadly, modernists felt and argued that the traditional forms of art (architecture, literature, music), science, philosophy, theology and social organisation were no longer relevant to the new economic, social and political environments of a widely industrialised world

– a critique whose essence is captured by Ezra Pound's injunction to 'Make it new!'[72] In so far as modernism is an aesthetic introspection, it could be said that modern psychotherapy itself is the applied psychology of modernism.

There are many theories within modernism (for instance, different forms of Marxism and feminism), the most famous of which – and the most relevant for our current examination – is critical theory.

Generally, critical theory refers to any theory that takes a critical stance on its subject, with the implication that it has an underlying alternative metaphysics or meta-theory on, and by which it critiques, its subject: for example, Marxism, feminism, critical race theory, queer theory etc. More specifically, the term 'critical theory' is also used to describe the neo-Marxist philosophy of the Frankfurt School, which was developed in Germany in the 1930s, especially by Max Horkheimer (a philosopher, sociologist and social psychologist), Theodor Adorno (a philosopher, sociologist and musicologist), Erich Fromm (a psychoanalyst), and Herbert Marcuse (a philosopher). This critical theory is of specific interest to psychotherapy because of Fromm's involvement in the Frankfurt School and the influence of psychoanalytic – and, more broadly psychotherapeutic – thinking on its development: an influence that was echoed in subsequent work, notably that of Juliet Mitchell in *Psychoanalysis and Feminism*.[73]

Aspects of contemporary psychotherapy that may be traced back to the influence of modernism and, specifically, critical theory, include the following.

- With regard to a theory of human nature:

    – that human beings have the power to create, improve and reshape their environment(s)

    – that this is best explained in terms of critical theories of self as a self-in-social-context.[74]

- With regard to a theory of human development:

    – that childhood has been pathologised.[75] Elsewhere, I have critiqued TA for its pathologising of the critical and the rebellious (in the terms 'Critical Parent' and 'Rebellious Child'),[76] and here I would add its reification of what is deemed to be free (as in the 'Free Child').

- With regard to a theory of health:
  – that healthy human beings can and should master their environment.[77]

- With regard to a theory of illness:
  – that neuroses are social diseases[78]
  – that it is based on a theory of alienation[79]
  – that groups become subjects and categories.[80]

- With regard to a theory of human change and ways in which change can be facilitated:
  – that this is and should be undertaken by a combination of individual psychotherapy and social action[81]
  – that this is best done in groups, so as to avoid the individualising effect of individual therapy.

- With regard to a theory of therapy:
  – that human beings can make decisions, and redecisions,[82] that, with regard to diagnosis,

  > ... it is time to dethrone diagnosis as the flower of mental health and stop using the excuse that we misdiagnose to get paid. The only reason we use it for reimbursement is because we haven't articulated the pitfalls of diagnosis to funding sources, nor have we offered anything different.[83]

  – that, in the same spirit, it is time to dethrone 'resistance'. In psychoanalysis and psychoanalytic psychotherapy, resistance refers to any action, or inaction, that opposes the possibility of making conscious that which is unconscious, and therefore requires interpretation. However, given the power differential between the analyst and the patient, it is easy to overinterpret resistance, a perspective that has led to a number of critical responses to the term and concept. For example, Thomas Szasz defines resistance as 'the term the psychoanalyst uses to register his disapproval of the patient who talks about what he himself wants to talk about rather than about what the analyst wants him to talk about'.[84] From a person-centred perspective, Gert-Walter Speierer argues that resistance is 'an error of empathy on the therapist's side'.[85]

- With regard to a theory of the role of both therapist and client:
    - that the therapeutic relationship is co-created and informed by a relational, two-person psychology.

Postmodernism

Postmodernism is a broad movement across philosophy, the arts (architecture, design, literature, and music) and criticism. As its name suggests, it marks a departure from modernism. It is associated with deconstruction and poststructuralism, and, as such, is hard to define. It is more definable or known by the critical attitude and process it proposes, which is one of scepticism, deconstruction, irreverence and uncertainty, all of which are brought to bear on Enlightenment rationality, Romantic essentialism and Modernist novelty. It is broadly characterised by epistemological relativism and pluralism.

In Chapter 1, I refer to 'Southern Theory', a concept developed by Connell, who argues that the dominant intellectual tradition is not only 'Western', it is also 'Northern'.[86] She argues that the 'Northernness' of general theory is expressed in four, related 'characteristic textual moves':[87] the claim of universality; reading from the centre (for example sociology *in* Australia) – a move or manoeuvre that presupposes that sociology or psychology has a centre and that this centre is 'neutral'; gestures of exclusion – ie. the exclusion of ideas originating in the 'periphery', such as Aboriginal or Māori concepts of health and healing, and 'grand erasure' – ie. the erasure of key experiences such as colonisation, one of the most infamous examples of which was the declaration by colonists that Australia was '*terra nullius*' (empty land).[88]

In order to counter these textual and political 'moves', Connell argues that, we need, from a 'Southern' perspective: a) theories that are specific and contextual; b) theories that are generated from and that reflect readings from the periphery, the edge and the margins; c) theories that are inclusive, and specifically inclusive of ideas from the periphery, and d) theories that present and represent experiences from the periphery and, therefore, that reclaim erased wisdom, knowledge and experience. These moves represent a deconstructivist and, therefore, postmodern critique. They are similar to Totton's argument in favour of local knowledge,[89] and I have applied them myself to what I identify as 'Southern psychotherapies'[90] (see also Chapter 8).

Aspects of contemporary psychotherapy that may be traced to the influence of postmodernism include the following.

- With regard to a theory of human nature:
  – that we are contextual and reflexive beings, and, moreover, as Foucault argues:

  > The critical ontology of ourselves has to be considered not, certainly, as a theory, a doctrine, nor even as a permanent body of knowledge that is accumulating; it has to be conceived as an attitude, and ethos, a philosophical life in which the critique of what we are is at one and the same time the historical analysis of the limits that are imposed on us and an experiment with the possibility of going beyond them.[91]

- With regard to all theories of human development, health, illness, change, therapy, and relationship:
  – that they may be discovered by an active process of elucidation, which Heidegger refers to as the 'hermeneutic circle'[92] – and that our understanding of the whole person

is established by reference to individual parts, and our understanding of the parts by reference to the whole. Heidegger's theory seeks to recover the original question or openness to *Dasein* (Being or Being there, which was present in pre-Socratic philosophy).

– that they represent a concept of a de-centred self, facilitated by mindfulness (see pp89–90 above).

– that they focus on health and illness as a condition of possibility, which Nick Fox refers to as 'arché-health'.[93]

- With regard to a theory of illness:

  – that it is based on ways in which we have been and still are violated and/or excluded – a perspective that is informed especially by the work of Foucault on sexuality and psychiatry.[94]

  – that, as Barnes puts it in typically deconstructive terms, 'there is no psychopathology until psychotherapy is invented to generate it'.[95]

  – that this is reflected in what Jerome Bernstein refers to as the 'borderland personality', which describes the person who 'straddles the split between the developed, rational mind and nature in the Western psyche'.[96]

- With regard to a theory of human change and ways in which change can be facilitated:

  – that this occurs by elucidation and social practice.

- With regard to a theory of therapy and of the role of both therapist and client:

  – that there is a shift from a focus on the (reified) therapeutic relationship to therapeutic relating, by which therapist and client co-create new, emergent relational possibilities.[97]

From this brief critical examination of theory, it may be seen: a) that theories of psychotherapy draw on a number of intellectual traditions; b) that, in some instances, opposing theories draw on the same intellectual traditions (eg. different emphases on the conscious and unconscious, both from the Enlightenment), and c) that, in many instances, the theories and models of a particular theorist have their roots and philosophical assumptions in different traditions. While philosophical congruence may be desirable from an Enlightenment perspective, it may not be possible from a Romantic perspective, and would not be sought from a postmodernist view.

Finally, writing about theory, Terry Eagleton suggests that it emerges 'when the traditional rationales for social or intellectual practice have broken down *and new forms of legitimization for it are needed*' (my emphasis).[98] This offers an important link between and support for the development of theory and criticism – namely, that we need to develop critical theory to legitimate new social and intellectual practice – and praxis, especially when we are applying old theory on new or different ground.

Endnotes

1. Lewin K (1951). *Field theory in social science: selected theoretical papers by Kurt Lewin* (D Cartwright ed). NY: Harper & Row (p169).
2. Reiff P (1959). *Freud: the mind of the moralist*. New York, NY: The Other Press (p3).
3. Lake F (1966). *Clinical Theology: a theological and psychiatric basis to clinical pastoral care*. London: Darton, Longman & Todd.
4. Tudor K, Worrall M (2006). *Person-Centred Therapy: a clinical philosophy*. London: Routledge.
5. Rangell L (1985). On the theory of theory in psychoanalysis and the relation of theory to psychoanalytic therapy. *Journal of the American Psychoanalytic Association 33*: 59–92.
6. Barnes G (2000). Retrieving a flourishing psychotherapy: a transactional cybernetic meditation on transactional analysis. *Transactional Analysis Journal 30*(3): 233–247. Also Barnes G (2005). Acceptance speech on receiving the 2005 Eric Berne Memorial award: transgressions. *Transactional Analysis Journal 35*(3): 221–239; Barnes G (1974). *Justice, Love and Wisdom: linking psychotherapy to second-order cybernetics*. Zagreb: Medicinska Naklada. The other is in the title of an article that considers the principles of model building: Stewart I (2001). Ego states and the theory of theory: the strange case of the Little Professor. *Transactional Analysis Journal 31*(2): 133–147.

7. Fonagy P, Gergely G, Jurist E, Target M (2002). *Affect Regulation, Mentalization, and the Development of the Self.* New York, NY: Other Press (see chapter 3).
8. Lecours S, Bouchard M-A (1997). Dimensions of mentalisation: outlining levels of psychic transformation. *The International Journal of Psychoanalysis* 78: 855–875.
9. Stern D (1985). *The Intersubjective World of the Infant.* New York, NY: Basic Books (p138).
10. Siegel D (1999). *The Developing Mind: toward a neurobiology of interpersonal experience.* New York, NY: Guilford Press.
11. Stern (1985) (p124).
12. Stern D (2000). *The Intersubjective World of the Infant* (revised ed). New York, NY: Basic Books.
13. Rangell (1985) (p60).
14. See Kelly G (1955). *The Psychology of Personal Constructs, vol 1.* New York, NY: WW Norton & Co.
15. Duncan BL, Miller SD, Sparks JA (2004). *The Heroic Client: a revolutionary way to improve effectiveness through client-directed, outcome-informed therapy.* San Francisco, CA: Jossey-Bass.
16. Hoch P (1955). Aims and limitations of psychotherapy. *American Journal of Psychiatry 112*: 321–327 (p322).
17. Berne E (1971). Away from a theory of the impact of interpersonal interaction on non-verbal participation. *Transactional Analysis Journal 1*(1): 6–13 (p12).
18. Rogers CR, Wood JK (1974). Client-centered therapy. In: Burton A (eds). *Operational Theories of Personality.* New York, NY: Brunner/Mazel (pp211–258).
19. Morgan S, Juriansz S (2002). Practice-based evidence. *Open Mind 114*: 12–13.
20. Rogers CR (1959). A theory of therapy, personality, and interpersonal relationships as developed in the client-centered framework. In: Koch S (ed). *Psychology: the study of a science. Vol 3: formulations of the person and the social context.* New York, NY: McGraw-Hill (pp184–256) (p191).
21. Kernberg O (1986). Institutional problems of psychoanalytic education. *Journal of the American Psychoanalytic Association 34*: 799–834 (p807).
22. Rangell (1985) (p81).
23. Mearns D (1997). *Person-Centred Counselling Training.* London: Sage (p146).
24. Lewin K (1951). *Field Theory in Social Sciences: selected theoretical papers by Kurt Lewin* (D Cartwright ed). NY: Harper & Row (p169).
25. See Cramer D (1992). *Personality and psychotherapy.* Milton Keynes: Open University.

26. Rangell L (1982). Transference to theory: the relationship of psychoanalytic education to the analyst's relationship to psychoanalysis. *The Annual of Psychoanalysis 10*: 29–56.
27. Rangell L (1985) (p60).
28. Illsley Clarke J (2000). A personal view from a parent educator. *Transactional Analysis Journal 30*(3): 219–218 (p221).
29. Riebel L (1996). Self-sealing doctrines, the misuse of power and recovered memory. *Transactional Analysis Journal 26*(1): 40–45 (p42).
30. Kramer R (1995). The birth of client-centered therapy: Carl Rogers, Otto Rank, and 'The beyond'. *Journal of Humanistic Psychology 35*(4): 54–110 (p78).
31. Jung CG (1976/1961). Symbols and the interpretation of dreams. In: Read H, Fordham M, Adler G, McGuire W (eds) (RFC Hull trans). *The Collected Works of CG Jung, vol 18*. Princeton, NJ: Princeton University Press (pp185–266; para 515).
32. Jung (1976/1961) (para 518).
33. McLeod J (2003). *Doing Counselling Research*. London: Sage.
34. The principal proponents of grounded theory are Glaser B, Strauss AL (1967).*The Discovery of Grounded Theory*. Chicago, IL: Aldine; and Strauss AL, Corbin J (1998). *Basics of Qualitative Research Techniques and Procedures for Developing Grounded Theory* (2nd ed). London: Sage.
35. Barnes G (2000). Retrieving a flourishing psychotherapy: a transactional-cybernetic meditation on transactional analysis. *Transactional Analysis Journal 30*(3): 233–247.
36. Barnes (2005) (p238).
37. Freud S (1964/1912). New introductory lectures. In: Strachey J (ed & trans). *The Standard Edition of the Complete Psychological Works of Sigmund Freud, vol 12*. London: Hogarth Press (pp1–182) (p143).
38. Rangell L (1985) (p69).
39. Karpman S (1968). Fairy tales and script drama. *Transactional Analysis Bulletin 7*(26): 39–43.
40. Although the term was first used in the 1880s when, commenting on a way to depart from French Impressionism, Watkins Chapman suggested 'a Postmodern style of painting'. Hassan I (1987). *The Postmodern Turn: essays in postmodern theory and culture*. Columbus, OH: Ohio University Press.
41. In their discussion of Che Guevara's pedagogy, Nathalia Jaramillo and Peter McLaren remind us of Guevara's reference to the Stalinist cult of authority as scholasticism. See Jaramillo N, McLaren P. Rethinking critical pedagogy: socialismo netpantla and the spectre of Che. In: Denzin NK, Lincoln YS (eds). *Handbook of Critical and Indigenous Methodologies*. Thousand Oaks, CA: Sage (pp191–210).

42. See Aron L, Starr K (2013). *Psychotherapy for the People: toward a progressive psychoanalysis*. New York, NY: Routledge (p186) (original emphasis).
43. Graham Richards relates the importance of this tripartite division of ways of seeing human being to the late 18th century German intellectual tradition. See Richards G (1992). *Mental Machinery: the origins and consequences of psychological ideas. Part I: 1600–1850*. London: The Athlone Press.
44. Sartre J-P (1958/1943). *Being and Nothingness: an essay on phenomenological ontology* (HE Barnes trans). London: Methuen & Co (p570).
45. Erikson EH (1950). *Childhood and Society*. New York, NY: WW Norton & Co.
46. See, specifically, Rogers CR (1969). *Freedom to Learn*. Columbus, OH: Charles E. Merrill. Also my own work with Worrall on supervision: Tudor K, Worrall M (eds) (2004). *Freedom to Practise: person-centred approaches to supervision*. Ross-on-Wye: PCCS Books; and Tudor K, Worrall M (eds) (2007). *Freedom to Practise II: Developing person-centred approaches to supervision*. Ross-on-Wye: PCCS Books.
47. Kaplan EA (ed) (1990). *Psychoanalysis and Cinema*. New York, NY: Routledge.
48. Freud A (1954). The widening scope of indications for psychoanalysis – discussion. *Journal of the American Psychoanalytic Association 2*: 607–620 (p618).
49. Freud (1954) (pp618, 619).
50. Ricoeur P (1970). *Freud and Philosophy: an essay on interpretation*. New Haven, NJ: Yale University Press (p27).
51. Fischer HJ (1991). *The Science of Psychotherapy*. New York, NY: Hemisphere.
52. Jones E (1957). *The Life and Work of Sigmund Freud*. New York, NY: Basic Books.
53. Caspar David Friedrich, cited in Novotny F (1971). *Painting and Sculpture in Europe, 1780–1880* (2nd ed). Yale, VT: Yale University Press (p96).
54. Berlin I (2013/1990). *The Crooked Timber of Humanity: chapters in the history of ideas* (H Hardy ed). London: John Murray.
55. Fay J (2013). 'The struggle to live and let live…': a review. *Ata: Journal of Psychotherapy Aotearoa New Zealand 17*(2): 173–181 (p178).
56. See Chapter 2 and Neville B (2013). *The Life of Things: therapy and the soul of the world*. Ross-on-Wye: PCCS Books.
57. Neville (2013) (p29).
58. See Rogers CR (1967/1961). *On Becoming a Person*. London: Constable; and Neville (2013).

59. Akhtar S (2005). *Freud along the Ganges: psychoanalytic reflections on the people and culture of India*. New York, NY: Other Press (p5).

60. Akhtar (2005) (p7).

61. Ramana CV (1964). On the early history and development of psychoanalysis in India. *Journal of the American Psychoanalytic Association 12*: 110–134 (pp125–126).

62. Akhtar (2005) (p8).

63. Aron L, Starr K (2013). *Psychotherapy for the People: toward a progressive psychoanalysis*. New York, NY: Routledge (p391). See also Strenger C (2005). *The Designed Self*. Hillsdale, NJ: The Analytic Press.

64. Berne E (1968/1964). *Games People Play*. Harmondsworth: Penguin.

65. Whelton WJ (2007). The enduring legacy of Carl Rogers: clinical philosophy and clinical science. [A review of *Person-Centred Therapy: a clinical philosophy* by Tudor & Worrall.] *PsychCRITIQUES 52*(12).

66. Frymer-Kensky T (2002). *Reading the Women of the Bible: a new interpretation of their stories*. New York, NY: Knopf (p353).

67. Orange D (2011). *The Suffering Stranger*. New York, NY: Routledge.

68. See Storr A (1990). *The Art of Psychotherapy* (2nd ed). London: Routledge.

69. Tudor K (2011). Understanding empathy. *Transactional Analysis Journal 41*(1): 39–57.

70. Fay (2013) (p178).

71. Schore A (2012). *The Science of the Art of Psychotherapy*. New York, NY: WW Norton & Co.

72. Pound E (1935). *Make it New: essays by Ezra Pound*. London: Faber & Faber.

73. Mitchell J (1974). *Psychoanalysis and Feminism: Freud, Reich, Laing, and women*. Harmondsworth: Penguin.

74. See Sève L (1978). *Man in Marxist Theory and the Psychology of Personality*. Hassocks: Harvester Press. Also Appel S (1996). *Positioning Subjects: psychoanalysis and critical education studies*. Westport, CT: Bergin & Harvey; and Tudor & Worrall (2006).

75. See Newnes C (2014). *Clinical Psychology: a critical examination*. Ross-on-Wye: PCCS Books.

76. Tudor K (2003). The neopsyche: the integrating adult ego state. In: Sills C, Hargaden H (eds). *Ego States*. London: Worth Reading (pp201–231).

77. See Jahoda M (1958). *Current Concepts of Positive Mental Health*. New York, NY: Basic Books.

78. Fenichel O (1945). *The Psychoanalytic Theory of Neuroses*. New York, NY: WW Norton & Co.

79. This was the principle contribution of radical psychiatrists such as Steiner. See Steiner C (1971). Radical psychiatry: principles. In: The Radical Therapist Collective. *The Radical Therapist*. New York, NY: Ballantine Books; see also Tudor and Worrall (2006), chapter 6.
80. See Barnes (2005).
81. See, notably, Holland S (1988). Defining and experimenting with prevention. In: Ramon S, Giannichedda MG (eds). *Psychiatry in Transition*. London: Pluto Press (pp125–137).
82. This is one of the basic assumptions of transactional analysis. See Goulding MM, Goulding RL (1978). *Changing Lives Through Redecision Therapy*. New York, NY: Grove Press.
83. Duncan BL, Miller SD, Sparks JA (2004) (p30).
84. Szasz T (1973). *The Second Sin*. London: Routledge & Kegan Paul (p82).
85. Speierer G-W (1990). Toward a specific illness concept of client-centered therapy. In: Lietaer G, Rombauts J, Van Balen R (eds). *Client-Centered and Experiential Psychotherapy in the Nineties*. Leuven: Leuven University Press (pp337–359) (p353).
86. Connell R (2008). *Southern Theory: the global dynamics of knowledge*. Crow's Nest: Allen & Unwin.
87. Connell (2008) (p44).
88. A declaration that was only revoked as recently as 1989 in the Mabo judgment. See Russell P (2005). *Recognizing Aboriginal Title: the Mabo case and indigenous resistance to English-settler colonialism*. Sydney: University of New South Wales Press.
89. Totton N (1999). The baby and the bathwater: 'professionalisation' in psychotherapy and counselling. *British Journal of Guidance and Counselling* 27(3): 313–324. In advocating local knowledge – or, more accurately, local knowledge*s* – Totton draws on the work of van der Ploeg. See van der Ploeg JD (1993). Potatoes and knowledge. In: Hobart M (ed). *An Anthropological Critique of Development: the growth of ignorance*. London: Routledge (pp209–227); and Wynne B (1995). May the sheep safely graze? A reflexive view of the expert–lay knowledge divide. In: Lash S, Szerzynzki B, Wynne B (eds). *Risk, Environment and Modernity: towards a new ecology*. London: Sage (pp44–83).
90. Tudor K (2012). Southern psychotherapies. *Psychotherapy and Politics International* 10(2): 116–129.
91. Foucault M (1984). *What is enlightenment?* In Rabinow P (ed). *The Foucault Reader*. New York, NY: Pantheon Books (pp32–50) (p50).
92. Heidegger M (1962/1927). *Being and Time*. New York, NY: Harper & Row.
93. See Fox NJ (1999). *Beyond Health: postmodernism and embodiment*. London: Free Association Books (p10).

94. Foucault M (1978–1986/1976–1984). *The History of Sexuality, vols 1–3* (Hurley R trans). New York, NY: Vintage Books; and Foucault M (2006/1961). *History of Madness* (J Khalfa ed, J Murphy trans). New York, NY: Routledge.
95. Barnes (2005) (p221).
96. Bernstein J (2005). *Living in the Borderland: the evolution of consciousness and the challenge of healing trauma*. Kensington: New South Wales University Press (p17).
97. See Tudor K, Summers G (2014). *Co-Creative Transactional Analysis: papers, responses and developments*. London: Karnac.
98. Eagleton T (2005/1984). *The Function of Criticism*. London: Verso (p90).

CHAPTER 5

Personal therapy and supervision

Ἰατρέ, θεράπευσον σεαυτόν (Physician, heal yourself)
(Luke 4:23)

Historically, supervision, personal therapy and continuing professional development (CPD) preceded more formal training education and training (which I discuss in Chapter 7). Freud, famously, analysed himself and then others, and in those days the practitioner's own analysis was seen as crucial to their ability to practise, and, in effect, formed an apprenticeship model of analyst training. In this chapter, I consider two aspects of the psychotherapist's development: personal therapy and supervision. I discuss a third aspect, that of continuing or sustaining professional development, in Chapter 7.

Personal therapy

Historically, most people who subsequently became psychoanalysts or psychotherapists were patients or clients first. Even people who knew they wanted to become psychoanalysts first engaged in their own analysis; indeed, their training was their analysis, and hence the term 'training analysis'.[1] The significance of this was not only that they gained insight into their own neuroses and the impact of their personal history on how they thought about and reacted to life, and, in particular, to their patients or clients, but also that they had the experience of being a patient or client. When I did my first therapy training course in the early 1980s, most, if not all, of my fellow trainees had first had experience of therapy – usually of the therapy in which we were training – and were still in therapy.

Until relatively recently, this was the widespread assumption of most training courses, which by and large did not need to make personal therapy a requirement of training. There was also an assumption, especially in more psychoanalytic and psychodynamic circles, that psychotherapy is, by definition, long-term, and that long-term, open-ended psychotherapy is preferable and better. Given this, it is interesting to note that many of the early psychoanalysts engaged in relatively short-term therapy, often moving to Vienna so that they could be in analysis with Freud for six months or so. Freud himself experimented with setting a definite end date for analysis,[2] and other early analysts, notably Ferenczi and Rank, followed this practice and discussed its implications for psychoanalytic method.[3]

A number of arguments have been advanced to explain why therapists should engage in personal therapy:

- that it supports practitioners to place greater attention on the therapeutic relationship with their clients – in one study therapists who had not experienced personal therapy were found to be more technique-oriented than those who had.[4]

- that it improves the emotional and mental functioning of the therapist; it provides the therapist-patient with a more complete understanding of personal dynamics, interpersonal elicitations and conflictual issues; it alleviates the emotional stresses and burdens inherent in the profession; it acts as a socialisation experience for a therapist; it places therapists in the role of the client and, therefore, gives them a better understanding of that role/position, and it provides an opportunity to experience clinical methods firsthand, and, therefore, provides experiential learning.[5]

- that it increases the therapist's effectiveness by 'teaching' (or demonstrating) genuineness, warmth, acceptance and empathy.[6]

- that it develops greater reflexivity in the therapist-client; it provides what Murphy refers to as 'validational experiences'[7] – ie. an experience that therapy is a valid form of psychological change, and it provides normalisation – ie. the therapist-client comes to experience themselves as fit for the role of being a therapist.[8]

- that it helps with unresolved personal issues, as well as issues arising from the training itself and, therefore, promotes awareness and understanding of the influence of personal issues (summarised by Murphy as 'the reflexivity phase'); it develops empathic understanding and awareness, thereby promoting understanding of aspects of self and environment ('the growth phase'); it offers a validation of self and of the approach, and thus matches inner and outer experiences ('the authentication phrase'); it establishes the therapist-client in the profession and develops their skilfulness, thereby demonstrating the usefulness of personal therapy and its potential as a longer-term option ('the prolongation phase').[9]

- that it improves self-esteem, work functioning, social life, emotional expression and symptom severity.[10]

The importance given to the requirement for personal therapy for psychotherapists varies across theoretical orientations (with psychoanalytic practitioners most likely to engage in personal analysis or psychotherapy, and behavioural therapists least likely[11]), professions and disciplines. Thus, generally, psychotherapists are expected to have personal therapy before, during and, from time to time, after training (for further details about which see pp148–149 below). Psychoanalysts in training are expected to be in analysis four times a week, although, as Aron and Starr point out,[12] this is not sustainable for many students and, in any case, does not reflect post-qualifying practice. There are varied expectations or requirements on counsellors to have some experience of personal counselling, although usually any formal requirement is for a limited time (for instance, 12 sessions over a one-, two- or even three-year training programme). For psychologists (clinical and/or counselling), predominantly there are no expectations of or requirements for them to have personal therapy.

However, while there is a general acceptance among therapists that personal therapy is important, and surveys reveal that most therapists feel that they have benefited both professionally and personally from personal therapy, there is a remarkable lack of evidence of the effectiveness of personal therapy in safeguarding or promoting therapists' health or wellbeing, or their consequent efficacy as therapists,[13] and there is no research to date that demonstrates a direct relationship between the therapist having their own therapy and their clients' outcomes.[14]

Despite this, one review of the literature estimated that three quarters of all mental health professionals have engaged in personal therapy.[15] Whatever the research findings do or don't suggest, I think that there are two compelling arguments for psychotherapists undertaking their own psychotherapy:

- desire – that psychotherapists or people interested in becoming psychotherapists would want to experience psychotherapy. Interestingly, this 'brand belief' (to use a marketing term) in their respective products is not the same across the psy professions – clinical or counselling psychologists who undertake personal therapy tend to do so with psychotherapists, not with other psychologists.

- mutuality – this refers to the argument that you would not ask somebody to do something that you haven't done yourself. Following on from the first point, it would appear both disingenuous and somewhat distanced for a psychotherapist to say that psychotherapy is well and good for others, but they wouldn't want, need, or use it themselves.

Of course, not all healing takes place in the context of, or as a result of, a therapeutic relationship. Thus, a critical perspective would suggest that, notwithstanding the point about belief in the brand, we would be open to what constitutes personal therapy. This was illustrated to me by a colleague who had had some previous experience of personal therapy but who, at a certain point in her training and professional and personal development, felt that she would gain more from some form of spiritual practice and/or direction. Fortunately, the particular requirements under which she was completing her training allowed for this. At one point in my own development post-qualification, I took regular singing lessons for two years, a weekly discipline and pleasure that had direct therapeutic benefits. I would argue that this flexibility was – and is – more useful than having to 'do' psychotherapy to conform to a particular definition of 'personal therapy' and/or to meet an inflexible requirement.

Personal therapy as a training requirement for psychotherapists

Possibly the key debate about personal therapy for therapists is the question of compulsion. For some, compulsory or mandated personal therapy is unproblematic because it can lead to positive outcomes in terms of professional development and validation of therapy as an effective psychological intervention.[16] For others, making personal therapy a mandatory requirement of training is philosophically problematic, professionally undesirable, and possibly unethical.[17] When, in 1998, the then British Association of Counselling introduced the requirement for 40 hours of personal therapy to achieve accreditation, a group of senior practitioners objected to this, referring to it as 'a financial scam'.[18] In one study that specifically considered the compulsory nature of personal therapy during counselling training, there was some criticism of this – that such a requirement discounted previous experience and hours of therapy, felt repetitive, and contributed to pressure on finances and time – although, interestingly, none of the participants suggested excluding therapy from the requirements of the training.[19]

A number of therapeutic approaches object to personal therapy being compulsory on the basis of the underlying value(s) of the particular approach. Thus, for instance, from a person-centred perspective, requiring or directing a trainee to be in therapy is clearly antithetical to the principle of non-directiveness. Mearns argues: 'Personal development for professional working is so crucial to the person-centred approach that it cannot be left to the vagaries of individual therapy.'[20]

At Temenos, a UK training organisation committed to person-centred education and training (of which I was a founding co-director),[21] we took the view that personal therapy was too important to be a course requirement. Our alternative was as follows:

- that, first, we preferred and expected that applicants had already undertaken some personal therapy – thereby, in effect, making it *an entry requirement.*[22]

- that, second, we outlined the United Kingdom Council for Psychotherapy (UKCP) requirements at the time so that students planning to seek UKCP registration were aware of them and their implications (along with other requirements for professional registration and/or accreditation) – thus making it *a matter of personal responsibility.*

- that, third, because we accorded such importance to the purpose and benefit of ongoing personal therapy, we felt it was our responsibility as trainers, at any point during the course, to initiate a conversation with a student, as a result of which we might recommend her/him to begin or resume personal therapy – thereby making it *a matter of dialogue.*

It has, for a long time, been a requirement of the UKCP that all psychotherapists seeking voluntary registration should undertake some personal work throughout their training: 'The Trainee must engage in a continuous process of analysis and self-examination, before, during and after training.'[23]

Interestingly, as this statement refers to analysis and self-examination *before* training, this suggests that some evidence of such analysis is or should be an entry requirement – and part of the assessment – for psychotherapy training – a point that the Council for Psychoanalysis and Jungian Analysis (CPJA) makes explicit by stating its requirement that 'Trainees should be in an appropriate psychoanalytically based psychotherapy for about twelve months before the commencement of the course.'[24] Beyond entry, the *UKCP Standards of Education and Training* contains a very broad statement, under the heading 'Supervised practice of training', that all training programmes should include 'arrangements to ensure that the students and trainees can identify and manage appropriately their personal involvement in and contribution to the processes of the psychotherapies that they practise'.[25] While this statement does not suggest training courses should *require* trainees to undertake personal psychotherapy – these requirements are left to the second tier of individual colleges, and the third tier of accrediting and training organisations themselves – it does imply a certain monitoring of student's personal involvement in and responsibility for their process(es). Informing this are the different policies of the 10 Colleges of the UKCP, which take very different approaches to the nature, and terms and conditions of such personal work, which I summarise below.

1. Regarding the different terms used

That the UKCP does not express the requirement for personal work as one of 'personal *psychotherapy*' reflects the fact that it is a broad church, although some might find it strange that its members (individual and organisational) do not regard such a requirement as a common denominator. Indeed, the terms used to refer to this vary according to the different Colleges of the UKCP, thus:

- 'experiential work' (the College for Sexual and Relationship Psychotherapy (CSRP))

- 'group personal work' (the College for Family, Couple and Systemic Therapy (CFCST))

- 'personal and professional development' (CFCST)

- 'personal involvement' (the Cognitive Psychotherapies College (CPC) and the Constructivist and Existential College (CEC))

- 'personal therapy' (the CEC, the CFCST, the College of Medical Psychotherapists (CMP) and the Universities Training College (UTC))

- 'personal psychotherapy' (the CEC, the CMP, and the Humanistic & Integrative Psychotherapy College (HIPC)).

For some, the use of such phrases is anathema (and represents one reason why some organisations did not originally join the UKCP); for others, it is an accurate description of a necessarily broad, professional church.

2. Regarding the requirement of personal work

- Required by the College for Hypno-Psychotherapists (CHP), the CMP, the CPJA, the CSRP, the HIPC, the Psychotherapeutic Counselling and Intersubjective Psychotherapy College (PCIPC), and the UTC. The CMP is the only College to use the word 'mandated' in this regard and to justify this mandate/requirement, arguing that: 'This is in response to the recognition that to be able to help others who come with minds in distress, awareness of one's own state of mind is needed.'[26]

- Not required by the CEC, the CFST and the Cognitive Psychotherapies College (CPC)), although the CFST does require trainees to experience 25 hours of 'group personal work' during training, usually facilitated by someone external to the training. Although these Colleges do not require their trainees to have personal therapy, they do qualify this. Behavioural and cognitive therapists 'must ensure that they can identify and manage appropriately their personal involvement in the process of cognitive and/or behaviour therapy'.[27] Commenting on the personal therapy requirement, and acknowledging that most members of the College will have had some psychotherapy, the CFST states, uniquely, that, in any case: 'We do not think that the training period is always the best time to do this.'[28]

3. Regarding the minimum requirement

This is rated as follows:

- twice weekly (the CPJA), throughout the duration of training

- weekly, throughout the course of training (the CMP), although this College also recognises that this is a 'minimum' requirement and 'that it will desirable for trainees to have a greater frequency of sessions'[29]

- 160 hours (ie. 40 hours per year for four years of training) (the HIPC and the UTC)

- 105 hours, of which a minimum of 50 hours must be undertaken during training

- 80 hours (the CHP and the CSRP), although the CHP recognises that 'most of our trainees do much more than this'[30]

- 50 hours (the UTC, for registration as a psychotherapeutic counsellor).

Further to this, the criteria and guidelines of the Humanistic and Integrative Psychotherapy College state that:

> For membership... it is a requirement of a training course that trainees have personal psychotherapy with an experienced psychotherapist as part of their training. This should be at least as intensive in terms of frequency and duration as the form of psychotherapy to be practiced.[31]

This is not unusual. Compare it with, for instance, this statement from the NZAP, which, interestingly, is published on a website page headed 'For the Public':[32]

> The task of psychotherapy is such that all psychotherapists are required to have been engaged in personal psychotherapy as part of their training. It is expected that this will be at least as intensive in terms of frequency and duration as the form of psychotherapy the trainee intends to specialise in. Consideration of further personal psychotherapy will subsequently become

part of the regular supervisory review of personal and professional development needs, which is a continuing requirement for all practising psychotherapists.

Experience of personal psychotherapy is likely to ensure that the nature and quality of the experience of being a client in psychotherapy is understood and appreciated.

It is also the most direct way that a psychotherapist, as the very instrument of therapy, is alerted to the operation of their conscious and unconscious patterns, which are likely to affect their own perceptions, judgements, needs and responses during the various phases of therapy.

The professional need for a high degree of awareness of one's own personal functioning in the prolonged, intimate and often stressful relationships that are the essence of psychotherapy, is a necessary prerequisite to the ability to assess and manage these relationships appropriately.

Together with supervision, the process of personal psychotherapy provides an experiential basis for maintaining a commitment to the process of observation and comment by one's peers, on professional practice.

NZAP supervisors... have an ethical and professional responsibility to ensure that their supervisees engage in, or continue with, appropriate personal psychotherapy, during the course of their supervisory relationship.

NZAP members in professional practice are required to maintain arrangements for their ongoing supervision... continuing education and personal and professional development – including personal psychotherapy where this is indicated.

This statement has a number of implications.

1. That a trainee should work with an experienced psychotherapist

Too often, in my experience, trainees work with inexperienced psychotherapists, often because they charge lower fees. This, however, is problematic for a number of reasons. Working with a trainee psychotherapist is quite complex, partly because there is a danger that they will be watching their therapist doing therapy to them, rather than being fully immersed in the therapy themselves (a defence that, in gestalt psychology, is described as egotism). This process may be further complicated by the therapy being compulsory. Also, the inexperienced therapist is likely to be closer to their own training experience, which can be a problem, especially if they have unresolved issues about their own experiences of training.

2. That the therapy should be of the same frequency, duration – and form – as that to be practised

While this makes sense intuitively, especially in terms of experiential learning, it is not always possible for the trainee to predict what form of therapy they will practise. For instance, the trainee may have experience of long-term individual psychotherapy over the four years of their training, but then, after completing their training, may find a job in which they are offering only short-term or time-limited therapy. Does this mean that their experience of therapy is invalidated? Should they, too, get some short-term therapy? Also, as most psychotherapy training is organised in terms of theoretical orientation or modality (see Chapter 7), this requirement is usually taken to mean that the trainee needs to experience personal therapy in that orientation. Again, while this makes some sense, this is less manageable and probably less desirable in a small community, in which case – and, perhaps, in any case – it is better for a trainee to have a good therapist of whatever modality.[33] Nevertheless, I think that the spirit of this expectation is better than having a numerical tariff, which, at worst, encourages an attitude of doing therapy by numbers.

3. That whether the qualified therapist needs further personal therapy is the purview of their supervisor – or supervision

For discussion of this see pp152, 154 and 165 below.

4. That the therapist is responsible for maintaining arrangements for their personal psychotherapy

This appears straightforward, although again, in a small community, and especially for senior practitioners, this can become more complex. In my experience, this requires the therapist to keep at a bit of a distance colleagues who might be suitable personal therapists (or supervisors), and/or to be open to working with colleagues in another country by telephone or online. This implication also raises the question of what happens when the therapist is or does not appear to be maintaining arrangements for their personal therapy – a situation that may require their colleagues, as well as their supervisor, to challenge and/or confront them.

As a result of an incident in a particular professional community in which a trainee had managed to qualify without undertaking the then required personal therapy, I wrote an article in which I made a number of suggestions for trainers.[34] Reviewing these nearly 10 years later, I realise, somewhat sadly, that they are still relevant. Here, I have reproduced and expanded them.

1. Prospective trainees need to know all the requirements, terms and conditions of training before they embark on a training programme

Thus, at some point in the application/recruitment process, trainers need to discuss all the elements of psychotherapy training, including the personal therapy requirement and the research about this. As trainees are increasingly being asked to undertake personal therapy, and as there is little supporting evidence to explain the benefits, David Murphy suggests that his phase model – reflexivity, growth, authentication, and prolongation (see p143 above) – is a good way to explain the benefits to prospective and beginning trainees. Those applicants who are already in therapy need to know if the course/programme requires them to engage with another therapist; those who aren't in therapy need to know of any limitations on their choice of therapist.[35] In this respect, I suggest that more open communication is needed from both trainers and training programmes/organisations, a point that is supported by the ethical principle of autonomy, which is widely enshrined in codes of ethics.[36]

2. Trainers need to be clear and open about their position on the personal therapy requirement

I suggest that this is important not only for their trainees but also for themselves as practitioners, as part of their ongoing process of professional development. In this respect, I suggest that greater congruence is needed from trainers.

3. Trainers need to be clear about their responsibilities and accountabilities with regard to their professional association/s, and to be informed about the requirements for accreditation and/or registration

With the increasing professionalisation of psychotherapy, trainers are often having to respond to the increasing demands for accreditation and/or validation of their courses, programmes and qualifications, as a result of which they need to keep abreast of the requirements that their trainees or students need or may wish to meet and fulfil. Also, as trainers, they themselves may well be members of accrediting organisations and/or regulatory bodies and, as such, will have responsibilities to ensure that their programmes and students meet these requirements or know about the implications of such requirements. Furthermore, these interests and/or memberships may represent a conflict of interest. In this respect, I suggest that greater clarity and declarations of interest are needed from both trainers and professional associations/bodies.

Reflecting on these suggestions, I think they represent the need for greater and open communication about the nature and purpose of personal therapy and development, in order to promote choice (autonomy) and engagement (homonomy), and to avoid requirements becoming power plays – an expression of 'power over' – on the part of educators or trainers.

Supervision

Supervision is often translated as 'oversight' or 'overview', which emphasises the (at least) implicit, 'top-down' hierarchical nature of the relationship between supervisor and supervisee. However, the word may equally be translated as 'wider vision', which carries a more collegial sense of the relationship, and links supervision more to a 'two-person psychology',[37] in which the relationship between supervisee and supervisor, including the power dynamics, is more likely to be addressed. As Mary Gail Frawley-O'Dea puts it, the relational supervisor is 'conscious of the necessary and ever-present tension between assumed and authorized power that infuses the work of the supervisory pair'.[38] For this reason, the practice is sometimes referred to as inter-vision or trans-vision – and, drawing on the concept of 'paragogy',[39] could also be viewed as 'paravision'.

A brief history of supervision

In the early days of psychoanalysis, and later psychotherapy, practitioners reflected on their practice in psychoanalysis/psychotherapy. This was partly because supervision was not recognised as a unique practice, distinct from personal therapy and training, until the 1980s,[40] and partly because, in some quarters, the therapist's responses to their patient(s) or client(s) were viewed as countertransference, which thus required analysis – a perspective that represents the treatment side of what is referred to as the teach-or-treat debate.

The origins of this debate go back to Freud, who did not differentiate his educative and therapeutic functions, often fulfilling both for his students – including his daughter, Anna. Joan Sarnat suggests that discomfort with the conflation or overlap of these functions and roles dates from the time when the training process in psychoanalysis became institutionalised,[41] when the two functions became strictly segregated and allocated, respectively, to the trainee's supervisor and to their training analyst. The rules for psychoanalytic training were established at the Berlin Congress of the International Psychoanalytic Association (IPA) in 1922 (and published two years later), and included the requirement that prospective analysts had a training analysis of at least six months' duration.[42] It is generally acknowledged that it was the Berlin Institute, under the direction of Karl Abraham, Max Eitingon and George Simmel, that first established the separate and distinct role of the supervisor. The influence of this distinction may be seen to this day when, as a result of the supervisee sharing something 'personal' in supervision, the supervisor says, 'Take that to therapy.'

At the same time as the Berlin Institute was establishing its model, Ferenczi and Rank, in Budapest, were developing a different educational approach in which the training (trainee) therapist would begin the treatment of an analytic patient while they were still themselves in analysis, where they would discuss their patient; thus the trainee-therapist's analyst was their first supervisor. What came to be known as 'the Hungarian model' (or method) had the advantages of fostering a deeper understanding of the origins of the therapist's reactions to their patients, and integrating this with their training, and the disadvantage of giving the training analyst too much control over the trainee/candidate's training. As Daniel Jacobs, Paul David and Donald Meyer put it: 'The Hungarian method emphasised what Freud had already noted: that an analysis cannot go further than the unresolved complexes of the analyst.'[43] Although the language is different, this focus is echoed in the distinction made between the supervisor being person-centred (ie. centred on the person of the supervisee/ therapist, who is here-and-now), and client-centred (ie. focused on the supervisee's clients, there-and-then).[44]

Janine Bernard and Rodney Goodyear credit Rudolph Eckstein and Robert Wallerstein as the first proponents of the psychodynamic supervision model that 'portrayed supervision as a teaching and learning process',[45] which placed the emphasis on the teaching and learning of the student/practitioner, rather than the analysis and, therefore, treatment of the student/ patient. Harold Searles is very clear that 'analysing the student's countertransference [should be done] sparingly, if at all'.[46]

While the teach–treat debate is largely historic, its echoes sometimes manifest in the nature and style of some supervisors and their interventions: for instance, when a hypothesis becomes an interpretation, when a specific interpretation offered in supervision becomes a 'treatment', or when an interview or a qualifying examination becomes therapy – all of which are forms of power plays, based on a redefinition (on the part of the supervisor, interview or examiner) of the purpose of the relationship.

Bernard argues that, while psychodynamic theory was addressing supervision directly, behavioural and humanistic therapists were doing so more indirectly, in that practitioners such as Rogers and John Krumboltz were not articulating a supervision theory or process separate from their respective therapies.[47] This raises the question as to whether an approach to psychotherapy is itself an approach to supervision, or whether it can be applied to a different practice – ie. supervision. If so, then all well and good; if not, that would suggest that it needs some additional theorisation. In a comment on the application of theory, Rogers suggests that the further away a theory is from its clinical origins, the greater the possibilty of the 'magnification of error'.[48] This philosophical point challenges psychotherapists to be explicit about the principles underpinning their clinical practice, and then, rather than assuming that they are transferable to other applications such as supervision, testing whether this is the case.[49]

Summarising the history of psychotherapy supervision, Michael Carroll identifies three stages in its development: the first, in the 1920s, was influenced by the psychoanalytic tradition; the second, in the 1950s, was influenced by the emergence of humanistic psychology and (later) the development of humanistic/existential therapies, and the third emerged the 1970s, when supervision began to be recognised as a learning activity.[50] In 2005, Bernard noted that, '[s]ince the explosion of the early 1980s, model development in supervision has been relatively low key',[51] and that, subsequently, practitioners and theorists have been involved in the refinement, exploration and, to a limited extent, testing of models. Under 'refinement', Bernard includes the contribution of constructivist theory and solution-focused approaches, and the 'infusion' (as she puts it) of ideologies such as feminism – and, I would add, other critical theories – into supervision.

To these I would further add the 'infusion' of particular models of therapy (or theoretical orientations/modalities) into the supervision of practitioners of those therapies, including cognitive,[52] dialectical behavioural,[53] person-centred,[54] gestalt,[55] transactional analysis,[56] and relational,[57] as well as the development of other influences in and on supervision, including play, art, metaphor and sandtray work. The 'exploration' of models of supervision includes their application to new contexts, populations and purposes, including practitioners from different disciplines and professions, and beyond that, supervision as a meta-skill, in different forms, such as group supervision and peer supervision, and through different media, such as e-technology. However, the 'testing' of supervision through research is still underdeveloped, and studies are somewhat scarce, and give mixed results.[58] Supervision is generally viewed as a good thing, and a number of explanations are advanced for its benefits, some of which are similar to those proposed for personal therapy (see pp142–143 above):

- that it supports practitioners placing greater attention on the therapeutic relationship with their clients, for instance, by understanding the parallel process[59]

- that it improves the emotional and mental functioning of the therapist by enhancing support and self-care[60]

- that it increases the therapist's ability to self-reflect[61]

- that it fulfils both an educative purpose, which Owen-Pugh and Symons regard as conformity to a theoretical approach, and a normative purpose, thereby ensuring that practice conforms to ethical standards.[62]

However, there is little or no evidence that supervision impacts measurably on the practitioner's client outcomes.[63]

Supervision has its own extensive literature and specialised training courses, so here I only briefly outline its scope(s), and examine two issues – choice, and responsibility – that lie at the heart of a (more) critical approach to this aspect of the practice of psychotherapy.

Scope

Based on a broad review of the literature, I summarise the main scope(s) of supervision,[64] and draw out some critical points.

The functions of supervision

Originally identified by Alfred Kadushin as 'educative, supportive, and managerial',[65] and subsequently popularised by Bridget

Proctor as 'formative, restorative and normative',[66] these words describe the functions of supervision succinctly. In my experience as a supervisor and as a trainer of supervisors, they are also useful as points of reflection, for both supervisor and supervisee, as to whether the supervision is providing the right balance between these different elements. Here, the critical point (in both senses of the word) is how the normative function is understood and, specifically, whether the supervisor thinks that they are responsible for it and for embodying and communicating 'the norms' to their supervisee, or whether the supervisor facilitates the supervisee's relationship to relevant norms – for example, of society, of the profession, and those enshrined in codes of ethics and practice (see also the point on ethics and legal matters, p160 below).

The respective roles of supervisor and supervisee

In a relatively early paper on supervision in transactional analysis, Marilyn Zalcman and Cornell identify the activities and focus of attention and functional modes in supervision for both the supervisor and supervisee.[67] Their emphasis on the bilateral nature of activities in supervision offers an important challenge to more unilateral and top-down ways of thinking about roles and responsibilities in supervision, which are becoming increasingly compromised by regulation (see also discussion on pp164–166 below).

The notion of development in supervision

There are several models of development and supervision – that is, the development of the supervisee as a therapist. These may be traced back to Richard Hogan's 1964 paper on supervision, where he identifies four stages in the development of the psychotherapist,[68] although Edward Watkins acknowledges an earlier paper by Fleming.[69] The concept of a stage model of professional development appears appealing – within 25 years of Hogan's paper, as many different developmental models were published.[70] The basis of any developmental model is 'process differentiation' – that is, the identification of the developmental stage, in this case, of the therapist – while the point of such models is that the stage then informs and directs how the supervisor supervises the therapist. While this has some merit, such models can become somewhat prescriptive, and can be insensitive to more mature practitioners and people who may be 'younger' in a second career in psychotherapy. Elsewhere, I and Mike Worrall articulate a number of criticisms of developmental models based on stage theories,[71] not least that they do not account for more recent developmental theories, such as Stern's,[72] which generally suggest a more unfolding and ongoing process of human development.

The process of supervision

A focus on and conceptualisation of the process of supervision is especially associated with the work of Casement,[73] and of Peter Hawkins and Robin Shohet.[74] Casement's work is itself a critique of over-reliance on the supervisor; as he puts it: 'Formal supervision alone does not adequately prepare the student to deal with the immediacy of the therapeutic present.'[75] He goes on to propose and describe a number of reflective processes that are developed not only through being supervised but also in personal analysis or therapy, and when working without formal supervision, with the primary focus on and interest in learning from the patient. Based on the overlapping of the therapy matrix comprising the client and therapist, and the supervisory matrix comprising the therapist and supervisor, Hawkins and Shohet's model identifies originally six, and now seven, levels or modes of supervision on which the supervisor focuses: the content of the therapy session, the therapist's strategies and interventions, the therapy relationship, the therapist's process, the supervisory relationship, the supervisor's own process, and the wider contexts in which supervision takes place. The authors' declared purpose in developing a model was 'to provide a framework for new levels of depth and new ways of creatively intervening in a supervision session'.[76] As a model, it is accessible and widely used across the helping professions and, while its origins are informed by psychodynamic concept and thinking, the authors have changed their language over the course of a number of editions of the book to be more inclusive of different theoretical orientations and professions.

Ethics and legal matters in supervision

The consideration of these matters generally falls under the normative function of supervision (as referred to above). However, when faced with a supervisee presenting an 'ethical dilemma' or a legal issue, it is all too easy for the supervisor to view her/himself – and to be viewed – as the purveyor of knowledge and/or the ultimate arbiter on these matters. From a critical perspective, it is more helpful that the supervisor helps the supervisee to know the foundations of their own morality (as ethics is the science of morality), and the implications of this, alongside those of the code(s) of ethics to which they subscribe. This is genuine education – a drawing or leading out of the practitioner's own value orientation that informs and guides their practice.

There is, in some quarters, an increasing – and, from a critical perspective, worrying – trend of supervision being used to carry out a more regulatory and monitoring role, which is justified by reference to professional insurance and the law. For example, as part of its auditing procedures, the British Association for Counselling and Psychotherapy (BACP) requires not only that its members have a 'supervision record' but also that its members 'provide details of how they have developed as a result of supervision'.[77] However, Peter Jenkins, an expert in the field of counselling and the law, observes: 'The law is, by definition, open to challenge, re-interpretation and change',[78] and goes on to demonstrate this by offering an alternative reading of some of BACP's guidance on contracts and contracting and supervisor third-part liability.

The organisation and tasks of supervision

In the literature on psychotherapy supervision, there are many contributions about what different authors and practitioners consider to be ways of organising supervision and the specific tasks of supervision.[79] While some of these theories and models are helpful, especially to the novice supervisor, many of them are too complicated to be of practical use in supervision,[80] and encourage supervision-by-numbers rather than relationality and creativity. One of the more useful of these models is Clarkson's 'brief supervision checklist', which includes fulfilment of the contract, identification of the key issues, minimisation of possibility of harm (to the client), increase in developmental direction (of the supervisee), modelling of the process, and equal relationship (between supervisor and supervisee).[81] While this is a good checklist, to which I and Mike Worrall have added ethics and context,[82] it has been somewhat reified in that it has been taken to form the basis of the international exam for supervising transactional analysts,[83] in which the supervisor is asked to demonstrate each element in a 20-minute presentation in which not all of the criteria may be relevant. In part, this is the problem of a *check*list, as it suggests that these items need to be checked, rather than that they are a useful *aide memoire* for practice and thinking about practice.

The context of supervision

This scope refers to the acknowledgement of – and an increasing interest in – the context of supervision, whether organisational or cultural, and its impact on supervision. The different contexts in which supervision takes place, or is organised, impact on the supervisee, the supervisor and the supervision itself: for instance, whether the supervision is clinical and or managerial; whether or not it takes place in the workplace and in worktime; whether it is paid for by the supervisee or by an organisation; whether the supervisor is chosen by the supervisee or allocated to the supervisee, and the impact on the supervisee of the supervisor being of a different gender, race, ethnicity, dis/ability, sexuality etc. In our book *Freedom to Practise*, I and Mike Worrall contributed to this scope of supervision by identifying time as a context, as well as a number of different domains in which issues, questions and dilemmas arise, from the micro to the macro: clinical, professional, ethical, personal, legal, social and cultural.[84]

Choice

These days, the practice of supervision and the person of the supervisor are usually introduced during training. As an element of training is supervised practice (see Chapter 7), trainers have certain supervision requirements associated with the practice component of training. These encompass the number of required supervision hours, usually in some ratio to practice hours – for instance, one hour of supervision for every four or six hours of practice, the frequency of supervision, which may vary from once a week to once a month,[85] and the choice of supervisor.

Different training programmes have different approaches with regard to whether the trainee can or should choose the supervisor, representing four different models, as follows.

1. Training programmes that require trainees to be in supervision with the trainer(s)

This has the advantage of a more integrated approach to the training of psychotherapists, whereby the trainer/supervisor is familiar with the trainee's practice, and, using recording technology, it is also possible for the trainer/supervisor to able to hear or watch the supervisee at work. The disadvantage of this model is a certain restriction on the trainee's choice of supervisor, and trainers who use this model and work in the private sector are open to the accusation that they are financially exploiting their trainees. In either context, trainers and training programmes again need to be clear in advance about the terms and conditions of such supervision. One variation of this model is that the trainee is in supervision with the trainer for, say, the first year of their practice, following which they are free to choose their supervisor.

2. Training programmes that require trainees to be in supervision with recommended supervisors

This has the advantage of giving students more choice, but the disadvantage of creating more work and potential problems for the trainer/programme with regard to establishing the criteria by which they, in effect, approve and recommend supervisors – and, by implication and practice, disapprove of others. This becomes very complicated if supervisors who are not recommended challenge the trainer/programme about their criteria. Again, clarity is crucial.

3. Training programmes that recommend supervisors to trainees

The distinction of 'recommendation' over 'requirement' has the advantage of giving the trainee further choice, although even informal recommendations can create the same complications as in the model above. One variation of this model (which we implemented at Temenos) is to ask potential supervisors to provide a curriculum vitae and a statement of their philosophy of supervision, which is then put on file and made available to all trainees. This has the distinct advantages of giving trainees the information to make informed decisions and of encouraging supervisors to be clear about the personal philosophy that informs their professional practice.

4. Training programmes that do none of the above

While this appears to have the advantage of offering trainees complete freedom of choice, it would also appear to be lacking in any duty of care towards them.

These models are particularly important in the light of a study by Nicholas Ladany and Deborah Melincoff, who found that over 97 per cent of psychotherapists in training had failed to disclose to their supervisors at least one thought, feeling or reaction – reactions that included negative ones towards their supervisor, personal issues, clinical mistakes, negative reactions to clients, and issues of attraction to clients.[86]

Further to this, the practitioner's choice of supervisor may also be influenced, or even determined, by accrediting bodies and/or regulatory authorities. In Aotearoa New Zealand (under the *Health Practitioners Competence Assurance Act 2003*), the title 'psychotherapist' has been protected since 2009 – a protection that is administered by the PBANZ, the 'responsible authority' under the Act. In 2011, the Board decided to extend its influence over registered psychotherapists to include approving their supervisors. Two experienced and senior practitioners who were not registered tested this by applying to the Board to be 'Board-approved supervisors' and were turned down – because of their criticism of the *Act*.[87] Such decisions compromise not only the freedom of psychotherapists to choose their supervisors but also the role of critique and criticism in the development of practice and the profession.

It is quite common for psychotherapists to have more than one supervisor, perhaps because they work in more than one context, such as a placement or an agency, or more than one modality. Some therapists have group supervision in addition to their individual supervision, which may be a group of peers. In some contexts, and especially for trainees, having more than one supervisor may be frowned upon, for fear that they will 'split' their supervisors in some way. However, it should be recognised that this perspective is based on a particular Kleinian model of psychoanalysis and, therefore, has limited value or application as a criticism of choice. In my experience, this view suggests a degree of self-interest (both psychological and financial) on the part of the trainer in holding on to what they see as 'their' trainees.

Responsibility

In my experience, supervisors take, are given, and are ascribed too much responsibility. Many operate an implicit model of supervision in and by which they are responsible for their supervisees' work – a model or perspective that seems to derive from the legal concept of vicarious liability, whereby the supervisor is viewed as liable for the impact and outcome of the supervisee-therapist's work with the client. Again, these views or perspectives are influenced by different therapeutic modalities, different professional requirements (in terms of codes of ethics and professional practice), different professions,[88] and different legal jurisdictions – and also by a certain prejudice, such as assumptions about responsibility, ignorance of the law, and, in some instances, power-plays, whereby supervisors take and maintain a certain responsibility and authority. Jenkins states very clearly that responsibilities are defined by law, policy or context, and, therefore, are not simply abstract or given – and so should not be assumed. He also argues that supervisors have *ethical*, as distinct from legal, responsibilities, and that, with regard to work with clients, there is – or should be – an emphasis on the responsibilities of the supervisee/therapist, not those of the supervisor.[89]

Thus, in a private practice setting, just as the therapist has a duty of care and a certain accountability (and liability) for their work with their client(s), so the supervisor has a responsibility to the supervisee-therapist, and *not* directly to the client. The supervisor's duty to the client is an ethical one, and a broad one at that. In addition, in the public and private sectors, an organisation that is offering therapy has a duty of care and liability to the client, as well as to its workers, which may include both the therapist and supervisor, and, while the supervisor is accountable to the organisation, again, their duty of care to the client is a broad ethical one, unless defined otherwise.

These points are important, not only in terms of encouraging accurate knowledge about professional, clinical, ethical and legal responsibilities (and the differences between them), but also as the assumption of responsibility they represent supports a hierarchical model of the supervisory relationship. One example of this is the view of the NZAP that supervisors 'have an ethical and professional responsibility to ensure that their supervisees engage in, or continue with, appropriate personal psychotherapy, during the course of their supervisory relationship'.[90] Apart from the question of how a supervisor can actually 'ensure' such engagement, the phrasing of this statement clearly makes it the supervisor's responsibility.

The critique here is of supervision as a one-person psychology, based as much on the anxiety of the supervisor/training institute/professional organisation as that of the supervisee/therapist. Like Sarnat, I suggest that viewing supervision from the basis of a two-person psychology is more accurate, more respectful, and more useful (see Chapter 2). Martha Stark herself regards one-person psychology as interpretive, one-and-a-half-person psychology as corrective, and two-person psychology as relational,[91] to which I would suggest that two-person-plus psychology is contextual.[92] Acknowledging her own emphasis on two-person views of the supervisory relationship, Sarnat argues that they 'more accurately capture the actual reality of the supervisory relationship, but also... transform the interpersonal meaning of focusing on the supervisee's problems, thus enabling the supervisor to become a more effective teacher/helper to the supervisee'.[93] One example of this perspective (on these views) is Tony Merry's description of supervision as a heuristic research enquiry.[94]

Some may argue that such relational views only apply to those supervisees who are qualified psychotherapists, and that supervisors of trainees/students should be more interpretive and/or corrective. I disagree. As Sarnat puts it: 'The two-person nature of the supervisory relationship creates a new theoretical context.'[95] Thus, if the education and training of psychotherapists is more andragogic than pedagogic (see Chapter 7), and more relational, then it appears to be more philosophically congruent to establish an andragogic and relational model of supervision from the start.

Endnotes

1. See Rawn ML (1991). Training analysis and training psychotherapy. *Psychoanalytic Psychology 8*(1): 43–57.
2. Freud S (1964/1937). Analysis terminable and interminable. In: Strachey J (ed & trans). *The Standard Edition of the Complete Psychological Works of Sigmund Freud, vol 23.* London: Hogarth Press (pp216–253).
3. For further reading on brief, time-limited (or what is sometimes referred to as time-conscious) therapy, see a number of books in the Sage brief therapy series, edited by Stephen Palmer and Gladeana McMahon. https://uk.sagepub.com/en-gb/eur/series/Series558 (accessed 17 January 2018).
4. Wogan M, Norcross J (1985). Dimensions of therapeutic skills and techniques: empirical identification, therapist correlates and predictive utility. *Psychotherapy 22*: 63–74.
5. Norcross JC, Strausser-Kirtland D, Missar CD (1988). The process and outcomes of psychotherapists' personal treatment experiences. *Psychotherapy: Theory, Research, Practice, Training 25*: 36–43.
6. Macran S, Shapiro DA (1998). The role of personal therapy for therapists: a review. *British Journal of Medical Psychology 71*: 13–26.
7. Murphy D (2005). A qualitative study into the experience of mandatory personal therapy during training. *Counselling and Psychotherapy Research 5*(1): 27–33 (p28).

8. Grimmer A, Tribe R (2001). Counselling psychologists' perceptions of the impact of mandatory personal therapy on professional development: an exploratory study. *Counselling Psychology Quarterly 14*(4): 287–301.
9. Murphy D (2005). A qualitative study into the experience of mandatory personal therapy during training. *Counselling and Psychotherapy Research 5*(1): 27–33.
10. Norcross JC (2005). The psychotherapist's own psychotherapy: educating and developing psychologists. *American Psychologist 60*: 840–850.
11. Norcross (2005).
12. Aron L, Starr K (2013). *Psychotherapy for the People: toward a progressive psychoanalysis*. New York, NY: Routledge.
13. See, for instance, Wheeler S (1991). Personal therapy: an essential aspect of counselor training, or a distraction from focusing on the client? *International Journal for the Advancement of Counselling 14*: 193–202. Also Macran & Shapiro (1998); Beutler LE, Malik M, Alimohamed S et al (2004). Therapist variables. In: Lambert MJ (ed). *Bergin and Garfield's Handbook of Psychotherapy and Behaviour Change* (5th ed). Chicago, IL: John Wiley & Sons (pp227–306).
14. Beutler, Malik, Alimohamed et al (2004).
15. Norcross (2005).
16. Grimmer & Tribe (2001).
17. See Atkinson P (2006). Personal therapy in the training of therapists. *European Journal of Psychotherapy, Counselling and Health 8*(4): 407–410.
18. Mearns D, Dryden W, McLeod J, Thorne B (1998). £1,200 personal therapy: financial scam. Letter to the editor. *Counselling 9*(2): 83.
19. Von Haenisch C (2011). How did compulsory personal therapy during counselling training influence personal and professional development? *Counselling and Psychotherapy Research 11*(2): 148–155.
20. Mearns D (1994). *Developing Person-Centred Counselling*. London: Sage (p35).
21. See www.temenos.ac.uk (accessed 12 December 2017).
22. Although we didn't know it at the time, this echoes the French model of psychoanalytic education, which, in contrast to the Eitingon model, proposes that personal psychoanalysis should precede entry into psychoanalytic training (see Kernberg (2000), and Chapter 7). Kernberg O (2000). A concerned critique of psychoanalytic education. *International Journal of Psychoanalysis 81*(1): 97–120.
23. UKCP (1990). *Special General Meeting Resolution*. (Document no longer available.)
24. UKCP AP-PPS (2004). S3.1.2, S4.3. (Document no longer available.)

25. UKCP (2012). *UKCP Standards of Education and Training: the minimum core criteria. Psychotherapy with adults.* London: UKCP.
26. See Royal College of Psychiatrists (2016). *A Competency Based Curriculum for Specialist Training in Psychiatry: specialists in medical psychotherapy (formerly known as psychotherapy).* London: Royal College of Psychiatrists. www.rcpsych.ac.uk/pdf/Medical_Psychotherapy_Curriculum_August_2016.pdf (accessed 12 December 2017).
27. UKCP Behavioural & Cognitive Psychotherapy Section (undated). S2.11. (Document no longer available.)
28. Lask J (2016). Personal e-mail communication, 4th October.
29. For further guidance and information about the financial support for such levels of personal therapy within each Local Education Training Board, see Royal College of Psychiatrists (undated). *Financial Support for Medical Psychotherapy Trainees' Personal Therapy.* [Online.] London: Royal College of Psychiatrists. www.rcpsych.ac.uk/pdf/Financial%20Support%20for%20Medical%20Psychotherapy%20Trainees%E2%80%99%20Personal%20Therapy2.pdf (accessed 12 December 2017).
30. Gawler-Wright P (2016). Personal e-mail communication, 20th October.
31. Humanistic & Integrative Psychotherapy College (undated). *Training Standards of the Humanistic and Integrative Psychotherapy College (HIPC) of UKCP.* www.ukcphipc.co.uk/public/training (accessed 24 April 2017).
32. New Zealand Association of Psychotherapists (2016). *About Psychotherapy.* [Online.] Porirna: NZAP. http://nzap.org.nz/about/psychotherapy (accessed 29 September 2016).
33. I am grateful to Jo Stuthridge for influencing my thinking on this point.
34. Tudor K (2008). To be or not to be in personal therapy, that is the question: part II. *ITA News 36*(1): 3–7.
35. Some programmes require their trainees to be in therapy with a therapist who is approved by the programme, a policy that raises questions of free choice and also the criteria by which therapists are approved and, by implication, not approved; for further discussion of which see Chapter 7.
36. See, for instance, European Association for Transactional Analysis (2006). EATA ethical code. *EATA Newsletter* 87: 13–21.
37. Stark M (1999). *Modes of Therapeutic Action: enhancement of knowledge, provision of experience and engagement in relationship.* Northvale, NJ: Jason Aronson.
38. Frawley-O'Dea M (2003). Supervision is a relationship too: a contemporary approach to psychoanalytic supervision. *Psychoanalytic Dialogues 13*(3): 355–366 (p358).
39. Herlo D (2014). Paragogy: a new theory in educational sciences. *Journal Plus Education 10*(4): 35–41. See also Chapter 7.

40. Holloway E (1995). *Clinical Supervision: a systems approach*. London: Sage.
41. Sarnat J (1992). Supervision and relationship: resolving the teach-treat controversy in psychoanalytic supervision. *Psychoanalytic Psychology 9*(3): 387–403.
42. Jacobs D, David P, Meyer DJ (1995). *The Supervisory Encounter*. New Haven, CT: Yale University Press (p14).
43. Jacobs, David & Meyer (1995) (p21).
44. See Tudor K, Worrall M (eds) (2004). *Freedom to Practise: person-centred approaches to supervision*. Ross-on-Wye: PCCS Books.
45. Bernard JM, Goodyear RK (2009). *Fundamentals of Clinical Supervision* (4th ed). Boston, MA: Allyn & Bacon (p82). See also: Eckstein R, Wallerstein R (1958). *The Teaching and Learning of Psychotherapy*. New York, NY: International Universities Press.
46. Searles H (1965/1962). Problems of psycho-analytic supervision. In: Searles H (ed). *Collected Papers on Schizophrenia and Related Subjects*. London: Karnac (p602).
47. Bernard J (2005). Tracing the development of clinical supervision. *The Clinical Supervisor 24*(1/2): 3–21.
48. Rogers CR (1959). A theory of therapy, personality, and interpersonal relationships as developed in the client-centered framework. In: Koch S (ed). *Psychology: the study of a science. Vol 3: formulations of the person and the social context*. New York, NY: McGraw-Hill (pp184–256) (p193).
49. For an example of this approach, see Tudor K, Worrall M (2004). Person-centred philosophy and theory in the practice of supervision. In: Tudor & Worrall (2004) (pp11–30).
50. Carroll M (2007). One more time: What is supervision? *Psychotherapy in Australia 13*(3): 34–40.
51. Bernard (2005) (p16).
52. Liese BS, Beck JS (1997). Cognitive behaviour supervision. In: Watkins CE (ed). *Handbook of Psychotherapy Supervision*. New York, NY: John Wiley & Sons (pp114–133).
53. Fruzzetti AE, Walz JA, Linehan MM (1997). Supervision in dialectical behaviour therapy. In: Watkins (1997) (pp84–100).
54. Paterson CH (1997). Client-centered supervision. In: Watkins (1997) (pp134–146). Also Tudor & Worrall (2004); Tudor K, Worrall M (eds) (2007). *Freedom to Practise II: developing person-centred approaches to supervision*. Ross-on-Wye: PCCS Books.
55. Yontef G (1997). Supervision from additional therapy perspective. In: Watkins (1997) (pp147–163).
56. Mazzetti M (ed) (2004). *La supervisione. Scambi di saperi. Quaderni di*

Psicologia, Analisi Transazionale e Scienze Umane 42. Milano: Edizioni La Vita Felice.

57. Hargaden H (ed) (2015). *The Art of Relational Supervision: clinical implications of the use of self in group supervision*. London: Karnac.

58. See Wheeler S, Richards K (2007). *The Impact of Clinical Supervision on Counsellors and Therapists, their Practice and their Clients: a systematic review of the literature*. Rugby: BACP. Also: Davies N (2016). *Research and Literature Overview of Supervision within the Counselling Professions*. Rugby: BACP.

59. Darongkamas J, John C, Walker M (2014). An eight-eyed version of Hawkins and Shohet's clinical supervision model: the addition of a cognitive analytic therapy concept of the 'observing eye/I' as the 'observing us'. *British Journal of Guidance and Counselling 42*(3): 261–270.

60. Vallance K (2004). Exploring counsellor percpetions of the impact of counselling supervision on clients. *British Journal of Guidance and Counselling 32*(4): 559–574. Also: West A (2012). Supervising counsellors and psychotherapists who work with trauma: a Delphi study. *British Journal of Guidance and Counselling 38*(4): 409–430.

61. Prasko J, Mozny P, Novotny M, Slepecky M, Vuskocilova J (2012). Self-reflection in cognitive behavioural therapy in clinical supervision: applying the fidelity framework. *Training and Education in Professional Psychology 8*(3): 149–157.

62. Owen-Pugh V, Symons C (2011). *Evaluation of Roth and Pilling's Competence Framework for Clinical Supervision*. Report to the British Association for Counselling and Psychotherapy. Leicester: University of Leicester Institute of Lifelong Learning.

63. See, for instance, Vallance K (2004). Exploring counsellor perceptions of the impact of counselling supervision on clients. *British Journal of Guidance and Counselling 32*(4): 559–574.

64. For further discussion of these scopes, see Tudor K, Worrall M (eds) (2004). *Freedom to Practise: person-centred approaches to supervision*. Ross-on-Wye: PCCS Books (chapter 3).

65. Kadushin A (1976). *Supervision in Social Work*. New York, NY: Columbia University Press.

66. Proctor B (1988). Supervision: a co-operative exercise in accountability. In: Marken M, Payne M (eds). *Enabling and Ensuring Supervision in Practice*. Leicester: Leicester National Youth Bureau/Council for Education and Training in Youth and Community Work.

67. Zalcman MJ, Cornell WF (1983). A bilateral model for clinical supervision. *Transactional Analysis Journal 13*(2): 112–123.

68. Hogan RA (1964). Issues and approaches in supervision. *Psychotherapy: Theory, Research, and Practice 1*: 139–141.

69. Watkins (1997). Also Fleming J (1953). The role of supervision and psychiatric training. *Bulletin of the Menninger Clinic 17*: 157–159.
70. Noted by Borders LD (1989). A pragmatic agenda for developmental supervision research. *Counsellor Education and Supervision 29*(1): 16–24. Perhaps the most referenced of these models is Stoltenberg CD, Delworth U (1987). *Supervising Counselors and Therapists*. San Francisco, CA: Jossey-Bass. See also Stoltenberg C (1981). Approaching supervision from a developmental perspective: the counsellor-complexity model. *Counselor Education and Supervision 43*: 326–335.
71. Tudor K, Worrall M (2004). Person-centred perspectives on supervision. In: Tudor K, Worrall M (eds). *Freedom to Practise: person-centred approaches to supervision*. Ross-on-Wye: PCCS Books (pp43–63).
72. Stern D (2000). *The Interpersonal World of the Infant* (revised edition). New York, NY: Basic Books.
73. Casement P (1985). *On Learning from the Patient*. London: Tavistock; Casement P (1990). *Further Learning from the Patient: the analytic space and process*. London: Routledge.
74. Hawkins P, Shohet R (2012/1989). *Supervision in the Helping Professions* (4th ed). Maidenhead: Open University Press.
75. Casement (1985) (p30).
76. Hawkins & Shohet (2012) (p87).
77. BACP (2016). *BACP Register Audit. Annual report 2015–2016*. Lutterworth: BACP (p20). www.bacp.co.uk/docs/pdf/15874_bacp%20register%20audit%20annual%20report%202015-2016.pdf (accessed 9 July 2017).
78. Jenkins P (2016). Chesnuts roasting on an open fire? Supervisor liability revisited. [Online.] *Contemporary Psychotherapy 8*(2).
79. Page S, Wosket V (1994). *Supervising the Counsellor: a cyclical model*. London: Routledge. Also: Carroll M (1996). *Counselling Supervision: theory, skills and practice*. London: Cassell.
80. Perhaps the prime example of this is Elizabeth Holloway's seven-dimensional systems model, which identifies a total of 29 elements of and for supervision. Holloway E (1995). *Clinical Supervision: a systems approach*. London: Sage.
81. Clarkson P (1992). *Transactional Analysis Psychotherapy: an integrative approach*. London: Routledge.
82. Tudor & Worrall (2004).
83. See EATA Professional Training Standards Committee (2017). *EATA Training and Examinations Handbook*. Konstanz: EATA. www.eatanews.org/training-manuals-and-supplements (accessed 9 July 2017). Also: International Association for Transactional Analysis (2013). *Training and*

Examinations Handbook. Pleasanton, CA: IATA. http://itaaworld.org/itaa-training-examinations-handbook (accessed 12 July 2017).
84. Tudor & Worrall (2004).
85. In the UK, the standard 'default setting' for supervision, even during training, is generally once a month. When I moved to Aotearoa New Zealand, I was surprised to find, and had to get used to, the expectation to have and offer supervision once a fortnight; for trainees or provisional members of NZAP, this expectation increases to supervision once a week.
86. Ladany N, Melincoff D (1999). The nature of counsellor supervisor non-disclosure. *Counselor Education and Supervision 38*(3): 161–176.
87. See Tudor K (2012). Ebb and flow: one year on from *The Turning Tide: Pluralism and Partnership in Psychotherapy in Aotearoa New Zealand. Psychotherapy and Politics International 10*(2): 170–177, and Chapter 9.
88. I was recently told by a group of counselling psychologists, as a *fact*, that they had clinical responsibility for their supervisees' clinical work.
89. Jenkins P (2007). Supervisors in the dock? Supervision in the law. In: Tudor & Worrall (2007).
90. New Zealand Association of Psychotherapists (2016).
91. Stark M (1999). *Modes of Therapeutic Action: enhancement of knowledge, provision of experience, and engagement in relationship*. Northvale, NJ: Jason Aronson.
92. Tudor K (2011). Understanding empathy. *Transactional Analysis Journal 41*(1): 39–57.
93. Sarnat J (1992). Supervision and relationship: resolving the teach-treat controversy in psychoanalytic supervision. *Psychoanalytic Psychology 9*(3): 387–403 (p396).
94. Merry T (2004). Supervision as heuristic research enquiry. In: Tudor & Worrall (2004) (pp189–199).
95. Sarnat (1992) (p387).

CHAPTER 6

Psychotherapy research

Life itself still remains a very effective therapist.
(Karen Horney)[1]

It is appropriate that this book considers psychotherapy research, for two reasons. The first is that research itself is a critical enquiry; the second is because, by and large, there is a gap in psychotherapy between research and practice, in that relatively few practitioners read or conduct research – indeed, in some parts of the profession there is an antipathy, and even antagonism towards, research and researchers.[2] In his discussion of this problem, John McLeod suggests 'reframing the relationship between researchers and practitioners'.[3] This includes, first, acknowledging that, in the field of psychotherapy and counselling, new ideas have tended to come from practitioners, and second, that for therapy researchers, there is no personal gap between research and practice – indeed, the experience of doing research is often enriching for the student or practitioner. McLeod goes on to argue that: a) it would be useful for researchers to find out what practitioners want to know; b) researchers could use their own experiences as practitioners to be truly reflexive, and to communicate that, and c) we – in the field, profession and discipline – need to consider the therapeutic value for clients of participating in research, which, studies suggest, clients tend to favour, but therapists do not.

By way of offering a critical examination of this area of critical enquiry, the first part of the chapter reviews four key areas of psychotherapy research: case study research, outcome studies, research into client factors, and research into common factors. The second part of the chapter addresses the question of evidence and, specifically, the problem of the privileging of certain 'evidence' over others, and, in doing so, offers a framework that clarifies the basis of this and other problems and questions about research. I conclude the chapter with a review of what might be considered to be critical methodologies and methods in and for psychotherapy research.

Researching psychotherapy

When it comes to research, it is particularly difficult to distinguish psychotherapy as a distinct discipline and practice, for reasons referred to in the Introduction. Thus, while there is a lot of research being conducted into psychotherapy, there are only two journals published in the English language that are specifically dedicated to psychotherapy research: *Psychotherapy Research*, the journal of the Society for Psychotherapy Research, launched in 1991 (published by Taylor & Francis), and *Counselling and Psychotherapy Research*, launched by BACP in 2001 (now published by Wiley-Blackwell). For a number of years, the generic journal *Psychotherapy*, published by the American Psychological Association (APA), had 'research' in its subtitle, but it dropped this in 2013.

As a result, most research that encompasses psychotherapy is published in a variety of academic and professional journals – in his book on *Counselling Research*, John McLeod lists some 45 such journals[4] – that are hard to access, especially for practitioners. Moreover, the overlap between the practice and fields of counselling, psychology and psychotherapy (which I note in the Introduction) makes it hard to distinguish research that is specifically concerned with psychotherapy (as distinct from counselling and clinical and counselling psychology).

Although research in psychotherapy may be viewed as the domain of the researcher and academic, it was practitioners who initiated the first research into the practice of psychotherapy. From Freud onwards, practitioners have been reflecting on their practice with a view to communicating and generalising it. Rogers' 'therapeutic conditions' were formulated, not on the basis of some *a priori* theorising, but from listening to recordings of therapy sessions and, using what might now be considered coding, in the tradition of grounded theory research, identifying what appeared (that is, sounded) to be helpful.[5] Despite the dominance of medically- and empirically-based models of research,[6] the bias of governments,[7] and a certain disengagement with research on the part of practitioners,[8] the facts from research and psychotherapy are, as Mick Cooper puts it, 'friendly'.[9] These facts include:

- that, compared with medical and surgical procedures, psychotherapy and counselling has a large positive effect[10]

- that more 'resistant' clients tend to do better in nondirective therapies[11]

- that psychotherapy is the most cost-effective form of treatment for severe psychological distress.[12]

Of course, it is impossible to summarise the findings of the past 160 years of research into psychotherapy, or even all the *areas* of psychotherapy research. Writing about the historical development of counselling research, McLeod makes the point that many of the current concerns in the research world have their echoes and, indeed, their antecedents, in earlier eras, although some of the concepts have changed. Thus, earlier research on 'non-directiveness' has been replaced by research on 'therapist reflection', and research into 'therapeutic conditions' has become research into the 'therapeutic alliance'. Here I examine four of areas of psychotherapy research – case study research, outcome studies, research into client factors, and research into common factors – from a critical perspective.

Case study research

Case study research has played an important part in the development of psychotherapy, from Freud onwards. In his case studies of 'Dora',[13] the 'Rat Man',[14] and 'Schreber',[15] Freud describes the techniques and assumptions of psychoanalysis;

in the case study of Little Albert, Watson and Rosalie Rayner illustrate their application of behavioural concepts to problems of emotional disturbance,[16] and, in what was the first fully recorded, transcribed and published psychotherapy case in history, the case of Herbert Bryan, Rogers demonstrates his work, including his own reflections on the process.[17] Clearly, psychotherapy and psychotherapists have gained enormously from the publication of such work; and, indeed, trainees/students and candidates the world over are required to write case studies for qualification and professional membership/accreditation.

However, it is also clear that, as a research method, the case study is most vulnerable to the criticisms of its subjective bias from the dominant research traditions of medicine/psychiatry and psychology, as well as its apparent lack of verification and generalisability, both of which are considered problematic and even unethical. In terms of levels of evidence for intervention – and funding – it is equally ill-considered (see discussion pp187–190 below and Table 6.3).

There are two related responses to this. The first is to assert that, by and large, psychotherapy operates from a different paradigm of practice and research than medicine or psychology (see discussion below, pp188–192), and, specifically, that we need to reclaim the methodologies that support our thinking and practice – and those that support critical thinking and practice. The second response has been to develop this particular research method, which now encompasses a number of different forms: narrative case studies, single-case experiments, single-case quantitative analyses, research-informed case studies, and combined qualitative/quantitative studies.[18] Also, from a critical perspective, it is clear that such case studies are enhanced by the involvement of the client.

Outcome studies

Psychotherapy outcomes research encompasses the efficacy of therapy, including change in the world outside therapy and ratings of clients by significant others; outcome expectation; whether clients get worse as a result of therapy; how much therapy clients need; what happens after therapy; how therapy compares with medication, and the cost-effectiveness of therapy.[19]

In 1992, Michael Lambert summarised the existing research in psychotherapy outcomes, grouping the factors of successful therapy into four areas, ranked by the percentage of change in clients as a function of the factors.[20] This showed that 40 per cent of change in clients is attributable to extra-therapeutic factors – that is, factors that are qualities of the client themselves (such as ego strength) or of their environment (such as fortuitous events and social support) and aid recovery 'regardless of participation in therapy'.[21] In his review, Lambert refers to the environmental qualities of the nature, strength and quality of social supports, and especially the marital relationship, to which I would add friendship and family support,[22] peer support,[23] and income.[24] In any case, given the significance of such extra therapeutic factors, it does seem important 'to examine the supportive aspects of the natural environment'.[25] Lambert notes a clear implication of this finding, which is for therapists '[to] draw upon the natural helping systems that are abundant in the environment to assist them in their efforts to improve psychological therapies'.[26] Moreover, if we regard the natural world itself as 'a natural helping system', then this implication provides a good basis for ecotherapy, and for research into its effectiveness as part of the 40 per cent change in clients.

The second most influential factor, which, according to Lambert, accounts for 30 per cent of change in clients, comprises factors that are common in and across therapeutic approaches (which I discuss below), and the therapeutic relationship (which I discuss in Chapter 4, pp124–125, 128, 131 and 133). In his review, Lambert makes an important historical point that particular systems or schools of therapy are generally developed 'long before empirical evidence supports their use'.[27] Lambert gives examples of common factors such as empathy, warmth, acceptance, encouragement etc, and groups them into support, learning and action factors (Table 6.1). Overall, this is an interesting and useful taxonomy that acknowledges practice across the psychotherapeutic spectrum, and, after 25 years, still stands up to scrutiny.

Table 6.1 – Sequential listing of factors across therapies that are associated with positive outcomes[28]

Support factors	Learning factors	Action factors
Catharsis	Advice	Behavioural regulation
Identification with therapist	Affective experiencing	Cognitive mastery
Mitigation of isolation	Assimilation of problematic experiences	Encouragement to face fears, take risks, and of mastery efforts
Positive relationship	Changing expectations of personal effectiveness	Modelling
Reassurance		Practice
Release of tension		Reality testing
Structure	Cognitive learning	Success experience
Therapeutic alliance	Corrective emotional experience	Working through
Therapist-client active participation	Exploration of internal frame of reference	
Therapist expertness	Feedback	
Therapist warmth, respect, empathy, acceptance, genuineness	Insight	
Trust	Rationale	

Of course, in many ways it is hard to separate these factors, or the fact that they are inter-related. In one study, clients were asked to rate what had been important in forming and strengthening a positive therapeutic relationship with their therapists in terms of technical activity, the therapist's self-disclosure, emphasising client expertness, and active listening.[29] The results showed that technical activity was rated the highest, which may seem surprising until we consider that one of the reported examples was the therapist asking the client to make a list of their goals. Commenting on this, Cooper suggests 'that technical and relational processes are often much more interlinked than we might imagine'.[30] It is also worth noting that this table is based on a development sequence that, by moving from support, through learning, to action, represents a movement from the inside out, as opposed to outside in.

The third factor, which accounts for 15 per cent of change in clients, is expectancy (or placebo effects) – that is, the improvement that results from the client's expectations of the help they are receiving and/or their belief that it will be helpful.

The fourth factor, which also accounts for 15 per cent of change in clients, is attributable to techniques – that is, factors unique to specific therapies, which are often tailored to the treatment of specific problems – although, as Lambert concludes, 'there is little evidence to suggest superiority of one school technique over another'.[31]

As Feltham points out in his discussion of common factors research, a similar review by Bruce Wampold in 2001 reported different percentages: extra therapeutic factors accounted for 87 per cent, common factors nine per cent, client factors three per cent, and specific therapeutic techniques a mere one per cent.[32] The findings of both Lambert and Wampold have significant implications, indicating the need for a more context-sensitive psychotherapy, and more education and training for psychotherapists with regard to the significance of context on client's lives (see Chapter 7) – and, indeed, with regard to the view that both clients and therapists are contextual beings (see Chapter 2). These findings also indicate that psychotherapists should think more broadly about their way(s) of working and question their allegiance to particular theoretical orientations, especially if they are reliant on and proposing the efficacy of highly specialised skills and techniques.

Some forms of psychotherapy, and especially psychoanalysis and psychoanalytic psychotherapy, propose regular therapy, ideally twice a week or more, and a long-term commitment and engagement over a number of years. This appears to be supported by research into the relationship between dose and effect. In their research on this, Kenneth Howard, Mark Kopta, Merton Krause and David Orlinsky found that between 60 and 65 per cent of people experienced significant symptomatic relief within one to seven visits; after six months, these figures rose to between 70 and 75 per cent and, at one year, to 85 per cent.[33] Commenting on this phenomenon, Cooper reports: '[r]esearch into the "dose–effect" relationship makes it clear that the more therapy clients have, the better they tend to get, and this has been shown in both the efficacy... [and] effectiveness... research.' He continues: 'It would not be true to say, however, that there is a direct relationship between the number of sessions and the degree of improvement. Rather, what the research tends to show is a "law of diminishing returns".[34] While there are some meta-studies that support the efficacy of psychodynamic psychotherapy – notably Shedler's[35] – and specifically of its long-term form – notably Falk Leichsenring and Sven Rabung's[36] – the findings on the relationship between dose and effect have serious implications for those who simply assume and assert the benefit of long-term psychotherapy, as well as for public sector provision: the public sector cannot, by and large, fund long-term psychotherapy.

While most clients improve as a result of psychotherapy, there are those who don't, and there is some evidence to suggest that therapists tend to underestimate this.[37] In a sense, this is not surprising as, understandably, professionals in any line of work are committed to their product. However, it would appear that psychotherapists need to take this aspect of psychotherapy outcome research more seriously and, for instance, attend to clients when they fail to turn up for a scheduled session or when they withdraw from therapy before the therapist thinks it advisable. They might also consider the implications of research into initial or intake interviews, with reference to long waiting times between the initial interview and first session, and the need for therapists to provide clarity, perspective and information, especially for clients who have not had previous experience of therapy.[38] In its treatment guide *Coping with Depression,* the Royal Australian and New Zealand Association of Psychiatrists advises consumers that the greatest contribution to a positive outcome from treatment comes from '[t]he person and their health professional developing a trusting relationship and working together to find a suitable treatment'.[39]

Client factors

Traditionally, these include a range of factors and characteristics, which, in his review of the literature, Cooper usefully divides into those that are inferred and those that are observed (Table 6.2).

Table 6.2 – Inferred and observed characteristics in client-factor research[40]

Inferred characteristics	Observed characteristics
Attachment and interpersonal style	Age
Level of social support, including close friendships, peer support	Ethnicity
	Gender
Motivation and involvement, including active participation in therapy and openness	Sexual orientation
	Socio-economic and employment status
Outcome expectation, including faith and hope	
Perfectionism	
Personality disorders	
Predilections, ie. the client's expectations of how change takes place and the congruence or fit between this and the treatment	
Preferences concerning type of therapy	
Process expectations, which are aided by clients having a relatively clear understanding of the process and goals of therapy	
Psychological functioning	
Psychological mindedness	
Stage of change	

The research on client factors raises a number of concerns from a critical perspective.

1. Regarding psychological functioning

A number of different research studies suggest that clients with higher levels of manifest, overt distress have better clinical outcomes, while those with high levels of psychosocial dysfunction get the least amount of therapy.[41] In other words, therapy is less effective in helping people compensate for their deficiencies, and is better at helping clients build on or capitalise their strengths. This is known, appropriately enough, as the 'capitalisation hypothesis',[42] and tends to support one criticism of psychotherapy, that it works more with and for the relatively well-functioning 'worried well', and is less helpful to those who are less well off, both in terms of functioning and finance. While this is of concern, it should also be considered in the context of a number of public sector projects that have provided psychotherapy for underprivileged and marginalised people and have reported success.[43] From an equity perspective that seeks to compensate for inequality (rather than to increase capital), one conclusion that may be drawn from this is that we need more such projects – and that we need them to be well researched.

2. Regarding attachment and interpersonal style

Echoing the previous point, research suggests that clients with secure early attachment tend to get more out of therapy,[44] the one exception to which is that clients with a dismissive, avoidant attachment style can do well in therapy.[45] These findings suggest psychotherapists need to intervene earlier, psychotherapeutically, psycho-educationally and organisationally, with young people, children and infants, and their parents, as well as in social and healthcare systems such as schools, nurseries and hospitals.

3. Regarding stages of change

In 1958, Rogers identified a number of stages of therapy, and argued that, when people are at stages one and two (where, among other things, they do not recognise or own their feelings, are somewhat remote from their experience, do not recognise that they have problems, and tend not to relate to others), there is only a modest degree of success with voluntary clients.[46] A more recent and popular model of change has been developed by James Prochaska and Carlo DiClemente,[47] which, similarly, identifies a number of stages of change (from pre-contemplation, through contemplation, preparation, action and maintenance, to termination). Research has shown that success rates for making behavioural changes, such as giving up smoking, increase across the stages,[48] and, conversely, that clients in the pre-contemplation stage are most likely to drop out of therapy.[49] On the basis that other forms of therapy can reach people before they are ready for psychotherapy, we can consider the benefits of 'pre-therapy', an approach to therapy with clients who are in some way 'contact-impaired'.[50]

4. Regarding 'observed characteristics'

While research indicates that outcomes are fairly similar across gender, sexual orientation and age, this is not the case with regard to ethnicity. Indeed, clients from ethnic minorities, which in countries such as Aotearoa New Zealand, Australia, Canada, the US and many others presumably includes indigenous clients, are generally less likely to be offered talking – or listening – therapies. In part, this is exacerbated by the low numbers of ethnic minority and indigenous psychotherapists, and, while I don't advocate necessarily 'matching' therapists to clients on the basis of ethnicity (or age, gender, sexual orientation and so on), it is clear that having more psychotherapists from such 'minorities' (which, in the profession of psychotherapy, includes men) would enhance the practice of psychotherapy and the profession – and, most likely, our critique of both.

Common factors research

The term 'common factors' was first used by Saul Rosenzweig in 1936,[51] in an article in which he challenged the view that a positive therapeutic result could be used as a test of the particular theory (or doctrine) being advanced, and, as an alternative, proposed three common factors that he viewed then as largely implicit in therapy. These were the therapist's effective personality; the therapist's 'formal consistency' with their approach,[52] and that the approach was adaptable to presenting problems of what he termed 'the sick personality'.[53] It was Rosenzweig who first referred to what has become known as the Dodo verdict when, in the epigram of his paper, he quoted from Lewis Carroll's *Alice in Wonderland*: 'At last the Dodo said, "Everybody has won, and all must have prizes".' In the context of psychotherapy research, this verdict refers to the fact that there is an overwhelming body of evidence on the comparative efficacy of the various therapies to suggest that there is little difference between them. There are, of course, critiques of the Dodo verdict and position, notably from John Hunsley and Gina Di Giulio,[54] and from Shedler, who, in effect, claims to have put the Dodo (verdict) to flight.[55]

Currently, there is an emerging view that both common factors and orientation-specific factors are likely to contribute to our understanding of effecting psychological change.

In 1950, John Dollard and Neal Miller published a book in which they emphasised that the psychological principles and social conditions of *learning* are the most important common factors, and identified four fundamentals necessary for instrumental learning: drive, cue, response and reward.[56] In a sense, their model anticipated more recent interest in common client factors.

In 1957, Rogers published the results of his research into what he termed 'the necessary and sufficient conditions of therapeutic personality change'[57] – therapeutic conditions and attitudes that I have discussed with regard to practice in Chapter 3, and which led to a plethora of research.[58] In the context of research, it is worth noting four points:

1. that Rogers presented these conditions as applicable to all types of psychotherapy, and not specifically client-centred therapy – an implication that led Jeanne Stubbs and Jerold Bozarth to refer to this as an 'integrative' statement,[59] and applicable to all types of clients.

2. that he did so in terms of necessity and sufficiency – a philosophical construction that, in Sol Garfield's view, distinguishes the common factors research of Rogers and Hans Strupp[60] from that of others, including Garfield's own.[61] His point is that common or non-specific factors are not necessarily the sole factors that account for change in psychotherapy, but that they may account for *some* of the change that takes place.

3. that, in effect, these conditions describe factors of the therapeutic process and relationship and, significantly, factors for both the therapist (psychological contact, congruence, unconditional positive regard and empathic understanding) and the client (psychological contact, incongruence, and perception of the therapist).

4. that the sixth condition – '[t]he communication to the client

of the therapist's empathic understanding in unconditional positive regard is to a minimal degree achieved'[62] – which, elsewhere, Rogers describes as the 'basic' or 'assumed condition',[63] is the most fundamental one, or litmus test of the efficacy of therapy. As Barry Duncan, Scott Miller and Jacqueline Sparks (2004) put it: 'Clients, not therapists, make therapy work.'[64]

This last point offers a theoretical or conceptual base for research that demonstrates the importance of the client's involvement in therapy. Indeed, one of the paradigm shifts in research in psychotherapy and counselling over the past 25 years, and one undoubtedly influenced by the user/survivor/consumer movement, has been the focus on the client factors that determine the outcome of therapy[65] – or, better perhaps, the focus on the client her or himself. As Miller, Duncan and Mark Hubble conclude: '[T]he research literature makes it clear that the client is actually the single most potent contributor to outcome in psychotherapy.'[66]

In 1961, Jerome Frank published a book that was entirely devoted to examining common factors across psychotherapies and related healing approaches. He proposed what might be described as a meta-framework,[67] which identified four factors: the importance of the expectation of help (an aspect of the placebo effect); the therapeutic relationship; a rationale or conceptual scheme that explains given symptoms and that prescribes a ritual or procedure for resolving them, and the active participation of both therapist and client/patient in carrying out that ritual procedure.

Since Frank's work, a number of researchers have proposed various different meta-frameworks for levels of intervention, in terms of theories of change (that is, therapists' theories about how change occurs); principles or strategies of change, and therapy techniques (that is, interventions that therapists suppose will be effective).[68] Meta-frameworks have also been put forward for what Marvin Goldfried and Wendy Padawer refer to as 'a generic model of psychotherapy', comprising five process variables: the therapeutic contract, therapeutic interventions, the therapeutic bond between therapist and patient, the patient's and the therapist's states of self-relatedness, and therapeutic realisation.[69] In their study, Lisa Grencavage and John Norcross reviewed 50 publications and a total of 89 common factors, selected the 35 most common, and grouped them into five areas: client characteristics, therapist qualities, change processes, treatment structure and therapeutic relationship.[70]

There is an emerging view that *both* orientation-specific factors *and* common factors are what effect psychological change. This is significant in that it supports an inclusive, diverse, non-sectarian and pluralistic approach to and across different psychotherapies, and implies and, therefore, hopefully promotes, a client-centred perspective on research: that is, one that focuses on and includes the client in the research. Further, it leads to an appreciation of the influence of other, environmental factors in and on therapy and on its outcomes, all of which are important both to research itself and in the politics of psychotherapy research,[71] and in psychotherapy education and training. However, we are not alone...

The question – and problem – of evidence

The question, or problem, of evidence that psychotherapy and psychotherapists face is manifested in three related phenomena: evidence-based practice, empirically-supported treatments (ESTs) and randomised controlled trials (RCTs) – phenomena that represent, respectively, the politics, the methodology and the method of traditional 'scientific' research.

Evidence-based practice

At first glance, the idea that psychotherapeutic practice is – or should be – based on evidence seems reasonable. However, when we examine this in more detail, we discover that it derives from a particular perspective in science, medicine and psychology, which is then applied to psychotherapy. A classic example of this concerns the work of the APA's Task Force on Promotion and Dissemination of Psychological Procedures,[72] which, in 1995, established a set of criteria for identifying ESTs and produced a list of psychosocial treatments for specific problems or disorders. The Task Force was appointed by Division 12 (Clinical Psychology) of the APA. Similar projects took place at the time in the UK and Germany, and, subsequently, in other countries. Notwithstanding that there are dissenting voices within clinical psychology,[73] there is an easy elision between the dominant discourse in psychology and the dominant discourse in psychotherapy – which is why I refer to this as the politics of and about evidence.

The issue here is that evidence-based practice (EBP) privileges certain evidence, as is clear from Table 6.3.

Table 6.3 – **Levels of evidence for intervention studies**[74]

Level of evidence	Type of evidence
1++	High quality meta-analyses, systematic reviews of RCTs, or RCTs with a very low risk of bias
1+	Well-conducted meta-analyses, systematic reviews of RCTs, or RCTs with a low risk of bias
1–	Meta-analyses, systematic reviews of RCTs, or RCTs with a high risk of bias*
2++	High-quality systematic reviews of case-control or cohort studies High-quality case-control or cohort studies with a very low risk of confounding, bias or chance, and a high probability that the relationship is causal
2+	Well-conducted case-control or cohort studies with a low risk of confounding, bias or chance, and a moderate probability that the relationship is causal
2–	Case-control or cohort studies with a high risk of confounding, bias or chance and a significant risk that the relationship is not causal*
3	Non-analytic studies (for example, case reports, case series)
4	Expert opinion, formal consensus

* Studies with a level of evidence (–) should not be used as a basis for making a recommendation

The emphasis here on meta-analyses and away from experience (through case material, opinion and consensus) is significant not only for its bias but also for its focus on research rather than on practice. An antidote to this view of evidence and focus has been offered by the concept of 'practice-based evidence', a phrase first coined by Steve Morgan and David Juriansz in an article that, significantly, was published in a mental health consumer magazine.[75] It is a concept 'that has a specific approach (practice development in mental health), is based on solid principles (a strengths approach), and works in important areas of practice',[76] and one that, over the past 15 years, has been well developed.[77]

Despite the best efforts of consumers and some professional associations that have lobbied for the inclusion of other evidence,[78] the politics are clear: governments and insurance companies who fund psychotherapy have a vested (financial) interest in only accepting research that specifies and limits treatment – a political bias that is supported by a methodological one.

Empirically-supported treatments

Again, the idea that we want and need to know what works, and, if possible, to know what works for whom, is reasonable. The problem comes when we consider the basis of that knowledge and knowing.

The 'treatments' in ESTs, sometimes also referred to as 'interventions' (thus, ESIs) and 'therapies', are, as the term suggests, based on empirical evidence and, beyond that, empiricism. The language of EST is that of 'pills', 'psychological placebo', 'treatment', 'experimental designs', 'treatment manuals', 'control groups', and so on – all of which are taken from the criteria for empirically validated treatments published by the APA Task Force.[79] The problem with this is not that this language or the approach it represents are wrong; it is that it's only one approach to studying humans, and, as Rogers argued some years ago, we need 'a *human* science'.[80]

Empiricism is a theory about knowledge that was originally expounded by British philosophers such as Locke, George Berkeley and David Hume, and proposes that knowledge is derived primarily from sensory experience (see Chapter 2). In terms of the philosophy of science, empiricism emphasises evidence, especially that which is discovered through experiments, and argues that hypotheses and theories must be tested against observations, rather than based on intuition or revelation – which explains why ESTs do not value case studies or client reports. In terms of their broader location within social science, ESTs are based on research methodologies that are nomothetic (or legislative), rather than ideographic (or symbolising). In terms of their epistemology or theory of knowledge, they are based on positivism, as distinct from anti-positivism, which is represented in different ways of knowing (such as personal and ethical, and through aesthetics[81] and nature, or contact with the land). With regard to human nature, they represent determinism rather than voluntarism (see Chapter 2), and, beyond that, they are based on an ontology (or essence of things) that is concerned with realism rather than nominalism. In short, they are on the 'objectivist' end of a subjectivist–objectivist continuum of approaches to science,[82] and, in effect, represent a modernist (although not a critical) ideology (see Chapter 4).[83] For empiricists and supporters of ESTs, evidence is objective, not personal.

The arguments for and against ESTs are closely linked to psychotherapy research into theoretical orientation, and, specifically, what therapies work for whom. On the basis of research that meets the criteria established by the APA Task Force, we can consider that some therapies have greater efficacy than others for specific forms of psychological distress, clinical disorders and personality disorders.[84] However, these criteria are specific, detailed and exclusive. For 'well-established treatments', they include:

1. that treatments have to be based on group design studies, and, in at least two of them, the treatment is demonstrated to be superior to a pill, psychological placebo or another treatment, *or* '[e]quivalent to an already established treatment and experiments with adequate statistical power (about 30 per group)',[85] or

2. 'a large series of single case design experiments (n>9) demonstrating efficacy', which must have 'used good

experimental designs... and compared intervention to another treatment'; and in any case, for either of these options, that:

3. a. 'experiments must be conducted with treatment manuals'
   b. 'characteristics of the client samples must be clearly specified', and
   c. 'effects must have been demonstrated by at least two different investigators or investigatory teams.'[86]

Unsurprisingly, these criteria exclude many therapies that would disagree, for instance, with the concept of working from the basis of a treatment manual, as well as many practitioner-scientists who simply don't have access to the resources necessary to undertake research that would meet these criteria. Due to this, only some therapeutic approaches have been researched on this basis. This wouldn't be a problem except that, as approaches that have not been researched on this basis do not appear on the lists of validated and therefore approved and supported treatments, they appear invalid. This is another example of a self-sealing system (discussed in Chapter 1).

In an article on the subject and discussing these criteria, Arthur Bohart, Maureen O'Hara and Larry Leitner argue that this clearly represents a 'disenfranchisement of humanistic and other psychotherapies'.[87] Discussing qualitative research in the context of what has been referred to as 'the conservative challenge', Ernest House refers to the bias represented by EBP and ESTs as 'methodological fundamentalism... [in which] only randomized experiments produce truth',[88] and, indeed, if EBP and ESTs are viewed as the 'gold standard' of research, RCTs are its golden method. RCTs may indeed be the gold standard research method for drug trials, but they are not necessarily applicable when comparing humans or human 'treatment'. The problems this presents in and for psychotherapy research are the subject of much debate and literature; however, the inappropriateness may easily be seen and heard in the language used by researchers who favour this method, when they routinely refer to 'waiting list control groups'.[89] Moreover, as Elizabeth Freire points out, 'the RCT is not a theory-neutral evaluative method but rather a research method shaped by assumptions that originate in behaviourist theories of therapy'.[90]

Another, broader issue is that this empirical approach to research is based on the notion that specific forms of psychological distress or disorder exist and that it makes sense to talk in terms of 'client groups' by diagnosis, both of which are challenged by more phenomenological approaches (encompassing both humanistic and psychodynamic approaches). Nine years after the APA clinical psychology task force published its criteria, another task force, from the APA's Division 32 (Humanistic Psychology), reported its practice recommendations for the provision of humanistic psychosocial services. Included in these recommendations were suggestions that research methods should:

- approach the person not just as a diagnostic category but as a whole
- consider therapy as an open dialogical process that is unpredictable and unmanipulable
- capture the non-quantifiable and the meaningful
- consider the participating individual as an agent and interpreter of the therapeutic situation, [and]
- focus descriptively and interpretively on individual people in depth.[91]

These are very different requirements and, in some respects, diametrically opposite to those of the clinical psychology task force, and it is significant that this report's subtitle is an '[a]lternative to mandated practices and treatment guidelines'. There is, however, no evidence to date that the recommendations of the humanistic task force have gained any traction, in terms of research funding, research projects, government policy or practice guidelines, all of which still favour and tend to focus on cognitive-behavioural therapies. In the UK, the government-funded Increasing Access to Psychological Therapies (IAPT) programme[92] in fact offers primarily and predominantly cognitive behavioural therapy, with the result that it has certainly increased access to this modality, but *decreased* access to the full range of well-recognised therap*ies*.

Despite widespread acknowledgement of the existence of research bias, the critique of the evidence base for cognitive behavioural therapy and the extensive evidence for equivalent effectiveness (the Dodo bird verdict), it appears that political exigencies trump research evidence. Some years ago, Jeremy Holmes offered a brief historical summary of how psychotherapy in the UK came to the awareness of mental health policy makers, concluding that:

> In each of these publications due homage is paid to psychotherapy as a multifaceted, pluralistic enterprise in which a range of therapies is required to meet patients' various needs. Yet, when detailed recommendations are examined, there is no doubt that cognitive behaviour therapy is promoted as the therapy of choice.[93]

Earlier, when discussing case study research (pp176 and 188 above), I referred to the response or strategy of reclaiming the methodologies that support critical thinking and practice. So, in the third part of this chapter, I discuss critical research methodologies and methods that can more accurately reflect the evidence from practice, and especially evidence from and about people (clients and practitioners) and practice that may be considered radical, marginal, peripheral or subversive.

Critical research methodologies and methods

Common sense would suggest that research into psychotherapy would be sensitive to, if not based on, principles and models derived from psychotherapy, and not those from medicine or psychology. However, from the literature and the discussion above, this sense is not at all common. Moreover, that psychotherapy itself could be considered a form of research[94] challenges dominant views of methodology and represents a critique of authority.

Psychotherapy is a human science and art; it is interested in the meaning that people make of themselves, their lives and their worlds, including other people. The data and evidence in which psychotherapy is interested are predominantly personal (although not necessarily individual), rather than general (as in 'client groups' by diagnosis) – another critique of its authority. This is supported by the more recent emphasis on client-centred and client-directed research, which, as Duncan, Miller and Sparks put it, recasts clients as 'the main characters, the heroes and heroines of the therapeutic stage'.[95]

The personal also applies to the researcher. Parker's point (referred to in Chapter 3) about 'understanding how we come to stand where we are'[96] suggests that it is important that the researcher considers their position and is mindful of their standpoint throughout the course of study – which is a critique of objectivity. I suggest that this starts – or should start – at the beginning of any study, such that the researcher considers the dynamic and dialogic relationship between their subject (ie. their research question or focus, as well as the subjects or people involved), themselves, and, where relevant, their supervisory team and the context of the research, as well as the methodology and the method they use – and, ideally, that these seven elements should be philosophically congruent with each other.

As with other forms of research at the more subjective end of the subjectivist–objectivist spectrum of social science, psychotherapy research tends to use different language: for instance, 'verification' might be assessed in terms of credibility, transferability, dependability and confirmability[97] – a critique of rhetoric. Another example is the shift from 'evidence-based practice' to 'practice-based evidence', and thence to a 'research-informed approach to therapy'.

As in the rest of the book, alongside a critical view of psychotherapy (in this case, psychotherapy research), I pose a critical praxis. In the final part of this chapter, I reclaim – or perhaps claim – a more critical approach to psychotherapy research, and consider methodologies that are clearly critical as well as other methodologies that may or may not be critical, depending on the philosophical assumptions that inform them. I first consider methodologies and then methods that are critical, following which I indicate possible relationships between the two.

Table 6.4 lists a number of methodologies and articulates the basis of their criticality.

Table 6.4 – Critical methodologies

Methodology	Basis of its criticality
Activist methodology	Based on reciprocity and dialogue,[98] or a critique of institutions through rhetoric[99]
Critical action research[100]	Based on the combination of critical theory with participatory action research that inverts the traditional hierarchy between 'subject' and researcher[101]
Critical or radical ethnography	Based on the researcher's advocacy for the emancipation of marginalised groups in society and/or cultures[102]
Critical indigenous methodology	Based on a dialogue between indigenous and critical scholars and, for instance, by drawing on Freire's pedagogy of the oppressed[103] and local indigenous contacts, an understanding that all enquiries are both political and moral[104]
Critical theory	Based on critical theory such as Marxism, feminism, and so on, which in turn is usually based on an analysis of alienation, power and oppression
Critical race theory	Based on the critical examination of society and culture and, specifically, the intersection of race and power (and, originally, law)
Emancipatory research	Based on an analysis that is emancipatory for both participants and researchers
Feminist research theory	Based on a critical analysis of patriarchy, patriarchal structures and gender relations
Indigenous, eg. kaupapa Māori research theory/methodology	Based on principles that assert or reassert the rights of indigenous peoples[105] and inform the purpose, aspiration and context of the research, as well as the relationships involved
Queer theory	Based on challenging the binary norm of heterosexuality and homosexuality, and the sexual categories, and decentring identity[106]
Transformatory research	Based on the principle that the subject and design of the research has the primary aim of achieving social and political change[107]

Although many of these methodologies are founded in the Western intellectual tradition, albeit a critical one, there are others that question and subvert this methodological hegemony. In Aotearoa New Zealand, the principles of *kaupapa* Māori research methodology lay the foundations for indigenous research that is not only emancipatory for Māori but can also be transformative for non-Māori. Wiremu Woodard identifies seven of these principles:

1. the principle of the *Te Tiriti o Waitangi* (the Treaty of Waitangi) – [the founding document of the New Zealand nation, which] provides a basis through which Māori may critically analyse relationships, challenge the status quo, and affirm Māori rights[108]

2. the principle of collective philosophy – the *kaupapa* – refers to the collective vision, aspiration and purpose of Māori communities

3. the principle of emancipation – *tino rangatiratanga* – relates to sovereignty, autonomy, control, self determination and independence

4. the principle of socio-economic mediation asserts a need for *kaupapa* Māori research to be of benefit to Māori communities

5. the principle of cultural aspiration, within a *kaupapa* Māori paradigm, [refers to] Māori ways of knowing, doing and understanding the world [being] considered valid in their own right

6. the principle of growing respectful relationships – *āta* – relates specifically to building, nurturing and maintaining wellbeing in relationships with Māori[109]

7. the principle of extended family structure – *whānau* – acknowledges the relationship the Māori have with the world around them and with one another. It also identifies the intrinsic connection between the researcher, the researched and the research.[110]

Parallel with critical methodologies and methodologies that can be critical, Table 6.5 considers the criticality of varied research methods.

Table 6.5 – Research methods that can be critical

Method	Basis of its criticality
Case study	When it accounts for personal, subjective – and, especially, subjugated – experience, and/or a critical study of that experience or situation[111]
Conversation analysis[112]	When it contributes to an understanding of the role of conversation and 'talk' in reproducing and maintaining dominant social conversations and arrangements.[113] Commenting on their approach to research with clients, Duncan, Miller and Sparks make a distinction between interviewing and what they call 'conversing'[114]
Co-operative enquiry	When it is based on collaborative research with people[115]
Critical hermeneutic method	When it resists polarised positions, considers a consciousness of those who are absent from the literature, and demands a commitment on the part of the researcher to attend to marginalised voices and neglected texts[116]
Discourse analysis	When it views language as a form of social practice
Focus groups	When both the focus of the group and the composition of the group itself reflect a critical analysis of power and oppression
Heuristic method	When it is based on critical self-examination and self-exploration
Interpretive phenomenological analysis	When it requires the naming of the basis of the interpretation and the interpreter[117]
Interview	When the focus of the interview reflects a critical analysis of power and oppression
Literature review	When the review of the literature is based on some critical theory and/or analysis
Narrative analysis	When it is based on an analysis of what is revealed about power inequities and positionings in the narrative or story told[118]
Participant observation	When it is based on the 'observer' being a participant and subject, and thus on some equalising of the inherent power of the position of the researcher

Questionnaire	When it offers a critical questioning of the subject of the research
Thematic analysis	When it is based on a critical analysis and theory of the text

Drawing together the content of Tables 6.4 and 6.5, I suggest *some* links between methods and critical methodologies. I emphasise *'some'* as the links are indicative rather than comprehensive, and I intend them to stimulate the reader and researcher to make their own links, based on the philosophical congruence between the subject of the research, method and methodology – and, in my experience, most people tend to think in this order. This is why Table 6.5 reads from method (left) to methodology (right). The lines are intended to be seen as travelling both ways, to indicate and encourage bi-directional thinking.

Table 6.6 – Links between methods and critical methodologies

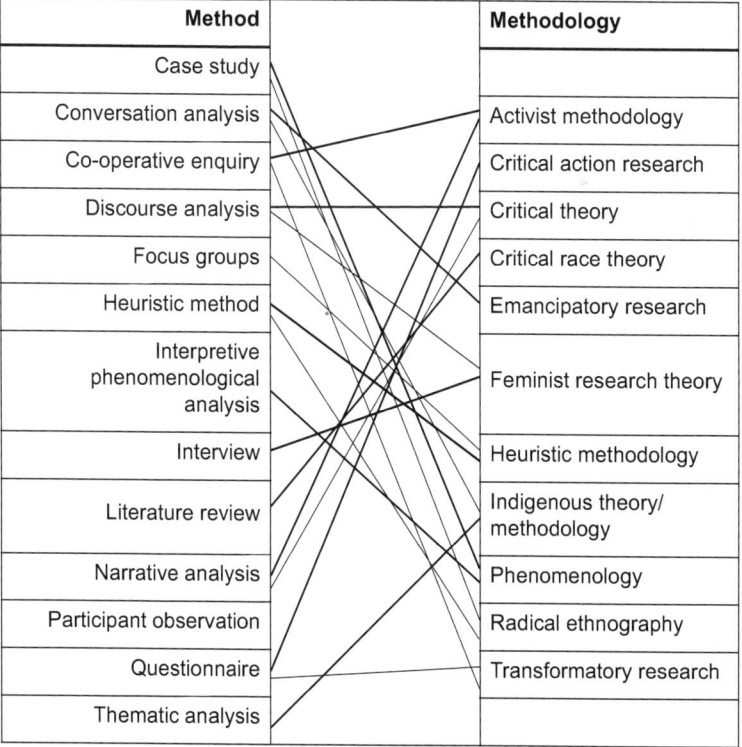

In terms of practice, and to conclude this chapter, I suggest some examples of a critical focus for psychotherapy research.

- Research question: What is the impact of **age differences** between psychotherapists and their clients, for instance with regard to changing attitudes to gender and sexuality?
  Research method: an interpretive analysis of recorded interviews (method), based on feminist research theory (methodology).

- Research question: To what extent are **client voices** present in psychotherapy research, and, if absent, how can they be more included in such research?
  Research method: a literature review (method), based on transformatory research (methodology).

- Research question: What is the relative allocation of **government funding** to public sector counselling, clinical psychology, counselling psychology and psychotherapy, respectively?
  Research method: a statistical analysis (method) of results, interpreted through the lens of critical theory (methodology).

- Research question: Does psychotherapy practice, theory and education/training reflect **institutionalised racism**?
  Research method: a conversation analysis (method) of groups of practitioners and students/trainees, based on critical race theory (methodology).

- Research question: Does the **statutory regulation** of psychotherapy and state registration of psychotherapists increase public protection and the public provision of psychotherapy?
  Research method: a questionnaire about public protection and a survey of the provision of public sector psychotherapy involving the (mixed methods of) thematic analysis of participants' responses and the interpretation of quantitative data, based on critical theory (methodology).

- Research question: What can we learn from the **suicide of psychotherapists**?
  Research method: a psychological autopsy of material written

by the deceased (method), drawing also on heuristic enquiry (methodology).

- Research question: What can we learn from **students/trainees/candidates** from psychotherapy education/training programmes? Research method: interviews or focus groups (method), with analysis focusing on dimensions of power and oppression (eg. regarding ability/disability, ethnicity, gender, race, and sexuality), informed by radical ethnography (methodology).

Endnotes

1. Horney K (1945). *Our Inner Conflicts: a constructive theory of neurosis*. New York, NY: WW Norton & Co (p240).
2. I have been told that at least one colleague has said: 'If you're studying for a PhD, you're not a proper psychotherapist.'
3. McLeod J (2003). *Doing Counselling Research*. London: Sage.
4. McLeod (2003) (p185).
5. In this I differ from McLeod's understanding of Rogers' research as based on and seeking to prove the pre-existing theory of client-centred therapy.
6. Deacon BJ (2013). The biomedical model of mental disorder: a critical analysis of its validity, utility, and effects on psychotherapy research. *Clinical Psychology Review 33*: 846–861 (p854).
7. As Gaie Houston observes: 'Political expediency and truthful accuracy are scarcely synonyms.' Houston G (1990). *The Red Book of Groups* (3rd ed). London: Rochester Foundation (p62).
8. Morrow-Bradley C, Elliott R (1986). Utilisation of psychotherapy research by practising psychotherapists. *American Psychologist 41*(2): 188–197.
9. Cooper M (2008). *Essential Research Findings in Counselling and Psychotherapy: the facts are friendly*. London: Sage.
10. Cooper (2008) (chapter 2).
11. Mohr DC, Beutler LE, Engle D et al (1990). Identification of patients at risk for nonresponse negative outcome in psychotherapy. *Journal of Consulting and Clinical Psychology 58*(5): 622–628. Also: Beutler LE, Malik M, Alimohamed S et al (2004). Therapist variables. In: Lambert MJ (ed). *Bergin and Garfield's Handbook of Psychotherapy and Behaviour Change* (5th ed). Chicago, IL: John Wiley & Sons (pp227–306).
12. Gabbard GO, Lazar SG, Hornberger J, Spiegel D (1997). The economic impact of psychotherapy review. *American Journal of Psychiatry 154*(2): 147–155.

13. Freud S (1953/1901). Fragments of analysis of a case of hysteria. In: Strachey J (ed & trans). *The Standard Edition of the Complete Psychological Works of Sigmund Freud, vol 7*. London: Hogarth Press (pp1–122).
14. Freud S (1955/1909). Notes upon a case of obsessional neurosis. In: Strachey J (ed & trans). *The Standard Edition of the Complete Psychological Works of Sigmund Freud, vol 10*. London: Hogarth Press (pp153–318).
15. Freud S (1958/1911). Psycho-analytic notes on an autobiographical account of a case of paranoia (dementia paranoids). In: Strachey J (ed & trans). *The Standard Edition of the Complete Psychological Works of Sigmund Freud, vol 12*. London: Hogarth Press (pp9–82).
16. Watson JB, Rayner R (1920). Conditioned emotional reactions. *Journal of Experimental Psychology 3*(1): 1–14.
17. Rogers CR (1942). *Counseling and Psychotherapy: new concepts and practice*. Boston, MA: Houghton Mifflin (part IV).
18. These categories were identified by Hillard RB (1993). Single-case methodology and psychotherapy process and outcome research. *Journal of Consulting and Clinical Psychology 61*(3): 373–380, and are discussed by John McLeod in: McLeod J (2003). *Doing Counselling Research*. London: Sage.
19. For an interesting and informative discussion of the historical development of psychotherapy outcome research, see McLeod J (2003) (chapter 8).
20. Lambert M (1992). Psychotherapy outcome research: implications for integrative and eclectic therapists. In: Norcross JC, Goldfried MR (eds). *Handbook of Psychotherapy Integration*. New York, NY: Basic Books (pp94–129).
21. Lambert (1992) (p97).
22. See Maluccio AN (1979). *Learning from Clients' Interpersonal Helping as Viewed by Clients and Social Workers*. New York, NY: Macmillan. Also: Zlotnick C, Shea MT, Pilkonis PA, Elkin I, Ryan C (1996). Gender, type of treatment, dysfunctional attitudes, social support, life events, and depressive symptoms over a naturalistic follow-up. *American Journal of Psychiatry 153*(8): 1021–1027.
23. See Glass CR, Arnkoff DB (2000). Consumers' perspectives on helping and hindering factors and mental health treatment. *Journal of Clinical Psychology 56*(11): 1467–1480.
24. See Clarkin JF, Levy KN (2004). The influence of client variables on psychotherapy. In: Lambert M (2004) (pp194–226).
25. Lambert (1992) (p99).
26. Lambert (1992) (p99).
27. Lambert (1992) (p99).
28. Lambert (1992).
29. Beutler LE, Malik M, Alimohamed S et al (2004). Therapist variables.

Lambert MJ (ed). *Bergin and Garfield's Handbook of Psychotherapy and Behaviour Change* (5th ed). Chicago, IL: John Wiley & Sons (pp227–306).
30. Cooper (2008) (p190).
31. Cooper (2008) (p103).
32. Wampold B (2001). *The Great Psychotherapy Debate: models, methods and findings.* Mahwah, NJ: Lawrence Erlbaum Associates.
33. Howard KI, Kopta MS, Krause MS, Orlinsky DE (1986). The dose effect-relationship in psychotherapy. *American Psychologist 41*(2): 159–164.
34. Cooper (2008) (p27).
35. Shedler J (2010). The efficacy of psychodynamic psychotherapy. *American Psychologist 65*(2): 98–109.
36. Leichsenring F, Rabung S (2008). The effectiveness of long-term psychodynamic psychotherapy: a meta-analysis. *Journal of the American Medical Association 300*(13): 1551–1565.
37. See Boisvert CM, Faust D (2006). Practising psychologists' knowledge of general psychotherapy research findings: implications for science–practice relations. *Professional Psychology: Research and Practice 37*(6): 708–716.
38. See Tryon GS (2002). Engagement in counselling. In: Tryon GS (ed). *Counselling Based on Process Research: applying what we know.* Boston, MA: Allyn & Bacon (pp1–26).
39. Royal Australian and New Zealand Association of Psychiatrists (2009). *Coping with Depression: New Zealand treatment guide for consumers and carers.* Wellington: Royal Australian and New Zealand Association of Psychiatrists (p21).
40. Developed from Cooper M (2008).
41. Mohr DC, Beutler LE, Engle D et al (1990). Identification of patients at risk for nonresponse negative outcome in psychotherapy. *Journal of Consulting and Clinical Psychology 58*(5): 622–628. Also: Castonguay LG, Beutler LE (2006). Principles of therapeutic change: a task force on participants, relationships, and techniques factors. *Journal of Clinical Psychology 62*(6): 631–638.
42. A term first coined by Cronbach LJ, Snow RE (1977). *Aptitudes and Instructional Methods.* New York, NY: Irvington.
43. See, for example: Holland S (1988). Psychotherapy, oppression and social action: gender, race and class in black women's depression. In: Perelberg R, Miller A (eds). *Gender and Power in Families.* London: Routledge (pp256–269); and Mills M, Topolski C (1996). Shanti: a women's therapy centre. *Counselling 7*: 108–112.
44. See, for example: Meyer B, Pilkonis PA, Proietti JM, Heape CL, Egan M (2001). Attachment styles and personality disorders as predictors of symptom course. *Journal of Personality Disorders 15*(5): 371–389.

45. See Fonagy P, Leigh T, Steele M et al (1996). The relationship of attachment status, psychiatric classification, and response to psychotherapy. *Journal of Consulting and Clinical Psychology* 64(1): 22–31.
46. Rogers CR (1967/1958). A process conception of psychotherapy. In: Rogers CR. *On Becoming a Person*. London: Constable (pp125–159).
47. Prochaska JO, DiClemente CC (1984). *The Transtheoretical Approach: crossing the traditional boundaries of therapy*. Homewood, IL: Dow Jones-Irwin.
48. See, for example: Ockene J, Kristellar JL, Goldberg R et al (1992). Smoking cessation and severity of disease – the Coronary-Artery Smoking Intervention Study. *Health Psychology* 11(2): 119–126.
49. See Brogan MM, Prochaska JO, DiClemente C (1999). Predicting termination and continuation status in psychotherapy using the trans-theoretical model. *Psychotherapy: Theory, Research, Practice, Training* 36(2): 105–113.
50. Prouty GF (1976). Pre-therapy, a method of treating pre-expressive, psychotic and retarded patients. *Psychotherapy: Theory, Research, Practice, Training* 13(3): 290–295; and Van Werde D (1994). An introduction to client-centred pre-therapy. In: Mearns D. *Developing Person-centred Counselling*. London: Sage (pp121–125).
51. Rosenzweig S (1936). Some implicit common factors in diverse methods of psychotherapy. *American Journal of Orthopsychiatry* 6(3): 412–415.
52. Rosenzweig (1936) (p413).
53. Rosenzweig (1936) (p415).
54. Hunsley J, Di Giulio G (2002). Dodo bird, phoenix, or urban legend? *Scientific Review of Mental Health Practices* 1(1): 11–22.
55. Shedler J (2010). The efficacy of psychodynamic psychotherapy. *American Psychologist* 65(2): 98–109.
56. Dollard J, Miller NE (1950). *Personality and Psychotherapy: an analysis in terms of learning, thinking and culture*. New York, NY: McGraw-Hill.
57. Rogers CR (1957). The necessary and sufficient conditions of therapeutic personality change. *Journal of Consulting Psychology* 21(1): 95–103.
58. For a summary of which, see Watson N (1984). The empirical status of Rogers' hypotheses of the necessary and sufficient conditions for effective psychotherapy. In: Levant R, Shlien J (eds). *Client-Centered Therapy and the Person-Centered Approach: new directions in theory, research and practice*. New York, NY: Praeger (pp17–40).
59. Stubbs JP, Bozarth JD (1996). The integrative statement of Carl R Rogers. In: Hutterer R, Pawlowsky G, Schmid PF, Stipsits R (eds). *Client-Centered and Experiential Psychotherapy: a paradigm in motion*. Frankfurt am Main: Peter Lang (pp25–33).
60. Strupp H (1973). On the basic ingredients of psychotherapy. *Journal of Consulting and Clinical Psychology* 41(1): 1–8.

61. Garfield S (1973). Basic ingredients or common factors in psychotherapy? *Journal of Consulting and Clinical Psychology 41*(1): 9–12.
62. Rogers CR (1957). The necessary and sufficient conditions of therapeutic personality change. *Journal of Consulting Psychology 21*(1): 95–103 (p96).
63. Rogers CR (1967). A process conception of psychotherapy. In: Rogers CR. *On Becoming a Person*. London: Constable (p130).
64. Duncan BL, Miller SD, Sparks J (2004). *The Heroic Client: a revolutionary way to improve effectiveness through client-directed, outcome-informed therapy* (2nd ed). San Francisco, CA: Jossey-Bass (p12).
65. Bohart AC, Tallman K (1999). *How Clients Make Therapy Work: the process of active self-healing*. Washington, DC: American Psychological Association.
66. Miller S, Duncan B, Hubble M (1997). *Escape from Babel: toward a unifying language for psychotherapy practice*. New York, NY: Norton (pp25–26).
67. Frank JD, Frank J (1961). *Persuasion and Healing: a comparative study of psychotherapy*. Baltimore, MD: The John Hopkins University Press.
68. Goldfried M, Padawer W (1982). *Converging Themes in Psychotherapy*. New York, NY: Springer.
69. Orlinsky DE, Howard KI (1986). Process and outcome in psychotherapy. In: Garfield S, Bergin A (eds). *Handbook of Psychotherapy and Behavior Change* (3rd ed). New York, NY: Wiley (pp311–381).
70. Grencavage LM, Norcross JC (1990). Where are the commonalities among the therapeutic common factors? *Professional Psychology: Research and Practice 21*(5): 372–437.
71. Rodgers B, Tudor K (eds) (2017). The politics of psychotherapy research [Special issue.] *Psychotherapy and Politics International 15*(3).
72. Task Force on Promotion and Dissemination of Psychological Procedures (1995). Training in and dissemination of empirically validated psychological treatments: report and recommendations. *The Clinical Psychologist 48:* 3–23.
73. See Newnes C (2014). *Clinical Psychology: a critical examination*. Ross-on-Wye: PCCS Books.
74. With reference to SIGN (the Scottish Intercollegiate Guidelines Network), see Harbour R, Miller J (2001). A new system for grading recommendations in evidence-based guidelines. *BMJ Clinical Research 323*(7308): 334–336. Although this framework is some 16 years old, it remains a good summary of the ranking. A more recent framework reduces the number of levels (to six), and elucidates each with regard to diagnostic category, prognosis, aetiology, and screening intervention, in addition to the type of intervention itself – see National Health and Medical Research Council (2009). *NHMRC Levels of Evidence and Grades for Recommendations for Developers of Guidelines*. Canberra: Australian Government.

75. Morgan S, Juriansz D (2002). Uncovering creative capability. *Mental Health Today* July: 25–28.
76. As developed by Morgan S (2004). Strengths-based practice. *OpenMind 126*: 16–17.
77. Barkham M, Hardy GE, Mellor-Clark J (eds) (2010). *Developing and Delivering Practice-Based Evidence: a guide for the psychological therapies*. London: Wiley-Blackwell. Also: Green D, Latchford G (2012). *Maximising the Benefits of Psychotherapy: a practice-based evidence approach*. London: Wiley-Blackwell. Also: Clement P (2013). Practice-based evidence: 45 years of psychotherapy's effectiveness in a private practice. *American Journal of Psychotherapy 67*(1): 23–46.
78. Rowland N (2007). BACP and NICE. *Therapy Today 18*(5): 27-30 (p 27).
79. Task Force on Promotion and Dissemination of Psychological Procedures (1995).
80. Rogers CR (1964). Toward a science of the person. In: Wann TW (ed). *Behaviorism and Phenomenology: contrasting bases for modern psychology*. Chicago, IL: University of Chicago Press (pp109–140).
81. Carper B (1978). Fundamental ways of knowing in nursing. *Advances in Nursing Science 1*(1): 13–23.
82. Burrell G, Morgan G (1979). *Sociological Paradigms and Organizational Analysis*. London: Heinemann.
83. Bohart AC, House R (2008). Empirically supported/validated treatments as modernist ideology I: Dodo, manualization, and the paradigm question. In: House R, Loewenthal D (eds). *Against and for CBT*. Ross-on-Wye: PCCS Books (pp188–201).
84. These are well summarised by Cooper M (2008) (chapter 3).
85. Elliott R (1998). Editor's introduction: A guide to the empirically supported treatments controversy. *Psychotherapy Research 8*(2): 115–125 (p117).
86. Elliott (1998) (p117).
87. Bohart A, O'Hara M, Leitner L (2010). Empirically violated treatments: disenfranchisement of humanistic and other psychotherapies. *Psychotherapy Research 8*(2): 141–157.
88. House ER (2006). Methodological fundamentalism and the quest for control(s). In: Denzin NK, Giardina MD (eds). *Qualitative Inquiry and the Conservative Challenge: confronting methodological fundamentalism*. Walnut Creek, CA: Left Coast Press (pp93–108) (pp100–101).
89. Elsewhere, I discuss the inhumanity of this with reference to a psychiatrist who thought that he could research the efficacy of counselling in a street agency by randomly turning away clients. He proposed that the researchers would follow them up to see how they'd fared without counselling. See Tudor (2016).
90. Freire ES (2006). Randomised control clinical trial and psychotherapy

research: an epistemological controversy. *Journal of Humanistic Psychology* 46(3): 322–335 (p323).

91. Task Force for the Development of Practice Recommendations for the Provision of Humanistic Psychological Services (2004). Recommended principles and practices for the provision of humanistic psychosocial services: alternative to mandated practices and treatment guidelines. *Humanistic Psychologist* 32(1): 3–25 (pp16–17).

92. Department of Health (2009). *Improving Access to Psychological Therapies: policy and guidance.* London: Department of Health.

93. Holmes J (2002). *The Search for the Secure Base: attachment theory and psychotherapy.* London: Routledge (p288).

94. For instance, from a phenomenological perspective, psychotherapy may be viewed as a heuristic enquiry on the part of the client, facilitated by the psychotherapist.

95. Duncan, Miller & Sparks (2004) (p52).

96. Parker I (ed) (1999). *Deconstructing Psychotherapy.* London: Sage.

97. Lincoln YS, Guba EG (1985). *Naturalistic Inquiry.* Newbury Park, CA: Sage.

98. Cushman E (2006/1999). The public intellectual, service learning, and activist research. In: Etzioni A, Bowditch A (eds). *Public Intellectuals: an endangered species?* Lantham, MA: Rowman & Littlefield (pp101–110).

99. Porter JE, Sullivan P, Blythe S, Grabhill JT, Miles L (2000). Institutional critique: a rhetorical methodology for change. *College Composition & Communication* 51(4): 610–642.

100. Some argue that action research is not a methodology so much as an approach to enquiry. See Burns D (2007). *Systemic Action Research: a strategy for whole system change.* Bristol: The Policy Press.

101. Carr W, Kemmis S (1986). *Becoming Critical: education knowledge and action research.* London: Falmer Press.

102. Thomas J (1993). *Doing Critical Ethnography.* Newbury Park, CA: Sage.

103. Freire P (1972). *Pedagogy of the Oppressed.* Harmondsworth: Penguin.

104. Denzin NK, Lincoln YS (2008). Introduction. In: Denzin NK, Lincoln YS (eds). *Handbook of Critical and Indigenous Methodologies.* Thousand Oaks, CA: Sage (1–20).

105. United Nations (2008). *United Nations Declaration on the Rights of Indigenous Peoples.* New York, NY: United Nations.

106. Plummer K (2005). Critical humanism and queer theory: living with the tensions. In: Denzin NK, Lincoln YS (eds). *The Sage Handbook of Qualitative Research* (3rd ed). Thousand Oaks, CA: Sage (pp357–373).

107. Dona G (2007). The microphysics of participation in refugee research. *Journal of Refugee Studies* 20(2): 210–229.

108. Pihama L (2001). *Tihei Mauri Ora, Honouring our Voices: mana wahine as a kaupapa Māori theoretical framework*. Unpublished doctoral dissertation. Auckland: University of Auckland.
109. Pohatu TW (2004). *Āta: growing respectful relationships*. Wellington: Massey University.
110. Woodard W (2008). *Entering the void: exploring the relationship between the experience of colonisation and the experience of self for indigenous peoples of Aotearoa and the implications for clinical practice*. Unpublished master's dissertation. Auckland: AUT University (p12).
111. See Janesick V (2004). *Stretching Exercises for Qualitative Researchers* (2nd ed). Thousand Oaks, CA: Sage. Rubin H, Rubin I (2005). *Qualitative Interviewing: the art of hearing data* (2nd ed). Thousand Oaks, CA: Sage. See, for example, Cunningham I, Hyman J (1999). The poverty of empowerment? A critical case study. *Personnel Review 28*(3): pp192–207.
112. Sacks H (1984). Notes on methodology. In: Atkinson M, Heritage J (eds). *Structures of Social Action: studies in conversation analysis*. Cambridge: Cambridge University Press (pp21–27).
113. Kitzinger C (2005). Heteronormativity in action: reproducing the heterosexual nuclear family in after-hours medical calls. *Social Problems 52*: 477–498.
114. Duncan, Miller & Sparks (2004).
115. Heron J (1996). *Co-operative Inquiry: research into the human condition*. London: Sage. Reason P (2003). Doing co-operative inquiry. In: Smith J (ed). *Qualitative Psychology: a practical guide to methods*. London: Sage (pp205–231).
116. Kinsella EA (2006). Hermeneutics and critical hermeneutics: exploring possibilities within the art of interpretation. [Online.] *Forum: Qualitative Social Research 7*(3): http://nbn-resolving.de/urn:nbn:de:0114-fqs0603190 (accessed 21 January 2018).
117. Schott argues that a hermeneutic philosophy of interpretation must take on a critical position: '... groups whose discourses, histories, and traditions have been marginalised need to struggle for the self-affirmation that is both a condition and consequence of naming oneself as an interpreter.' Schott R (1991). Whose home is it anyway? A feminist response to Gadamer's hermeneutics. In: Gadamer H-G, Silverman H (eds). *Gadamer and Hermeneutics*. New York, NY: Routledge (pp202–209) (p209).
118. See Souto-Manning M (2014). Critical narrative analysis: the interplay of critical discourse and narrative analyses. *International Journal of Qualitative Studies in Education 27*(2): 159–180.

CHAPTER 7

Education, training and sustaining professional development

Hate dogma. Love learning. Love art.
(Camille Paglia)[1]

Although, in the title of this chapter, I have privileged the word 'education', it is true to say that 'training' is more commonly used when referring to the formation of psychotherapists. I think this is significant, in that education, from the Latin *educare*, meaning to lead or to draw out, suggests a more engaged, and, to some extent, more equal or level relationship between teacher and student than is implied by the word training, with its connotations of instruction and exercise.

I begin this chapter with a critical reflection on psychotherapists as educators. I follow this with a brief discussion of the education and training of psychotherapists, their historical basis on an apprenticeship model of learning, and how this has been compromised by the impact of neoliberalism on and in education and, specifically, an audit culture, as well as those private training institutes and educational/training programmes in the public sector that promote a closed culture. I then summarise the common constituent elements of psychotherapy training, and follow this with discussions of particular models of psychotherapy education and training, the role of the academy (ie. academic institutions) in psychotherapy education, and that of continuing professional development (CPD). Throughout this chapter, I take up the points I make in earlier chapters, and especially Chapter 1 (regarding education and training, doctrine, conformity and purity, acculturation, and freedom), that have implications for education and training.

Teaching, treating or leading out?

Very few of the founding fathers or mothers of psychotherapy were either themselves educationalists or articulated a model of education and/or training. This is significant in (at least) three ways.

Psychotherapists as educationalists

The first is, that, while all psychotherapy trainers are clinicians, most are not trained or qualified as teachers or educationalists. Apart from colleagues who previously trained as teachers, the exceptions to this are qualified clinicians who are members of professional associations that have a teaching and supervising membership and some pathway (via an apprenticeship and/or further formal training) to achieving such membership.[2] The point here is that, if trainers do not identify as educationalists, they are less likely to be familiar with theories and models of education and the distinction between education and training, let alone critical models or contemporary debates in education, including its role in wider society.

A notable exception to this dislocation of psychotherapy education and training from education is Rogers, who, nearly 50 years ago, wrote what was to become a groundbreaking book on education, *Freedom to Learn*.[3] In it, he outlines the various aspects of what he suggests is a necessary 'climate of freedom' to promote learning, including the educator's attitude, beliefs, philosophy, theory and skills.[4] He goes on to identify a number of considerations for the person- or student-centred educator, including the importance of trust and relationship(s); the deconstruction of previous unhelpful educational or schooling experiences; the centrality of contact;[5] the responsibility for establishing the space for learning and holding external requirements, and the significance of the educator's openness and willingness to live 'the uncertainty of discovery'.[6] Importantly, Rogers situated his approach to education in the context of debates in the world of education at the time, referring both to AS Neil, who had founded the groundbreaking Summerhill School in Suffolk, UK, and Paolo Friere, the Brazilian educationalist and revolutionary, whose ideas about deconstructing pedagogy remain relevant to this day.[7]

Educational theory for education and training

Rogers' point about previous educational experiences has been picked up by contemporary educators. For example, Giles Barrow suggests that, 'in the absence of a deconstruction of early schooled experiences, clinician trainers are often simply replaying the archaic teacher-pupil relationship'.[8] Barrow frames this, in transactional analysis terms, as a particular dimension of a person's life-script as it relates to learning and teaching and education and schooling,[9] and he and others argue that such deconstruction needs to be done from and conceptualised within an educational rather than clinical framework.

The implicit model of education by which many psychotherapy trainers operate, however, is not one based on educational theory, but, rather, on clinical practice theory – a perspective and practice that dates back to Freud and, as discussed in Chapter 5, to the 'the teach-or-treat debate'. The point here is that such trainers will tend to draw on therapeutic models of relationship and development, and, specifically, on a pedagogical approach, which refers to a parent–child relationship, rather than an andragogical one, which refers to an adult–adult relationship and which is more appropriate to adult learning.[10] More recently, Dorin Herlo discusses the term 'paragogy' to describe 'alongside' peer learning.[11] He draws a distinction between this and angragogy, as he argues that 'paragogy deals with a very different challenge, that of *analyzing and co-creating the educational environment as a whole*' (original emphasis).[12] These distinctions are significant for, as Barrow argues, teacher–trainee relationships based on a parent–child pedagogy can lead to a 'blurring of the boundary between the clinic and the classroom',[13] and the infantalisation of adult trainees (see also Chapter 1).

Otto Kernberg writes about infantilisation of psychoanalytic candidates, which he attributes in part to the effects of the isolation of education institutions from intellectual developments in other disciplines.[14] Aron and Starr similarly contend that 'this infantilization of candidates [is] a direct result of separating psychoanalysis from psychotherapy'.[15] Elsewhere, I and Summers have discussed the infantilisation of students.[16]

In his book *Where Have all the Intellectuals Gone?*, Frank Füredi questions what he refers to as the patronising underpinning of contemporary education – and of cultural politics – and concludes that:

> This process of infantilisation expresses a pessimistic and anti-democratic account of people... Ideals of democratic participation presuppose citizens who possess the intelligence and responsibility to act autonomously and exercise their rights. They are able to criticize and take criticism... In an era of the infantilisation of culture, treating people as grown-ups has become one of the principal duties of the humanist intellectual.[17]

This is important for those who think that the education of the public and politicians about psychotherapy needs to be on the basis of 'arguing up', and not 'dumbing down'.

For some, education is about developing critical thinking; indeed, it constitutes critical thinking. As Tavris puts it: 'It does seem ludicrous that we have something called education and something else called critical thinking. There was a time when they were synonymous, or should have been. So, of course, we are talking about good teaching'[18] – or good facilitation of learning.

The social/political context of education and training

The third point relates to an understanding of the social and economic context of education. We, at least in the Western world, live in neoliberal times in which economic rationalism has a significant impact on education programmes, systems and processes – and, ultimately, on the quality and standard of education. This includes, among other things, an increasing focus on rating and audit systems, and on performance-based funding, and more use of adjunct staff and graduate students as lecturers. All these represent neoliberal beliefs about the economic role of the university. The consequences include generally more compliant (and/or disaffected) staff and students, both of which groups are focused more on achievement and results than on educational processes and learning. Moreover, the increasing costs of education are passed on to the student, resulting in a widespread increase in student debt. In the neoliberal world, education is not thought of in terms of pedagogy or andragogy, let alone paragogy, but in terms of economics, of cost–benefit analysis. However, as Ronald Coase put it in his classic article, 'The Problem of Social Cost':

> If we assume that the harmful effect of the pollution is that it kills the fish, the question to be decided is: is the value of the fish lost greater or less than the value of the product which the contamination of the stream makes possible?[19]

Coase's own response to the question he posed was: 'It goes almost without saying that this problem has to be looked at in total *and* at the margin.'[20] Thus, we cannot – or should not – think about education without considering, for instance, the impact of poverty, which has a greater effect on student performance than poor schools and universities or poor teaching,[21] as well as the impact of various forms of discrimination, such as racism and sexism.

Neoliberalism is, of course, also the backdrop to education and training in the private sector, where the majority of psychotherapy training programmes are located (see also the discussion of the academy, pp 225–231 below). The issue here is whether people who have been trained as psychotherapists (predominantly in the private sector), and who have little or no background or experience as teachers or educators, have enough knowledge about education – its theories, practice and context – to work as educators.

Psychotherapy education and training

The very earliest training in psychoanalysis and psychotherapy was based on an apprenticeship model of learning whereby a student/candidate (apprentice) studied with a psychoanalyst/supervisor/

trainer (master). As I discuss in Chapter 5, initially this took the form of the student's own analysis or personal psychotherapy, as well as their own study through attending seminars and conferences and supervision of their own analysands, patients or clients. At the same time, as early as 1913, individuals and groups were establishing training institutes at which a more formal course of study was offered, some of which had associated clinics in which students/trainees offered analysis and psychotherapy under supervision.

The first of these was the Budapest Psycho-Analytic Institute, established in 1913 under the direction of Ferenczi. In 1920, the Berlin Psycho-Analytic Institute was established, together with a Psycho-Analytical Poliklinik, under the direction of Abraham and Eitingon. From the 1920s onwards, psychoanalytic institutes were founded in other countries: Russia (Moscow, 1922), UK (London, 1924), US (New York, 1931; Boston, 1933; Washington-Baltimore, 1933; San Francisco, 1941), Australia (Melbourne, 1941), and so on.

In 1945, the first training to be located in a university was established at the Columbia University Centre for Psychoanalytic Training and Research in New York, by Sandor Radó, George Daniels, David Levy, Abram Kardiner and Nolan Lewis. From 1953–1964, Jacques Lacan held his seminars at the Sainte-Anne Hospital, Paris, presenting case histories of patients. In 1959, Albert Ellis founded his own institute in New York, promoting rational emotive therapy. In the early 1960s, Aaron Beck established training in cognitive behaviour therapy at the University of Pennsylvania, Pittsburgh.

In 1966, the first humanistic training programme was established in the Psychology Department, Sonoma State College by Eleanor Criswell, Rollo May, Clark Moustakas and James Bugenthal.

In 1985, the Centre for Freudian Analysis and Research was founded in London, with the aim of promoting and developing psychoanalysis in the UK from within a Freudian and Lacanian perspective. The last 25 years have seen a rise in numbers of psychotherapy training institutes with increasingly formalised training programmes.

Even though students/trainees/candidates were associated with or were members of an institute, their training was still based on an apprenticeship model, in that their application for full membership (which, in effect, indicated completion and graduation, if not qualification) was based on readiness, as assessed by a combination of – depending on the theoretical model – their trainers, training analysts/therapists, peers and themselves, and not on having completed a certain number of years or hours of training, supervised practice and personal therapy. While the apprentice model of education perhaps relied too much on an acceptance of external authority (of the trainer, and/or the training analyst), the concept of psychotherapist training as a journey that will take different individuals different lengths of time is, I think, a healthy and realistic one.

The move to framing psychotherapy education and training in terms of hours (see Chapter 5 and pp219–220 below) reflects more of an audit culture,[22] in which the achievement of education – and, to a certain extent, competence and knowledge – is measured by standard units of hours of theory, supervised practice and personal development, rather than personal and professional readiness and preparedness for practice.

Moreover, these days, most psychotherapy training – across all theoretical orientations/modalities – takes place at private training institutes, in which students are generally encouraged to complete a particular course. This in itself is not a problem, as long as trainees are informed about the terms and conditions and implications of how they proceed, including accruing and 'counting' training hours. If institutes are not informing students of their options or, indeed, if they are closing down their options, these institutions are, in effect, operating and maintaining a closed system and contributing towards a wider closed system with regard to the training of psychotherapists. An example of this took place in 2013, when the UK's Institute of Transactional Analysis (ITA) introduced a scheme whereby the training hours of psychotherapy trainees would only be recognised if they undertook them at a 'registered training establishment'.[23]

Also, if institutions only recommend and appoint from their own trainees or graduates, they are open to accusations that they are operating a 'closed shop' and of 'pyramid selling', both of which also support a 'pure' and closed, rather than open, system (see Chapter 1).

As psychotherapy has developed and grown, so professional associations have been founded at both national and international levels, some of which act as federal, umbrella organisations. These umbrella organisations can provide both a degree of protection for students' interests and a sense of being part of a wider professional community, but can also impose further terms and conditions on their member organisations that, directly or indirectly, restrict choice.

These days, most psychotherapy training is based in institutes, apart from in some countries where psychotherapy is less well established or where geographical distance makes it difficult to commit to a specific training programme, and the apprenticeship model still exists. For example, training in transactional analysis, including its application in psychotherapy, is still based on this model (although not in the UK). Apart from the 40 hours the candidate must have with their contractual supervisor, they are free to undertake training and supervision with whomever they like, as long as that person is accredited by one of the international TA accrediting organisations.

The main advantage of the apprenticeship model is that it maximises the apprentice's freedom of study. It is also more demanding in that it requires the student/trainee to design their course of study, and to negotiate their own way through qualification, accreditation, membership and other regulatory systems – and we live in an era of increasing regulation.

The constituent elements of psychotherapy education/training

Psychotherapy training predominantly comprises three elements: theory, practice and some form of personal development. This tripartite model reflects the different elements of an archetypal apprentice model of education/training that is centuries old – in psychotherapy, it dates back to the early 1920s, when the Berlin

Psycho-Analytical Institute and its poliklinik, under Eitingon's directorship, established the elements of psychoanalytic training as theoretical and clinical seminars, training analysis and supervision of control cases (referred to as the Eitingon model of training).[24]

Theory

Freud's argument in favour of lay (ie. non-medical) analysis and lay analysts was based on his views about the nature of psychoanalysis, and, from that, the knowledge a person needs in order to be a psychoanalyst, which he described as 'a great deal of psychology and a little biology or sexual science'.[25] He also argued that training should include 'elements from the mental sciences, from psychology, the history of civilization and sociology, as well as from anatomy, biology and the study of evolution'.[26] I suggest, that, with notable exceptions, current psychotherapy training programmes are generally light on the history of civilisation and sociology, and, possibly, anatomy, biology and the study of evolution.

Each psychotherapy educator/trainer has their own ideas about what is necessary and/or sufficient for their curriculum, and, if they are working in the private/independent sector, may have a high degree of autonomy in setting and teaching this, although, as noted in Chapter 1, such programmes are likely to – and should – be at a postgraduate, master's level. However, these days, many training programmes and institutes are accountable to some external authority. This might be a professional association, for whose membership the programme or institute will also be preparing their trainees/candidates, and/or an accrediting or registering authority, whether professional and/or academic.

In this context, such authorities usually determine a requisite number of training hours for membership and/or accreditation/registration, and may also set other criteria, including those governing the content of curriculum. For example, the UKCP sets out a minimum curriculum that, as far as theory and practice is concerned, should comprise:

- a model of the person and the human mind

- a model of gendered and culturally-influenced human development
- a model of human change and ways in which change can be facilitated
- a set of clinical concepts to relate theory to practice
- an extensive literature, which includes a critique of the core model
- awareness of safeguarding issues in relation to clients and those likely to be affected by their actions.[27]

Additionally, the UKCP's HIPC requires that member organisations should have a curriculum that includes and addresses:

- exploration of the philosophical foundations of the approach being studied
- an introduction to the range of psychotherapies and counselling
- basic research technique
- experience in both long and short-term modalities
- familiarisation with concepts of serious mental illness
- familiarisation with ethical and legal issues in relation to psychotherapy.[28]

I would think that most educators/trainers would accept these as fairly standard and relatively uncontroversial areas of knowledge to be covered in some way on a psychotherapy education/training programme. What is interesting, in the light of the present enquiry, is the reference to the inclusion of a critique of the 'core model' offered by the training, which, of course, encourages the development of independent thinking and reflexivity – including thinking and practising beyond a particular core model. Such praxis would not only challenge dogmatism (as outlined in Chapter 1), but would also positively encourage anti-dogmatism and non-dogmatism.[29] In this context, it is challenging to think about what criteria we might use to assess psychotherapy students' anti-dogmatism.

To this list, I would add 'a theory of theory' (see Chapter 4), as this encourages reflexivity and the identification of the underlying epistemology of the particular – and, indeed, any – theory of psychotherapy. It also encourages students to think theoretically, to become adept at playing with theory, and to think about methodology, which, in turn, underpins research.

Supervised practice

All psychotherapy education/training that leads to a qualification and, thereby, provides a licence to practise, comprises some element of supervised practice.[30] As with the other elements, there are differences in how this is viewed and organised. In Chapter 5, I discuss the nature of supervision (pp153–161), and the parameters of choice and responsibility in and about supervision (pp161–166). Here, I mention a few of the critical issues regarding supervised practice in the context of psychotherapy training.

The timing of supervised practice

It is generally recognised that it is important for students to be practising alongside their theoretical study of psychotherapy, as this facilitates greater integration of theory with practice, and, indeed, tests the theory they are learning against their experience of practice. The trainee/student may be experienced as a practitioner in another helping profession (as a counsellor, doctor, nurse, psychologist or social worker), but most psychotherapy training courses or programmes require students to practise their skills on each other before they undertake psychotherapy with clients. Indeed, many courses do not allow students to work with clients until they have completed a certain amount of this peer practice and have been approved to begin practising with clients. Some courses require students to have a certain number of clients in order to enter a second year of training. However, difficulties for students in getting clients, and for institutes in retaining students (and ensuing financial pressures), can lead to such requirements being waived. While this may not be a problem in any one year, or for certain students, I have known situations in which students have completed their formal training (over four years) without having seen many clients at all. This not only makes the student's experience of training less rich and rigorous, but leaves them having to complete a lot of client/practice hours without the support of ongoing training, in order to qualify.

The context of supervised practice

Generally, supervised practice during training takes place in a clinic run by or associated with the training institute and/or by placements in the public or voluntary/independent sector, which are either organised by the training programme or negotiated by the trainee. Both kinds of placement, I think, have value, both in terms of gaining experience of diverse clients and in encouraging trainee psychotherapists to experience public sector practice.

Most programmes (and accrediting bodies) discourage students/trainees from gaining practice experience through private practice, as this is seen as less protective, both for the student/trainee and for their clients, although it has to be said that some voluntary/independent sector placements are not terribly protective and, moreover, can exploit what is in effect students'/trainees' free labour.

The supervision of supervised practice

In the model of the clinic associated with an institute, the supervision, or a proportion of the supervision, is provided by the staff of the institute and/or a specialist clinical supervisor or educator. This arrangement further facilitates the integration of theory and practice, as well as research and practice – and, in this, I agree with the point that Feltham makes about supervisors being or becoming more 'research aware'.[31] On placements, trainees are usually supervised and/or mentored by placement supervisors who are in some way linked to the training programme – for instance, by means of an agreement or contract. It is important that the terms and conditions of this three-way relationship are clear, especially with regard to the expectations (of all parties), responsibilities (clinical and academic), accountability (clinical), assessment (of the student, the supervisor and the placement itself), and communication (between student, supervisor and the programme).

Personal development

This aspect of psychotherapy training is usually translated as meaning 'personal (psycho)therapy', a term that refers to the process and form of personal development. Interestingly, in referring to 'reflexivity', the Constructivist and Existential College of the UKCP emphasises the process and outcome of personal development (see Chapter 5 for a discussion of various aspects of personal psychotherapy and its role in the training of psychotherapists). Here, however, I focus on the relationship of personal development with the other aspects or elements of training.

Again, different educators/trainers, training institutes and professional bodies have different views about the relative importance of personal therapy and the degree to which it should be controlled: when, for instance, this takes place (ie. before, during or even after training); the amount (including frequency and duration, and, indeed, whether there should be a specified quantity), and with whom (for discussion of which see Chapter 5).

There is no agreed ratio between these three different elements, and training programmes differ as to the number of hours allocated to these and, indeed, other components, as well as the necessary, sufficient or desirable duration of the programme. In terms of the HIPC, these three requirements are as follows:

- training – 900 hours. This includes direct training (ie. tutor contact time of around 700 hours), 75 hours of supervision (at a ratio of one supervision hour to every six client contact hours), and a 20-day psychiatric familiarisation placement (say, 120 hours)
- supervised practice – 450 hours
- personal therapy – a minimum of 160 hours (based on 40 hours of therapy per year, multiplied by four years of training).[32]

Expressed as a ratio, for every 5.63 hours of training and 2.81 hours of supervised practice (a total of 8.45 hours), the humanistic and/or integrative trainee is required to have a minimum of one hour's personal therapy, which suggests that personal therapy is viewed as a significant proportion of the trainee's experience *and reflection* on their education/training. Of course, significance is in the eye of the beholder: for some, this hour will be too little, and for others too much. Another factor is that most training also includes, as part of its 'tutor contact time', personal development, usually in the form of some group process, which may be facilitated by the programme staff or an external person brought in for the purpose. In this way, the ratio of personal development to training and supervised practice will be much larger.

Finally, on this, it should be noted that none of these hours includes private study. Taking a university model, all study is accounted for in terms of a ratio of staff contact time (eg. lectures, tutorials and supervision) to private study, which in my own university, at master's level, is usually 1:5.25 hours. Applying this to the HIPC model outlined above, its total training commitment of 1,510 hours (over, usually, four years) would entail 7,928 hours of private study, which, based on a 40-week working/studying year over four years, works out at 50 hours per week. This is clearly unrealistic, especially for those studying part-time (which is probably the most common basis on which psychotherapy education/training is undertaken). However, it does raise a question about the expectations that psychotherapy training programmes, especially those in the private sector, have of their trainees regarding the amount of private study needed to support their engagement with and completion of the programme. It also, again, suggests that clarity about the expectations of students/trainees is essential – and good and ethical practice.

Models and the organisation of psychotherapy education and training

Just as students' ability to critique the core theoretical model of any psychotherapy training encourages an anti-dogmatic stance, so an andragogical teacher–learner relationship encourages – or, at least, is more likely to encourage – critical thinking.

Over some 25 years, Kernberg, a psychoanalyst, professor of psychiatry and past president of the IPA, has offered a consistent critique of psychoanalytic training, arguing that: 'Psychoanalytic education today is all too often conducted in an atmosphere of indoctrination rather than of open scientific exploration.'[33] The symptoms of this conduct, which Kernberg likens to an illness affecting educational structures of psychoanalytic societies and institutes, include:

- the disproportionate amount of time and energy given to Freud
- an undue focus on the study of the work of the institute's teachers
- an ignorance or only superficial study of alternative and contemporary psychoanalytic approaches
- a lack of transparency about the faculty/staff's own analytic work/practice
- a sheltering of trainees from disagreements within the institute
- an over-reliance on the learning of techniques from the trainee's own analysis
- a bias towards reading clinical data that only reports successful treatment
- an implicit priviledging of the training analysis over the other elements of education/training
- the lack of accountability of the faculty for their evaluation of candidates
- the paranoid atmosphere of such training
- the apparent or real arbitrariness of appointments (of junior faculty, training analysts and supervisors)
- the lack of explicit, public policies and criteria (for selection of candidates, appointment of faculty and of decision-making)
- the 'diminished creative thinking and scientific productivity on the part of faculty, students, and graduates', and what he refers to as 'cross-sterilisation'.[34]

Ten years later, Kernberg encapsulated these criticisms in his identification of 30 methods that destroy the creativity of psychoanalytic candidates.[35]

In exploring the causes of the symptoms of the illness of the educational structures of psychoanalytic training institutes, Kernberg presents and discusses four different models of education, which I summarise here and apply more generally to psychotherapy, and especially the role of the educator/trainer (Table 7.1).

Table 7.1 – Four models of education and their Implications (developed from Kernberg, 1986)

Primary task of psychotherapy education	Assumptions	Implications
Model: Art academy		
To train expert craftsmen/women – and artists	That psychotherapy is a craft and an art, and that there is an ideal technique to be mastered, 'as a basis for subsequent creativity within that art'[36] – a model of education based on andragogy	That 'discussion of theories would be circumscribed by the need to establish their relation to the ideal technique perfected in [a given] institute',[37] a point consistent with training in a specific theoretical orientation/modality That students would be able to observe, critically analyse and learn from the psychotherapy carried out by their 'masters' That the trainers themselves are artists, creative, and open to reflexivity, especially of their own practice
Model: Technical trade school		
For students to learn to define a skill or trade	That teachers focus more on the documentation, training and assessment of those skills, and less on personal inspirational creativity, a model of education based on andragogy	That such institutes would be 'highly specialised trade schools with a program of efficient training, monitoring of students' progress and, once the optimal level of skill has been reached, graduation'[38] – a model that highlights the advantages of an ...

			... organisation that has explicit criteria and standards of professional practice and functioning – for both students and teachers – but which minimises the heart and soul of the practice of psychotherapy and of educative relationships. This is also a form of education that, as Füredi puts it, 'is more interested in giving students a sense of achievement than in educating them'[39]
Model: Monastery/religious retreat			
For students to develop a sense of conviction about psychotherapy, connected to 'the discovery of the unconscious in oneself and the experience of psychological change following this discovery'[40]	That psychotherapy education is a 'deeply transforming emotional experience… [c]arried out in the context of an intense relation to another person, idealized and experienced as a spiritual guide'[41] – a model of education that is closer to that of the theological college, and based on pedagogy		That the guide as mentor is complemented by other colleagues who tend to look out for and/or focus on the limitations, shortcomings and inadequacies of the student, a combination that is reflected in some training programmes in which the trainee/student has a formal mentor or tutor who tends to advocate for their student(s) with other staff, and mediate the feedback of those other staff to the student. On this point, Kernberg favours more open discussion of students' progress among the faculty or teaching staff
Model: University/college			
For students 'to be exposed to and educated with a critical sense regarding all theories',[42] and to learn *contemporary* theory and practice	That psychotherapy is as much a science as an art, and the institution is one for 'the transmission, exploration, and generation of knowledge, including the transmission of methodological tools for the generation of …		That the faculty would be able and willing 'to expose their theories and actual clinical work to the critical analysis of the students,[43] and to tolerate – and, indeed, promote – rigorous and robust debate with regard to theory and practice That the selection/ appointment of faculty …

	... new knowledge'[44] – a model of education that is close to the training programmes of medical schools and other helping professions, and based on andragogy	... would be made according to agreed and public criteria and processes, and that the institute would be accountable for this
		That both faculty and student bodies would have independent organisations

Most psychotherapy educators/trainers – and students – will recognise some elements of these different models, and will have their own views about the pros and cons of these different models of education. Kernberg's own conclusion (in 1986) was that:

> ... a serious discrepancy exists between the prevalent, explicitly formulated or implicitly acknowledged aims of psychoanalytic education and the dominant organisational structures that characterise psychoanalytic institutes... While psychoanalytic educators think they are transmitting what is both an art and science, they have structured their institutes so they correspond most closely to a combination of the technical school and the theological seminary.[45]

The fervour and content of Kernberg's critique have not diminished with the passing of time. In an article written in 2010, he asserts: 'that the educational stagnation and underlying authoritarian structure of psychoanalytic education derive largely from the present-day training analysis system is a major source of inhibition of the educational process.'[46]

It is no surprise that Kernberg himself favours a model combining aspects of the art school and university college. While I agree with Aron and Starr's criticism of Kernberg's maintenance of the distinction between psychoanalysis, psychoanalytic psychotherapy and supportive therapy, I disagree with their assertion that his recommendations for models of education are dependent on these distinctions. Nevertheless, like Aron and Starr, I support Kernberg's call for a more diverse student body; for the freedom to challenge authority, and for the nurturing of the spirit of scientific enquiry, including (I would add) an emphasis on research, as well as, in effect, a greater philosophical congruence between a particular model and the aims of psychotherapy education and the administrative structure(s) of the institute and/or institution within which it is located.

Moving beyond the advocacy of a particular model of education, and, again, in the context of the current critical examination, the critical question is, which model or combination of models supports critical thinking and critical research, on what methodologies are they based, and what methods and practice follow from and support critical, reflexive practice? Denzin and Lincoln's description of critical indigenous pedagogy describes this well: 'It values the transformative power of indigenous, subjugated knowledges. It values the pedagogical practices that produce these knowledges... and it seeks forms of praxis and inquiry that are emancipatory and empowering.'[47]

The academy

From the beginnings of psychoanalysis, its training, first by apprenticeship and later by programmes within institutes, has been located in the private sector, outside public universities, and this legacy has impacted on psychotherapy training across all modalities. For example, of the current 62 training institutes or institutions that are organisational members of the UKCP, only seven are are university-based programmes.[48] According to Robert Wallerstein,[49] Freud's vision for psychoanalytic education, including 'a college of psychoanalysis',[50] was a 'university-like conception'[51] that would only have been possible in the context of full-time study at a university. That psychoanalysis did not find a home in academia was linked, according to Wallerstein,

> ... in part, with the revulsion of organized medicine and of organized academia against the scandalous childhood sexual doctrines expounded by this new psychoanalysis in a Victorian world, and, in part, with the almost official anti-semitism of the Austro-Hungarian Empire that denied Freud and his new 'Jewish science' the official posts and the academic recognition to which he lifelong aspired.[52]

It wasn't until 1945, some six years after Freud's death, that the Columbia University Centre for Psychoanalytic Training and Research, founded by Radó and his colleagues, became the first psychoanalytic institute affiliated with the American Psychoanalytic Association to be established in a university and, moreover, in its prestigious Department of Psychiatry. This initiative, however, did not open the door to psychotherapy education/training in the public sector; it wasn't until the 1960s that the first cognitive behaviour therapy training was established in a university, at the University of Pennsylvania, and only in 1966 that the first humanistic training programme was established in the further education sector, at Sonoma State College, California.

Kernberg argues that, in the US, it was 'the self-destructive isolationism of psychoanalytic institutions [that led]... to the separation of psychoanalysis from most psychiatric university settings in the 1970s and 1980s',[53] and that similar developments took place later in Germany and in Scandinavian countries. It is true that some universities have – or have had – somewhat restrictive policies that have limited the professional activities of their academic staff, such as maintaining their own psychotherapy practice, and, thereby, have discouraged the integration of psychotherapy and academia. But, equally, some psychotherapy institutes and professional associations have marginalised academics, who by definition (and contract) can only maintain a limited psychotherapeutic practice. While extolling both the development of psychoanalytic knowledge that took place in the UK in the 1940s and 50s and the cultural impact of French psychoanalysis in the 60s, Kernberg bemoans '[t]his isolation, retreat or expulsion from university settings [that] reinforced the narrowing of intellectual pursuits and psychoanalytic institutions',[54] and argues that:

> It is important to re-establish the links of psychoanalysis to academia, particularly with the university departments of psychiatry and clinical psychology, where interdisciplinary interests may facilitate creative interchange, and with the humanities and social sciences at large. It

may well be that the initial steps in such joint approaches require the incorporation... of scientists from other fields.[55]

There are a number of advantages to psychotherapy education being located in a university.

Culture

Universities both represent and shape culture and, at best, also challenge culture and cultural and social norms. According to John Stuart Mill (1806–1873), their object 'is not to make skilful lawyers physicians or engineers. It is to make capable and cultivated human beings'.[56] This objective represents the bedrock of a liberal education philosophy and the broader education reflected, notably, in and by the *literae humaniores* (human literature) developed at the University of Oxford, in contrast to *res divinae* (theology) that was the main field of study when the university began, in 1096. It also represents the view that a first or foundation degree should provide and engage the student in a broad field of study.

As a university houses many disciplines, it provides a unique opportunity for meeting, engaging with and drawing from other 'cultures', in the form of disciplines. This means that an education in psychotherapy is – or could be – enriched by professions such as anthropologists, biologists, ecologists, philosphers, psychologists and scientists teaching on its programme, with the result that it would look as much outwards to society as inwards to psyche.[57] Such interdisciplinarity – or even transdisciplinarity – is crucial not only for facilitating contact between students in different disciplines who will be working alongside each other as professionals in the service of clients and patients, but also, and more broadly, for establishing a psychotherapy that, as a discipline and a profession, is open, outward-looking and known. In this sense, the public academy is a challenge to professional training programmes that, in effect, represent the private sector, in which, as Barrow observes, 'the maintream business of therapy is tied into a private exchange as distinct from a public service'.[58]

However, universities are not neutral spaces and are subject to the challenges and problems of any large organisation, especially when they are part of a neoliberal economy that regards them more as businesses than academies. As well as teaching (and supervising), researching, and doing a certain amount of administration, scholars also need to address the politics of academic insitutions. Writing about critical indigenous pedagogy, Denzin and Lincoln put this well: '... it embraces the commitment by indigenous scholars to decolonize Western methodologies, to criticize and demystify the ways in which Western science *and the modern academy* have been part of the colonial apparatus' (my emphasis).[59] Given the presence of institutional racism, sexism, disablism and so on, there is still much to do to decolonise and deconstruct many aspects of the neoliberal university.

Research

Universities are major sites for research; indeed, for Karl Popper, the university's main purpose is research.[60] As discussed in Chapter 6, a common criticism of psychotherapy and its practitioners is that we are not sufficiently interested or involved in research. By contrast, universities provide the intellectual environment as well as opportunities, support and funding – and certain expectations – to research, write and publish. From his (psychoanalytic) perspective, Kernberg is very clear about the necessity of research: 'I believe that the research function and scholarship in psychoanalytic education are absolutely essential to the survival of psychoanalysis as a profession and a science.'[61] Whether or not psychotherapy is an autonomous scientific discipline (for discussion of which see Chapter 8), as a practice, discipline and a profession, it benefits from research, and from its practitioners being involved in research.

Academic freedom

Traditionally, and certainly since the collapse of scholasticism in the 15th century, universities have been places that have embodied 'academic freedom'. As Kernberg puts it: 'A university model implies open scientific discussions.'[62] With rare exceptions and under exceptional circumstances (such as living in a totalitarian state), universities are committed to freedom of enquiry, and to critical enquiry. In New Zealand, this is enshrined in the *Education Amendment Act 1990*, which outlines the characteristics of universities, including that 'they are primarily concerned with more advanced learning, the principal aim being to develop intellectual independence',[63] and that 'they accept a role as critic and conscience of society'.[64] Thus, by definition and purpose, a university-based psychotherapy education encourages free and critical thinking about psychotherapy and its practice and purpose.

Public

Psychotherapists predominantly work in the private sector – in one country, as many as 93.51 per cent.[65] If, as psychotherapists, we think more public sector provision of psychotherapy would be a good thing, then we need to prepare trainees/students for work in the public sector. One way of doing this is through trainees/students undertaking placements in the public sector; another way is to locate the training itself in the public sector – ie. in a university. In his book *Tools for Conviviality*, Ivan Illich critiqued the institutionalisation of 'specialised' knowledge and elite professional groups that exert, or seek to exert, a radical monopoly on basic human activities.[66] The location of psychotherapy in a public institution that contains multiple knowledge challenges the institutionalisation and privatisation of specialist knowledge in the private sector, which, by definition, is only available to those who can afford it. As most universities are located in the public sector, they often have, and engender, a strong sense of public ethos and public service. Along with this comes certain other advantages, such as funding (whereby student enrolments are subsidied by government), and accountability (in terms of well-developed systems for assessment, appointments etc). Given his advocacy of the university college model of (psychoanalytic) education, it is no surprise that Kernberg is positive about universities, especially their commitment to their basic (public) task: that of 'high level education and generation of new knowledge', which he views as 'a genuine, ongoing effort in a competitive world'.[67]

At the same time, some colleagues are sceptical, even antagonistic, to psychotherapy training taking place in an academic institution. Having worked as a trainer/educator in the private sector for 17 years, and in the public sector for nine years (to date), I see a certain similarity and an overlap between the research gap between practitioners and researchers (discussed in Chapter 6) and what I would refer to as 'an academic gap', some features of which include:

- that most psychotherapists have trained at institutions in the private sector, thereby gaining a professional qualification, and may be somewhat resentful and/or envious of colleagues who study on a programme at an academic institution and gain both a professional qualification and a university degree.

- that most psychotherapists who read the psychotherapy literature consult professional journals and magazines and books. Students and academics and universities have almost unlimited access to academic as well as professional journals, and so are generally reading quite a different literature, which, moreover, is often inaccessible to their professional colleagues.

- that most academics in psychotherapy spend more of their time in academia than in their psychotherapy practice, as a result of which they can be seen as more interested in ideas and teaching than in practice.

- that few practitioners in private practice have or make time to research, write and publish, which most academics do (or are expected to do), and this creates a potential divide between the private sector practitioner and the (predominantly) public sector academic.

In recent times (by now nearly 20 years), some private training institutes have sought academic validation for their programmes from universities. This development has in part been driven by market and consumer demand – ie. from trainees who want an academic degree in addition to a professional qualification. There are, of course, many implications of this, not least in terms of cost, but also with regard to the influence on and requirements of the academic institution from the training institute – for instance, with regard to curriculum and academic processes. I know of instances both where this has worked very successfully and where the compromises have been too great.

From a critical perspective, the litmus test of any psychotherapy education – and it is likely to be an education, as distinct from a training – is whether its students and graduates are critical thinkers and practitioners. In an open letter to the committee of the then UK ITA on the subject of TA and politics, Chris Turner questions the motivation of some TA training programmes that are, in his view, overly concerned with maintaining 'comfortable' relationships between management and workers and 'positive' customer-client programmes. He contends that, 'unless fundamental questions of power, political manipulation and alienation are dealt with, then such programmes, while apparently encouraging Adult behaviour, are developing Adaptive Child behaviour at the political level'.[68] He goes on to ask the 'crunch question': '[D]oes any particular TA programme enable this country to move towards a more just society, or does it reinforce the injustices, inequalities, and oppressions of capitalist society?'[69] Taking this further, he argues that TA 'must address itself to the cruelty, oppression, nastiness and injustice of the society in which we live, its national and international perspectives. TA should be out on the streets of Southall and St. Pauls, on the picket lines, in the refugee camps'. I suggest that Turner's call is no less true today, more than 35 years later.

Continuing education or professional development

Professional development begins at the beginning of professional training, and so the development of the professional is initially the concern of their trainer and/or supervisor – and/or their personal therapist.

Following training, practitioners may become members of a professional organisation (or a number of such organisations), a process and an experience that, to some extent, forms part of an acculturation to the profession. Obviously, people have different experiences of their membership of such organisations and associations; from a critical perspective, the issue is whether such acculturation is conservatising or not. The fact that many of these organisations allow students to join is to be welcomed, although the restrictions that some of them impose – for instance, when attending a conference, not allowing students to stay at the same hotel as the trainers – suggests a certain pedagogy that promotes a parent–child, developmental model of membership.

It used to be the case that, once someone had qualified, their further development was primarily their own responsibility. However, in the context of the increasing professionalisation of psychotherapy (see Chapter 8), and the accountability and audit culture,[70] there is a growing focus on what is generally referred to as 'continuing professional development' (CPD). Increasingly, this is taking the form of CPD policies and requirements for the practitioner's continuing membership(s) of professional associations, and/or accreditation or registration and re-accreditation. The UKCP is clear about this, considering CPD 'to be a compulsory, not optional, requirement of all its registrants, in line with maintaining current best practice'.[71] Here I first discuss what constitutes CPD, and second, explore three aspects of what could constitute critical professional development.

Most professional accrediting bodies justify their policies in terms of their overall aims and, beyond that, the protection of the public through the maintenance and improvement of professional standards, and this is no less true of those concerning CPD. However, CPD can be framed in more aspirational terms, as, for instance, does the UKCP's HIPC:

> Just as importantly, CPD is about an ongoing ethical belief in, and commitment to, our growth, freshness and development as practising psychotherapists. Implicit in this statement is an assumption that effective psychotherapists have a sense of liveliness and curiosity about their work, are critically reflective about psychotherapy itself, and regularly ask questions about their, and the, work. We believe, therefore, that any activity or experience that can be shown to alert us to new dilemmas, or new ways of thinking about and engaging in clinical work, should be included as

continuous professional development. This includes not only experiences with clients, or formal structures for further learning, but also all of our experiences outside the consulting room or seminar room.[72]

I appreciate the emphasis in this statement on growth, freshness, liveliness, curiosity, critical reflection, questioning, engagement and experience outside as well as inside the consulting room, and the HIPC's acknowledgement of the autonomy of the registrant in presenting their own portfolio of CPD activities. Other organisations and accrediting bodies are requiring and specifying more concrete evidence of a practitioner's CPD, such as signed certificates from training courses and events, evidence of the practitioner's consultation with the supervisor, and audit procedures etc.

As people are living longer, at least in the Western world, so psychotherapists are practising longer, and the profession is greying. One of the implications of this is that, in order to maintain currency with developments in the profession and related research and practice, CPD becomes even more important, as does the relationship between CPD and some form of monitoring, especially for colleagues who continue but don't develop and, in some cases, refuse to retire. In a 2008 article on ethical governance in which she discusses CPD, including the implications for elderly members of professional organisations, Ann Casement notes that: 'Age itself could not be a universal reason for retirement... [and] fitness to practise was actually the priority.'[73] She reports on the position of the UK's Health Professions Council (now the Health and Care Professions Council), which 'is *not* to impose retirement on registrants. The main emphasis within HPC is on professional self-management of fitness to practise'.[74]

In the context of a discussion about practitioners who are ageing and those who are the subject of a complaint, Herbert Hahn makes following point: 'In following current trends and nailing the challenging flag of "continuing professional development" to our mast, we perhaps need to give serious and careful consideration to what best *sustains*, as well as develops psychotherapists.'[75] Given the emphasis in psychotherapy on the use of self (however we may conceptualise that), and on self-awareness, self-knowledge and self-development during training, Hahn's point is particularly well made: we need to have ways of sustaining ourselves throughout our career.

In the context of this examination of psychotherapy, my interest is in proposing how continuing professional sustenance and/or development includes – or might include – the development, continuing or otherwise, of the practitioner as a critical thinker, supported by supervision or consultancy about cultural practice, and by research.

Critical thinking

Between 1976 and 1977, I worked as a temporary probation officer. Some clients told me, in confidence, that they had been beaten up by the police. When I proposed doing something about it, they told me that they would deny it. I had, of course, read in the media about this happening, but had not been confronted with it personally. This, and some other personal experiences, radicalised me; I knew that I wanted to learn more about injustice, critical theory and thinking and radical perspectives on practice. At the end of my temporary contract, I applied to a social work course that I knew took a radical perspective. I was not disappointed, and for the following two years I was exposed to and undertook further reading in critical thinking, especially Marxism and feminism, and critical and radical social work practice. The course encouraged critical reflection or reflexivity, which I used, among other purposes, to reflect on and critique the pedagogy of the training course.[76]

Just as we learn from our mistakes,[77] so we learn from gaps or perceived gaps in our formal education and training, which, usually, we make up for through further study. Having now been involved in the education and training of a number of counselling and psychotherapy trainees and students for more than 25 years, I have noticed that what begins as a complaint about a gap in the training, which is often an area of the student's own interest, becomes the subject of their further study and, sometimes, contribution to the field. In this sense, I propose that part of sustaining and continuing professional development (SCPD) could – and, arguably, should – be the (continuing) development of critical thinking, along the lines outlined in Chapter 1. Thus, for instance, and following the tenor of the argument in this chapter, and, indeed, this book, enrolling in a philosophy class could – and, I'd hope, would – be seen as part of a psychotherapist's SCPD.

Cultural supervision/consultancy

As is discussed in Chapter 2, psychotherapy arose in a particular Western – and Northern – intellectual tradition, and, by and large, the psychotherapy profession is predominantly white, middle class and female. Despite some quite sophisticated analyses of the interplay between race and culture and psychotherapy, there is still a sense from the literature that, in psychotherapy, 'culture' means being sensitive to the culture of clients and the other/Other, and that this is assessed in terms of the practitioner's cultural competence in working with the other. This approach, however, smacks of the superficial multiculturalism critiqued some years ago as the three Ss of liberal education: 'saris, samosas and steel bands'.[78]

A more critical and reflexive approach is one that, first, requires – or, from a political perspective that seeks to deconstruct power, demands – the subject to consider their own culture and the assumed neutrality of (their) dominant culture identity or identities,[79] and, second, requires them to subject themselves and their practice to the super (wider and different) vision of the other. Personally, I have had and still have experience of working with therapists and supervisors of different gender, sexuality, race and culture to my own, and consider that this has made a profound and significant difference to my understanding not only of myself but also of cross-cultural work and, in the context of Aotearoa New Zealand, bicultural engagement. As Margaret Poutu Morice and Fay put it: 'The working assumption of our approach to cultural supervision and cultural competence is that individual psychology and culture coexist and co-determine each other. Culture is the public face of psyche and psyche the private face of culture.'[80] With regard to sustaining and developing ourselves, I would hope that qualified psychotherapists, however experienced, would want to explore this co-existence through SCPD, whether in personal therapy, supervision or through supplementary education and training.

Research

Clearly research can itself be a form of SCPD (see Chapter 6). This could take the form of enrolling in further education or on a higher-degree programme, such as a master's in philosophy or a doctoral degree; indeed, the former may be particularly attractive to those practitioners who have undertaken their training at an institute in the private sector (at master's or 'M'-level), and who wish to study for and gain a master's degree. Whether or not a practitioner's research is conducted as part of a degree programme, it could take various forms, and there are a number of methodologies that support personal research. These include heuristic enquiry,[81] autoethnography,[82] intuitive enquiry[83] and integral inquiry[84] (see also Chapter 6). As McLeod reflects: 'Personal experience research can represent a powerful means of personal development.'[85]

Given the client-centred influence in this critical examination, it seems appropriate to leave the last word of this chapter with a client. In 1969, at the age of 25, Ronald Bassman was admitted to a psychiatric hospital, where he was given a range of diagnoses and treatments. He eventually returned to graduate school, gained a doctorate, and became a licensed psychologist. Having hidden his psychiatric history for over 20 years, he finally chose to 'come out' and identify as a psychiatric survivor. In 1999, he wrote an article that originally appeared in the American *Psychotherapy Bulletin*. Although he refers to psychologists, his conclusion stands equally for psychotherapy and psychotherapists:

> I urge psychologists to learn how they can use their education, talents, and skills in new ways by engaging in an exciting collaborative journey of creativity and personal growth where people support each other as equals and speak of what is in their hearts. To be effective in the service you provide for a consumer/survivor, it is imperative that you see the individual and value that special individual by engaging in a collaborative search to find understanding, meaning, and connection in this person's unfolding life narrative.[86]

Endnotes

1. Paglia C (1995). *Vamps and Tramps*. Harmondsworth: Viking.
2. This is still the case, for instance, in transactional analysis, for the requirements for which see EATA (2017). *EATA Training and Examinations Handbook*. Konstanz: European Association for Transactional Analysis. www.eatanews.org/training-manuals-and-supplements/ (accessed 9 July 2017); and International Association for Transactional Analysis (2013). *Training and Examinations Handbook*. International Association for Transactional Analysis. http://itaaworld.org/itaa-training-examinations-handbook (accessed 12 July 2017).
3. Rogers CR (1969). *Freedom to Learn*. Columbus, OH: Charles E Merrill. Subsequent editions were published in 1973 and, posthumously, in 1994.
4. Rogers (1969) (part II).
5. Rogers quotes Martin Buber's phrase: 'Contact is the primary word of education.' Buber (p101). Although Rogers himself didn't reference Buber's work, this quote comes from Buber M (1967). On contact. In: Buber M. *A Believing Humanism: my testament 1902–1965* (M Friedman trans). New York, NY: Simon & Schuster (p102).
6. Rogers (1969) (p115).
7. For further details of which, see: Embleton Tudor L, Keemar K, Tudor K, Valentine J, Worrall M (2004). *The Person-Centred Approach: a contemporary introduction*. Basingstoke: Palgrave (chapter 10); and Tudor K (2007). Training in the person-centred approach. In: Cooper M, O'Hara M, Schmid P, Wyatt G (eds). *The Handbook of Person-Centred Psychotherapy and Counselling*. Basingstoke: Palgrave (pp379–389).
8. Barrow G (2017). Personal e-mail communication; 9 May.
9. See Barrow G (2009). Teaching, learning, schooling and script. *Transactional Analysis Journal 29*(4): 298–304; and also Newton T (2006). Script, psychological life plans and the learning cycle. *Transactional Analysis Journal 36*(4): 186–195.
10. See Kapp A (1833). *Platon's Erziehungslehre, als Paedagogik für die Einzelnen und als Staatspaedagogik [Plato's Educational Theory as a Pedagogy for the Individual and as State Pedagogy, or its Practical Philosophy]*. Minden und Leipzig, Germany: Ferdinand Essmann; and Knowles MS, Holton EF, Swanson RA (1998). *The Adult Learner* (5th ed). Houston, TX: Gulf.
11. Herlo D (2014). Paragogy: a new theory in educational sciences. *Journal Plus Education 10*(4): 35–41.
12. Herlo (2014) (p36).
13. Barrow G (2017). Personal e-mail communication; 9 May.
14. Kernberg O (2000). A concerned critique of psychoanalytic education. *International Journal of Psycho-Analysis 81*: 97–120.
15. Aron L, Starr K (2013). *Psychotherapy for the People: toward a progressive*

psychoanalysis. New York, NY: Routledge (p22).
16. Most recently in Tudor K, Summers G (2014). *Co-creative Transactional Analysis: papers, responses and developments*. London: Karnac.
17. See Füredi F (2004). *Where Have all The Intellectuals Gone? Confronting 21st century philistinism*. London: Continuum (pp145, 156).
18. Tavris C (1993). Conversation. In: Esterle J, Cluman D (eds). *Conversations with Critical Thinkers*. San Francisco, CA: The Whitman Institute (pp113–127) (p119).
19. Coase RH (1960). The problem of social cost. *The Journal of Law & Economics 3*: 1–44 (p2).
20. Coase (1960) (p2).
21. See, for instance, Jenson E (2009). *Teaching with Poverty in Mind: what being poor does to kids' brains and what schools can do about it*. Alexandria, VA: ASCD.
22. King L, Moutsou C (2010). *Rethinking Audit Cultures: a critical look at evidence-based practice in psychotherapy and beyond*. Ross-on-Wye: PCCS Books.
23. Institute of Transactional Analysis (2013). *Code of Practice for Psychotherapy Trainers and Training Establishments*. Cambridge: Institute of Transactional Analysis. For a critique of this, see Tudor & Summers (2014).
24. See Eitingon M (1923). Report of the Berlin psycho-analytical policlinic. *Bulletin of the International Psycho-Analytic Association 4*: 254–269.
25. Freud S (1959/1926). The question of lay analysis: conversations with an impartial person. In Strachey J (ed & trans). *The Standard Edition of the Complete Psychological Works of Sigmund Freud*. London: The Hogarth Press (pp177–250).
26. Freud (1959/1926) (p252).
27. United Kingdom Council for Psychotherapy (2012). *UKCP Standards of Education and Training: the minimum core criteria. Psychotherapy with adults*. London: UKCP (p5).
28. Humanistic and Intergrative Psychotherapy College (undated). *Training Standards of the Humanistic and Integrative Psychotherapy College (HIPC) of UKCP*. London: UKCP.
29. The only specific anti-dogmatic training I have come across is an anti-dogmatic design course at Eindhoven University of Technology, The Netherlands: www.idemployee.id.tue.nl/g.w.m.rauterberg/lecturenotes/DG413(Anti%20Dogmatic%20Design).htm (accessed 30 October 2017).
30. There are, of course, academic programmes and courses that lead to a qualification in the *study* of psychoanalysis or psychotherapy, which have no practice component.
31. Feltham C (2013). *Counselling and Counselling Psychology: a critical examination*. Ross-on-Wye: PCCS Books (p122).

32. Interestingly, in the context of the argument about the audit culture with regard to hours, this requirement came about due to the fact that one student hadn't met the previous requirement but had still passed their qualifying examination, as a result of which the then Humanistic and Integrative Psychotherapy Section of the UKCP clarified the requirement by setting a tarif for hours.
33. Kernberg O (1986). Institutional problems of psychoanalytic education. *Journal of the American Psychoanalytic Association 34*: 799–834.
34. Kernberg (1986) (p806).
35. Kernberg O (1996). Thirty methods to destroy the creativity of psychoanalytic candidates. *International Journal of Psycho-Analysis 77*: 1031–1040.
36. Kernberg (1986) (p807).
37. Kernberg (1986) (p807).
38. Kernberg (1986) (p808).
39. Füredi (2004) (p144).
40. Kernberg (1986) (p810).
41. Kernberg (1986) (p810).
42. Kernberg (1986) (p811).
43. Kernberg (1986) (p811).
44. Kernberg (1986) (p811).
45. Kernberg (1986) (p812).
46. Kernberg O (2010). A new organisation of psychoanalytic education. *Psychoanalytic Review 97*(6): 997–1020 (p998).
47. Denzin NK, Lincoln YS (2000). Introduction: the discipline and practice of qualitative research. In: Denzin NK, Lincoln YS (eds). *Handbook of Qualitative Research* (2nd ed). Thousand Oaks, CA: Sage (pp1–29) (p2).
48. They are at Birmingham City University, Brighton University, Newman University Birmingham, New School of Psychotherapy and Counselling London, Oxford University, Roehampton University, and the Southern Association for Psychotherapy and Counselling London, all of which comprise the UKCP's Universities Training College. See www.psychotherapy.org.uk/about-ukcp/how-we-are-structured/ukcp-colleges/universities-training-college (accessed 31 October 2017).
49. Wallerstein RS (2009). Psychoanalysis in the university: a full-time vision. *International Journal of Psychoanalysis 90*(5): 1107–1121.
50. Freud S (1959/1926). The question of lay analysis: conversations with an impartial person. In: Strachey J (trans & ed). *The Standard Edition of the Complete Psychological Works of Sigmund Freud.* London: The Hogarth Press (pp177–250) (p246).

51. Wallerstein (2009) (p1108).
52. Wallerstein (2009) (p1109).
53. Kernberg O (2006). The coming changes in psychoanalytic education: part I. *International Journal of Psycho-Analysis* 87(6): 1649–1673.
54. Kernberg (2006) (p1657).
55. Kernberg O (2007). The coming changes in psychoanalytic education: part II. *International Journal of Psycho-Analysis* 88(1): 183-202 (pp189–190).
56. Mill JS (1867). *Inaugural Address Delivered to the University of St. Andrews*. London: Longmans, Green, Reader & Dyer (pp 4–5).
57. The Oxbridge system still allows for any student to attend any lecture.
58. Barrow G (2017). Personal e-mail communication; 9 May.
59. Denzin NK, Lincoln YS (2000). Introduction: The discipline and practice of qualitative research. In: Denzin NK, Lincoln YS (eds). *Handbook of Qualitative Research* (2nd ed). Thousand Oaks, CA: Sage (pp1–29) (p2).
60. In 1945, Popper and some colleagues wrote: 'We do not accept the point of view that teaching is the main function of the University. The two activities of the University, teaching and research, should be co-ordinated and combined… The commonly held view that the University is primarily a teaching institution should be abandoned.' See Allan R, Packer J, Eccles JC, Parton HN, Forder HG, Popper KR (1945). *Research and the University: a statement by a group of teachers in the University of New Zealand*. Christchurch: Caxton Press (p1).
61. Kernberg O (2000). A concerned critique of psychoanalytic education. *International Journal of Psycho-Analysis* 81: 97–120 (p108).
62. Kernberg (1986) (p832).
63. *Education Amendment Act 1990*, §4(i).
64. *Education Amendment Act 1990*, §4(v). For further discussion of which, see Tudor K (2017). *Conscience and Critic: the selected works of Keith Tudor*. London: Routledge.
65. Tudor K (2018). *Psychotherapy in the Public Sector: alternative and other facts*. (Submitted for publication.)
66. Illich I (1973). *Tools for Conviviality*. London: Fontana.
67. Kernberg O (2007) (p188).
68. Turner C (1981). TA and Politics. Part I: an open letter to the Committee of the Institute of Transactional Analysis. *Transactions* winter: 19.
69. Turner (1981) (p19).
70. King L, Moutsou C (2010). *Rethinking Audit Cultures: a critical look at evidence-based practice in psychotherapy and beyond*. Ross-on-Wye: PCCS Books.

71. UKCP (2015). *UKCP Policy for Continuing Professional Development*. London: UKCP (p1).
72. Humanistic and Integrative Psychotherapy College (2004). *Continuing Professional Development Requirements and Minimum Standards*. London: UKCP HIPC.
73. Casement A (2008). Ethical governance. *British Journal of Psychotherapy* 24: 407–428 (p420).
74. Casement (2008).
75. Hahn H (2004). F***ing, failing and finding out. [Review of the book *Disgrace* by JM Coetzee.] *British Journal of Psychotherapy* 18: 537–542 (pp539–540).
76. A critique which led to my first peer-reviewed publication: Brown K, Tudor K (1981). Social work education and practice: reform and revolution – a theory for change. *Contemporary Social Work Education* 4(2): 101–112.
77. See Casement (2002). *Learning from our Mistakes: beyond dogma in psychoanalysis and psychotherapy*. New York, NY: Guilford Press.
78. See Troyna B (ed) (1987). *Racial Inequality in Education*. London: Tavistock. Also: Troyna B (1993). *Racism and Education*. Maidenhead: Open University Press.
79. See, for instance: Naughton M, Tudor K (2006). Being white. *Transactional Analysis Journal* 36(2): 159–171.
80. Morice MP, Fay J (2013). Cultural supervision and cultural competence in the practice of psychotherapy and applied psychology. *Ata: Journal of Psychotherapy Aotearoa New Zealand* 17(1): 89–101.
81. Moustakas C (1990). *Heuristic Research: design, methodology and applications*. Thousand Oaks, CA: Sage.
82. Ellis C, Flaherty M (eds) (1992). *Investigating Subjectivity: research on lived experience*. Thousand Oaks, CA: Sage. Also: Ellis C, Bochner AP (2000). Auto-ethnography, personal narrative, reflexivity: researcher as subject. In Denzin NK, Lincoln YS (eds). *Handbook of Qualitative Research* (2nd ed). Thousand Oaks, CA: Sage (pp733–768).
83. Anderson R (1998). Intuitive inquiry: a transpersonal approach. In: Braud W, Anderson R (eds). *Transpersonal Research Methods for the Social Sciences: honouring human experience*. Thousand Oaks, CA: Sage (pp69–94).
84. Braud W (1998). Integral enquiry: complementary ways of knowing, being and expression. In: Braud & Anderson (1998) (pp35–68).
85. McLeod J (2003). *Doing Counselling Research*. London: Sage (p84).
86. Bassman R (1999). The psychology of mental illness: the consumers'/survivors'/ex-mental patients' perspective. *Psychotherapy Bulletin* 34(1): 14–16.

CHAPTER 8

Discipline, profession and social criticism

> Always the more beautiful answer who asks a more beautiful question.
> (ee cummings)[1]

Throughout this book, I have referred to psychotherapy as a practice involving various methods (see especially Chapter 4); as a profession; as a discipline, and, overall, as a field. To end this critical examination of psychotherapy, I briefly discuss various historical and contemporary debates about psychotherapy as an art or a science, the role of the academy and of professional associations, and professionalisation, under the three headings of psychotherapy as a discipline, psychotherapy as a profession, and psychotherapy as social criticism.

In their book on *Change*, Paul Watzlawick, John Weakland and Richard Fisch develop the concept of 'position', which they use to refer to those beliefs of the client that influence the presenting problem and the client's participation in therapy.[2] In this chapter, I draw on this concept analogously also to consider the beliefs psychotherapists have about themselves and about psychotherapy that, in effect, influence how they present and participate in society.

Psychotherapy as a discipline

Psychotherapy as an autonomous discipline

In the history of ideas, new thoughts and, ultimately, disciplines usually arise by distinguishing themselves from previous thoughts or disciplines. In Chapter 2, I acknowledge the influence of a number of different traditions on the practice of soul healing (p62–63), from which it is clear that it was primarily doctors – Walter Cooper Dendy, Daniel Hack Tuke, Hippolyte Bernheim, Charles Lloyd Tuckey, Frederik van Eeden, Albert Willem, Josef Breuer and, of course, Freud himself – who influenced the development of what can be called modern *psycho therapeia*.

In a rare and interesting article discussing the question of whether psychotherapy is an autonomous scientific discipline, Emmy van Deurzen-Smith and David Smith suggest that what characterises an autonomous discipline is that it '1)... must be theoretically distinct from any adjacent discipline... [and] 2)... must possess a theory which is irreducible to any adjacent theory'.[3] To this I would add a third criterion: that it must also have practitioners and theoreticians who identify primarily with the discipline. In this sense, the discipline of psychotherapy can be dated precisely from 21 October 1811, when Johann Heinroth was appointed as Professor of *Psychische Therapie* at Leipzig University (a position he held until his death in 1843): that is, Professor of Psychic (Psycho) Therapy, a title and a chair that represented a discipline that was seen as distinct from others, including psychology.

While Freud himself was very interdisciplinary in his interests and scope,[4] and was clear that he did not want psychoanalysis to be subsumed under medicine, he did see it as a form of psychology – a position and positioning that, I suggest, has been a problem for its development as a profession and a practice that is distinct from psychology. Arguably, this has been further compounded by the development of counselling psychology, with the result that psy professionals are faced with explaining the differences between counselling, counselling psychology, clinical psychology, psychotherapy and psychiatry, not only to the public but to other professionals.

Psychotherapy as an art and/or a science

Freud himself wanted to be seen as a neutral scientist and for his discoveries to be accepted by the scientific community. This was one of the reasons that he distinguished psychoanalysis from any form of religion, as he didn't want that to contaminate his new 'science'. As part of this, he took – or claimed to take – an objectivist approach, predicated on the view that nature and humans could be observed objectively, and that the observer was neutral in this process. As Aron and Starr comment: 'Given Freud's positivist vision and scientific aspirations, it is not surprising that he insisted he had made universal discoveries, rather than publicly acknowledge any subjective influence, let alone a particularly Jewish one.'[5]

In their article, van Deurzen-Smith and Smith echo Freud's concern, and, in their discussion of psychotherapy as a *scientific* discipline, discount any consideration of the view that psychotherapy is an art – or, at least, also an art. To claim the art and artistry of psychotherapy appears important if we are to honour that part of our tradition that derives from drama (from Moreno onwards), which includes, for instance, intuition (which was the subject of Berne's early work), and which encompasses the arts, ie. art, dance and movement, drama, and music, all of which have given rise to forms of creative and expressive therapies. Interestingly, a Google search (conducted in April 2017) on the terms 'MA in Psychotherapy' and 'MSc in Psychotherapy' produced almost twice as many results for the arts degree.

At the same time, there are different views about what constitutes 'science' (for a discussion of which, with regard to research, see Chapter 6). How psychotherapists position themselves in this respect is strategic. If we accept that psychotherapy is (only) an art, there is a sense in which we give up on science and, in effect, accept the view that it only encompasses certain disciplines and, more fundamentally, only specific methodologies, informed by certain philosophical traditions, such as empiricism. If, on the other hand, we argue that psychotherapy is a science, we can either position it as conforming to more traditional, objectivist views of science (as, generally, does psychology), or we can argue that science encompasses other and more subjectivist approaches to knowledge.[6] An early example of this is Rogers' work as a researcher in the field of psychology, counselling and psychotherapy and, specifically, his call for a more 'human science' of the person[7] (see also Chapter 4). A more contemporary example is the number of research methodologies that support enquiry into and exploration and examination of subjectivity (see Chapter 6, pp193–197). The European Association for Psychotherapy is clear about its position on this, and in 1990 published a declaration that asserted: 'Psychotherapy is an independent scientific discipline, the practice of which represents an independent and free profession.'[8]

However, viewing psychotherapy as either an art or a science is, in effect, subscribing to binary thinking and, ultimately, perpetuating a false polarity. It is, in postmodern parlance, a wicked problem – ie. one that is difficult to solve due to incomplete, contradictory, or, perhaps more significantly, changing requirements. In responding to the changing challenges of our complex world, I suggest we need a psychotherapy – or, rather, psychotherapies (plural) – that offer a range of methods, based on different methodologies, such that 'psychotherapy' encompasses and is recognised as encompassing many forms of and ways to facilitate 'soul healing'. In the way it has developed most specifically as a distinct discipline, practice and field over the past 200 years, psychotherapy is now a very 'broad church', holding a wide variety and variation of practice(s), based on a similarly wide range of theory, from across what would be regarded as both art(s) and science(s). In a world in which there is an increasing number of wicked problems, I suggest that we need a greater acceptance of the pluralism of psychotherapy, and the development of more wicked, wild, and subversive practice and theory.

Psychotherapy as an academic discipline

One of the ways in which a subject generally comes to be viewed or accepted as a discipline is if it has a distinct academic presence, and, as noted in Chapter 2, psychotherapy has had that since Johann Heinroth's appointment in 1811. However, it is also true to say there are very few university departments of psychotherapy that are distinct from departments of psychology or psychiatry, and, currently, there are very few professors of psychotherapy in the world,[9] while there are many professors of psychology who are also psychotherapists or who practise psychotherapy.

In Chapter 7, I discussed certain advantages to locating psychotherapy education/training within an academic context and setting, and cited Kernberg's work on this. As all university teaching should be research-informed, this places the responsibility on psychotherapy academics to be reading, researching, writing, publishing and generally advancing the field – as well as reporting and, thereby, accounting for this work. This is important if the academic wing of the profession is to help develop and advance concepts that are distinctly based in the psychotherapeutic understanding of the person and the world, rather than psychological and medical/psychiatric ones. Robert Young puts this robustly:

> I also hope that the desiccated and scientistic concept of personality which academic psychology has developed as a pale shadow of the concept we had before and need again, will give way to the concept of character, and that psychoanalysis will re-enter psychology departments through that door. Finally, I hope that the paltry and embarrassing dynamics of our profession will be transformed for the better. Since we no longer march under the banner of the medical and biological scientists which prevailed when I was training to be a psychiatrist so I could practice psychoanalysis, I hope we will enrich our world view from the arts and from humanism, good ole humanism.[10]

Psychotherapy as a profession

The various historical influences on psychotherapy – healing, medicine, ministry, psychology and social work (as noted in Chapter 2) – have had different impacts on the development of psychotherapy as a profession, and, indeed, how its practitioners have thought about and questioned this development. Thus, psychotherapists with a background in ministry, and some coming from social work, tend to think of psychotherapy as a vocation and its practice as a form of service;[11] those with a background in medicine and nursing generally think of psychotherapy as a health profession and practice allied to medicine; those with a background in political activism and/or community work emphasise psychotherapy as a form of liberation – Totton, for instance, argues that psychotherapy is best regarded as 'a spiritual and political practice',[12] a perspective that may also find resonance with indigenous practitioners of soul healing.

Caplow identifies four steps to professionalisation: the formation of a professional association; changing the association's name to reduce its identification with any occupations considered of lower status; the promulgating of a code of conduct, and regulation.[13] Here I use these four steps to frame some brief discussions about psychotherapy as a profession.

Professional association

Interestingly, and with perhaps some prescience, Freud referred to psychoanalysis as the third impossible profession (the other two being pedagogy and governance), in which, he reflected, 'one can be sure beforehand of unsatisfying results'.[14]

In 1902, Freud began to meet weekly with a group of colleagues to discuss his work, and thus what became known as the Psychological Wednesday Society was born.[15] In April 1907, this was reconstituted as the Vienna Psychoanalytic Society. By 1908, there were regular members, who included both analysts and lay people,[16] although the group also welcomed visitors.[17] In 1907, Ernest Jones suggested to Jung that an international meeting should be organised. Freud welcomed the suggestion, and a meeting took place in Salzburg on 27 April 1908, which Jung named the First Congress for Freudian Psychology. At the next congress, held in Nuremburg in March 1910, and following a proposal by Ferenczi, the IPA[18] was founded, with Jung as President and Rank as Secretary. Freud considered an international organisation as essential to advancing his ideas, and in 1914 he published a paper on the history of the psychoanalytic movement (which was published in English two years later).[19]

Currently, the IPA is the world's leading accrediting and regulatory body for psychoanalysis; it has more than 12,000 psychoanalysts as members, three regional organisations and some 60 constituent organisations, organises a biennial congress, and fosters provisional societies, study groups and allied centres. Its current aims include creating new psychoanalytic groups, stimulating debate, conducting research, developing training policies and establishing links with other bodies. It is, however, not without its critics: in 1975 Eric Fromm questioned its dictatorial standards,[20] and in 1999 Elizabeth Roudinesco wrote in support of French Lacanian colleagues who viewed the IPA as having 'betrayed psychoanalysis in favor of an adaptive psychology in the service of triumphant capitalism',[21] and herself criticised it for its homophobia.

Since 1910, many other such international associations have been established on the basis of theoretical orientation. These organisations of course have their strengths and weaknesses, their peaks and troughs, their alliances and splits. For instance, as Makari reports it, at one point: 'Freud declared Adler's ideas as too contrary, leading to an ultimatum to all members of the [Psychological Wednesday] Society (which Freud had shepherded) to drop Adler or [themselves] to be expelled, thereby disavowing the right to dissent.'[22] This dynamic has continued, and is well analysed with regard to psychoanalytic institutes by Doug Kirsner in his study of what he refers to as 'Unfree Associations'.[23]

While there are benefits to such international associations, they are, however, limited in their capacity to govern the profession, or even their specific orientation or modality, due to local conditions: ie. the laws of specific national jurisdictions. Thus, while a psychotherapist may be a member of and even accredited by a specific international association, they may not be recognised or licensed to practise in their country of residence. Historically, there was, I consider, a second wave of professional association – the establishment of national member associations, ie. sections of the international associations, and also the establishment of generic national psychotherapy associations that brought together practitioners from different modalities. Such organisations are useful in providing a certain identity through association, the opportunity to pursue common interests and professional development across therapeutic modalities, and the critical mass to organise around and advocate for psychotherapy. However, these broad-based associations often suffer from becoming overly focused on fostering the organisation itself, as well as from splits and subsequent division. In 1942, Reich wrote about the consequences of the process of professionalisation in psychoanalysis: 'Slowly but surely it was cleansed of all Freud's achievements. Bringing psychoanalysis in line with the world... took place inconspicuously at first... [but gradually] form eclipsed content; the organisation became more important than its task.'[24]

A third wave of organisation has been the establishment of regional, and even global, umbrella organisations, such as the European Association for Psychotherapy (in 1991)[25] and the World Council for Psychotherapy (in 1996),[26] both of which are somewhat unwieldy – and, interestingly, quite conservative.

Changing and distinguishing the name

The second phase of professionalisation, as identified by Caplow, is characterised by associations distinguishing themselves in some way from others in order to reduce their identification with any occupations considered of lower status. Usually this involves changing the association's name. For example, in 1981, the New Zealand Association of Psychotherapists, Counsellors and Behaviour Therapists (Incorporated) changed its name to the New Zealand Association of Psychotherapists and Counsellors (Incorporated), thus dropping behaviour(al) therapists. Six years later, it changed its name again, to the New Zealand Association of Psychotherapists (Inc), thereby excluding counsellors.

Such distinctions in the field of psychotherapy have a long history. Aron and Starr summarise the events that set the stage for the way in which the psychoanalytic establishment defined psychoanalysis in contrast to psychotherapy, and show how these definitions and 'binary opposition' have moulded psychoanalysis and 'the psychoanalytic educational policies we live by today'.[27] Even within psychoanalysis, there are distinctions, most particularly between psychoanalysis proper and psychoanalytic psychotherapy.[28] However, as far as Aron and Starr are concerned, '[d]efining psychoanalysis in opposition to psychotherapy set up two poles "at far ends of a spectrum", creating two disciplines, rather than one discipline with a variety of applications'. They argue: 'This polarization has been detrimental to all aspects of psychoanalytic theory, practice, and education.'[29] I agree with Aron and Starr, and would extend this to other polarisations and pseudo distinctions, especially between psychotherapy and counselling. Taking up their challenge to polarised and binary thinking, and drawing on the influences identified earlier (in Chapter 2), I suggest a more integrated and pluralistic conceptual vision for the field of psychotherapy (Figure 8.1, to be read, as the arrow indicates, from the bottom up).

Figure 8.1 – A conceptual framework for the relationship(s) between different aspects of the field of psychotherapy

Contexts	Clinic/Consulting Room – Outside Free – Charged – Low cost Public – Private
Applications	Children – Adolescents – Adults
Forms of therapy	Individual – Couple – Filial – Family – Group (small, medium, large) – Community
Modalities	More than 1,000
'Disciplines'	Psychoanalysis (proper) – Psychoanalytic psychotherapy – Psychotherapy – Clinical psychology – Counselling psychology – Counselling
Influences	Healing traditions – Medicine – Psychiatry – Lay practice and the consumer movement – Ministry – Psychology – Social work

An early debate that exacerbated distinctions within psychoanalysis, and that still has some resonance today (in terms of relationships between those psychotherapists who are medically qualified and those who are not), was about lay analysis – and, indeed, in a number of countries, training in psychotherapy is still only open to medical doctors. This became a question when

American psychoanalysts proposed restricting analytic training to medical doctors. Freud, who supported lay analysts,[30] argued that this question should not be decided on practical considerations alone or on 'local conditions' (ie. in America), and referred to it as 'the medical fixation'.[31] This question had a number of aspects to it, including the (pre)dominance of medical doctors and the medical model, and gender: Aron and Starr suggest that 'because it was difficult for women to become physicians, the effort to marginalize and control lay analysts was simultaneously an effort to keep women in their place'.[32] Changing and distinguishing an association in order to become 'more professional(ised)' had – and still has – consequences.

Codes of conduct

Having established themselves and distinguished themselves from others, professional associations then tend to promulgate codes of ethics, conduct and professional practice, a characteristic of what Caplow identifies as the third phase of professionalisation. In a number of ways, this represents ways of self-regulating members and aligns with the least restrictive of the six models of regulation identified by Anna Macleod and Bernadette McSherry.[33] At the same time, such codes tend to grow, gain more clauses and generally become more legalistic and restrictive – a process that represents a defensive rather than progressive psychotherapy.[34] In response to this, some professional associations have developed frameworks or guidelines based on ethical and moral principles, rather than rules,[35] which are designed to help the practitioner and, usually, their supervisor, to think about a particular ethical or professional situation or dilemma. Usually, these reflect commonly held principles about dignity, equality, freedom and so on. However, while these are important, they represent absolute 'rights', usually based on the Western Enlightment tradition, rather than relational responsibilities. A different approach to such principles is represented by and in the work of Margaret Poutu Morice, who articulates Māori ethical values and principles as applied to the practice of psychotherapy.[36] They are:

1. *manaakitanga* – the process whereby *mana* (roughly translated as power or authority) is translated into actions of generosity

2. *whanaungatanga* – the principle that binds individuals to the wider group and affirms the value of the collective

3. *kotahitanga* – the principle of unity, unity of purpose, intention and direction

4. *kaitiakitanga*[37] – which represents the embracing of the spiritual and cultural guardianship of *te Ao Marama* (roughly translated as the natural world)

5. *rangatiratanga* – the expression of the attributes of a *rangatira* (or leader), particularly humility, as well as leadership by example

6. *wairuatanga* (roughly translated as spirituality) – which recognises spiritual existence parallel to and interwoven with physical existence

7. *tohungatanga* – which refers to the role of the expert

8. *ūkaipō* – which refers to the experience of receiving a mother's milk in the night, and is a metaphor for the nourishing that derives from unseen places and spaces.

These principles, I suggest, represent a framework for a relational ethics that goes beyond the codification of behaviour and required responses.

One issue for members of professional associations that have such codes and a complaints system is that, when a client complains against them, the association tends to take the side of the client and to view the practitioner as guilty until proved innocent. While supporting the person in the least powerful position is to be welcomed, especially from a critical perspective, this approach represents an 'either/or' position – and, moreover, one that leads to the bizarre situation where the often-unsupported practitioner continues to pay fees to 'their' professional association to support a process whereby, in some instances, they are treated badly by their colleagues. Herbert Hahn puts this well and robustly:

> I wonder whether our psychotherapy profession, in trying to follow the example of the medical establishment, finds itself relating to its complained-of members in a way which lacks moral imagination. It seems as if, having acquired teeth, our organizations are eager to be seen to be using them to bite rather than to chew. While in no way exonerating the personal responsibility of those of us who exploit our patients, the solution of creating a struck-off underclass has its own problems. In washing our hands of 'them', we close our hearts to concern, and our minds to learning something about what might have gone 'wrong' during selection and training, and about our part in it.[38]

In response to this situation, some professional associations have established a parallel complaints authority/body that receives and hears complaints from clients, which leaves the professional association free and more able to support the therapist through the process.

Regulation

The fourth and final stage of professionalisation, according to Caplow, is regulation. There are different forms of regulation. Macleod and McSherry identify six models, from the least regulatory, that of self-regulation, to the most regulatory, in which an external authority, usually the state, restricts both the title (ie. 'psychotherapist') and the entire scope of practice (ie. psychotherapy) to members of the registered profession.[39] Freud himself was strongly against prohibition and any restriction of practice: 'If the prohibition were enacted, we should find ourselves in a position in which a number of people are prevented from carrying out an activity which one can safely feel convinced they can perform very well.'[40]

Much has been written about this subject, especially from a critical perspective.[41] There is no evidence that the state registration of psychotherapists and/or the statutory regulation of psychotherapy protect the public, and, despite calls for such evidence over many years, those who are in favour of such regulation simply tend to assert that it's a good thing. Here, rather than repeating the arguments for and against state registration and statutory regulation, I touch briefly on its psycho-political impact. Elsewhere, I distinguish between what I refer to as the '3 Rs', ie. recognition, regulation, and registration[42] – terms that I suggest are commonly confused and conflated.

Writing about this from a broader, cultural perspective, Füredi suggests that: 'The cumulative impact of the politics of recognition is the construction of a docile and conformist public.'[43] It also leads to a docile and conformist profession. In the post-regulation landscape of the psychotherapy profession in Aotearoa New Zealand, most trainees, following qualification, apply to the psychotherapists' registration board to be registered as psychotherapists. Some are sceptical about registration and wider regulation, but they register in order to get a job or to be marketable. In my experience, most are either ignorant of the historical and/or contemporary debates or simply uncritical of statutory regulation, let alone of the possibilities of a non-regulative praxis.[44] Nine years after the state registration of the title 'psychotherapist', I have noticed that a number of students/trainees say, 'I've worked hard to be registered.' This is understandable in a post-regulation society in which having the title psychotherapist requires you to be registered, but it is significant that the focus for students is not so much on psycho*therapy*, ie. its praxis, their identity with the history, organisation of the discipline, local professional associations etc, and more on being able to be a psycho*therapist*, which shifts their focus to registration, the Board, compliance, the state, the market etc.

Psychotherapy as social criticism

In Chapter 2, I quoted Aron and Starr as acknowledging that psychoanalysis was as much a social movement (for reform in education, social policy and culture) as it was a method of psychological treatment.[45] Similarly, Jeffrey Zeig reflects that: 'In the 1960s and 1970s… psychotherapy felt like a social movement, and you just wanted to be part of it.'[46] I don't think that contemporary psychotherapy can realistically be viewed as or claimed to be a social movement, let alone an active or influential mass movement. Nevertheless, I think it is reasonable to claim it as contributing to and, indeed, as a form of social criticism.

I see this as the psychotherapy *of* politics and the social world, one of the four categories that Totton identifies as elaborating the interplay between psychotherapy and politics.[47] For Totton, this comprises 'a range of attempts to understand and to evaluate political life through the application of psychotherapeutic concepts'.[48] From the perspective of this book, this would involve a critical understanding and evaluation of the social/political life.

Psychotherapists have contributed to such understanding, from Freud's work on *Civilization and its Discontents* (1930) and Reich's analysis of *The Mass Psychology of Fascism* (1933), through work in the 1960s on gender, sexuality and race, to work today on neoliberalism and austerity, global transformation, authoritarianism, Brexit, Donald Trump and post-truth politics.[49] These represent what we might refer to as social criticism at the macro level of politics.

The next aspect of the political/social world that I think psychotherapy could and should address is at the meso or intermediate level of analysis, which involves bringing psychotherapeutic knowledge, insights and understanding to specific areas of social issues and/or social policy. Such areas might include topics such as adoption, state childcare, circumcision, conflict, elder care, facial disfigurement, fostering, homophobia, immigration, maternity and paternity leave, misogyny, racism, self-help, self-hatred, social conflict, suicide, traumatic events, long-term unemployment and violence and its prevention. The knowledge, insights and understanding we can bring to bear on these areas and issues might include attachment styles, authoritarianism, defences, emotional literacy, empathy, internalisation, life scripts, the importance of play, projection, psychological games, regulation, transgenerational processes, trauma and violence etc. Making an impact in these areas also involves psychotherapists getting out of their clinics and into the public arena and media – as, for instance, the British psychiatrist Donald Winnicott did with his radio talks in the 1940s; other examples include psychotherapists having regular columns in local and national newspapers and slots on radio programmes.

The third aspect, the micro level, is when the psychotherapist works with the individual client (or clients) in a way that is informed by social criticism. For example, Neil Browne observes: 'When we recognise that critical thinking is something that is not broadly practised, we have some obligation to think in terms of "Why isn't it?"'[50] We might think about this as a broader social and educational issue; as psychotherapists, we may also work with a client to develop their critical capacity – and, thereby, be part of the project to move critical thinking and reflexivity into the mainstream. I consider this to be a useful way of thinking about psychotherapy as a form of social criticism.

However, although some view psychotherapy as, by definition, political, or it is not psychotherapy,[51] clearly it has not always been so progressive. Inspired by Fay's work on the political span of psychotherapy,[52] I have written elsewhere about transactional analysis encompassing practice and theory that is both liberal and radical, but also conservative;[53] psychotherapy has certainly been used in a reactionary and oppressive way. For example, Salman Akhtar writes about how two original members of the Indian Psychoanalytic Society, Owen Berkeley-Hill and Claude Dangar-Daly, both British Army officers, 'used psychoanalysis as a vehicle of cultural prejudice and oppression'.[54] This included a lack of curiosity about the experience of their Indian patients or positive aspects of Indian culture; promoting a split-self representation within the Indian psyche; publishing articles portraying Indians as inferior and infantile, and proposing that the British needed to take the role of enlightened parents for the Indian people. Akhtar comments: 'What is striking in all this is the utter lack of awareness of distortions arising from a racist countertransference, [the] confusion of group with individual psychology, and the disregard of actual sociopolitical variables in oppressed people's rebellion.'[55]

Another example of the abuse of therapy is the way in which the state medicalises – and medicates – distress. Thomas Szasz refers to the collaboration betwen psychiatry and government as the 'therapeutic state',[56] which:

> ... swallows up everything human on the seemingly rational ground that nothing falls outside the province of health and medicine, just as the theological state had swallowed up everything human on the perfectly rational ground that nothing falls outside the province of God and religion.[57]

This is why psychotherapists should be critical not only of medicine but also of the 'health' industry, 'health' professions, and the assumption that they themselves are best placed and understood as health professionals.[58]

Like Szasz, Füredi is critical of governments' attempts to act therapeutically towards their citizens, noting that:

> Therapeutic techniques are employed throughout the public sphere: since the early 1980s, when counselling emerged as a government policy directed at reintegrating the unemployed, therapeutic intervention has become a normal feature of social policy... In both the UK and the US, policies are increasingly represented as 'supporting', and 'empowering', if not quite treating, individuals.[59]

In order to embody this position, role and task of social criticism, I suggest that psychotherapy needs – and psychotherapists need – to be critical, and therefore peripheral, subversive and deconstructive.

We need to be critical, as I hope this contribution has demonstrated. As far as being peripheral is concerned, the history of psychotherapy reflects a tension between those who have sought to make it mainstream and those who promote psychotherapy as being on the margins of society. As Aron and Starr point out:

> Freud and the early analysts were at the margins of their society. Being at the margins gave them the edge and allowed for the intervention and development of psychoanalysis. Being at the margins is what allows for

reflexive self-awareness, the ability to look at oneself as both subject and object, without being caught up in one pole or another.[60]

Just as the shaman, wise elder or priest tended – and still tends – to live on the edge of the village, so, too, the therapist needs to be able to live on the periphery or margin and to take an inside/outsider perspective. This doesn't mean that therapists shouldn't work in the centre of society, metaphorically and literally (in town, in hospitals, schools and other public sector organisations, or even in large private corporations); it does, however, have implications for how therapists position, develop and organise themselves in relation to their clients, other professionals, and the state (see also p254). Psychotherapy is subversive, in the sense that it turns things upside down, overturns (turns over) the past as well as the present, and undermines old and unhelpful ways of thinking and being. From a critical perspective, it needs to be (more) subversive, in the sense of helping to turn and turn back, to convert and invert, and to transform and translate oppressive structures, dynamics and processes. It follows that psychotherapy is a deconstructive process – and not least about itself. As Glenn Larner puts it: '[P]sychotherapy is the subject of a radical critique *while* we do it. By deconstructing the cultural and discursive forces that shape or constitute its profession, it becomes a more powerful (and political) location for change.'[61]

Conclusion

A generation ago, in 1984, Terry Eagleton wrote a history and critique of the previous 200 years of cultural criticism, arguing that 'criticism today lacks all substantive social function'.[62] The same may be said of psychotherapy. However, and like Eagleton, I would say that this has not always been and need not now be the case. However, if a critical psychotherapy and psychotherapy as criticism are to develop a substantive social function and force, there is much to be done, starting with more public awareness about psychotherapy and its range and potential.

Leo Tolstoy is said to have said: 'Everyone thinks of changing the world, but no one thinks of changing himself.' Psychotherapists, on the other hand, have, traditionally, thought much more about changing people (and 'selves'), but not so much about changing the world. However, if the world is to be a more soulful and healing, and a more healthy and sustainable place for all, we might do well to broaden as well as deepen our focus, and take in those extra-psychotherapeutic factors that impact on the outcome of therapy (see Chapter 6). Paul dates the first reference to the concept of a 'critical society' as 1906 – and notes that we still don't have one.[63] As I mentioned in the Introduction, my hope is that, in some small way, this book contributes to critical thinking about psychotherapy, and promotes psychotherapy as a way of encouraging critical thinking and practice.

I hope that this book raises some interesting questions – in American poet ee cummings' words, some beautiful questions even – and encourages you, the reader, to question and continue questioning. That, at least, will ensure the continuation of the critical praxis that is psychotherapy at its best – and, of course, the continued critical examination of psychotherapy as a practice, theory, profession, discipline and form of social criticism.

Endnotes

1. cummings ee (1954). Poem. In: *Poems, 1923-1954*. New York, NY: Harcourt, Brace & Company.
2. Watzlawick P, Weakland JH, Fisch R (1974). *Change: problem formation and problem resolution*. New York, NY: WW Norton & Co.
3. van Deurzen-Smith E, Smith D (1996). Is psychotherapy an autonomous scientific discipline? *Inside Out 27*(winter). iahip.org/inside-out/issue-27-winter-1996/is-psychotherapy-an-autonomous-scientific-discipline (accessed 30 October 2017).
4. In that he drew on neuroscience, evolutionary theory, sexology, literature, the history of civilisation, ethnic psychology, mythology, linguistics, anthropology, sociology, child psychology, general psychology and psychiatry.
5. Aron L, Starr K (2013). *Psychotherapy for the People: toward a progressive psychoanalysis*. New York, NY: Routledge (p339).
6. As, for instance, indentified by Burrell and Morgan in their seminal work

on paradigms: Burrell G, Morgan G (1979). *Sociological Paradigms and Organisational Analysis*. London, UK: Heinemann.
7. Rogers CR (1985). Toward a more human science of the person. *Journal of Humanistic Psychology* 25(4): 7–24.
8. European Association for Psychotherapy (1990). *Strasbourg Declaration on Psychotherapy*. Vienna: European Association for Psychotherapy. www.europsyche.org/download/cms/100510/EAPLogo-Strassburg-Dekl-e_2015_new.pdf (accessed July 2017).
9. Currently, I number these as 25.
10. Young RM (1999). *The Curious Place of Ppsychoanalysis in the Academy*. [Online.] Talk delivered to the Programme in Psychoanalysis and the Humanities at the University of Toronto, 9 January. Robert M Young Online Archive. http://www.human-nature.com/rmyoung/papers/pap119h.html (accessed 20 April 2017).
11. See Taft's comment, quoted in Chapter 2, p43.
12. Totton N (1997). Not just a job: psychotherapy as a spiritual and political practice. In: House R, Totton N (eds). *Implausible Professions: arguments for pluralism and autonomy in psychotherapy and counselling*. Ross-on-Wye: PCCS Books (pp129–140).
13. Caplow T (1966). The sequence of professionalization. In: Vollmer HM, Mills DL (eds). *Professionalization*. Englewood Cliffs, NJ: Prentice Hall (pp20–21).
14. Freud S (1964/1937). Analysis terminable and interminable. In: Strachey J (ed & trans). *The Standard Edition of the Complete Psychological Works of Sigmund Freud, vol 23*. London: Hogarth Press (pp216–253).
15. This initially comprised Wilhelm Stekel (who is credited with the initiative for the meeting), Max Kahane and Rudolf Reitler, then Alfred Adler. Members who joined subsequently included Otto Rank, who in 1906 was appointed Secretary.
16. Sigmund Freud, Wilhelm Reich, Otto Rank, Karl Abraham, Sándor Ferenczi, Isidor Isaak Sadger, Victor Tausk, Hanns Sachs, Ludwig Binswanger, Carl Alfred Meier, Sabina Spielrein, Margarete Hilferding, Alfred Adler, and Wilhelm Stekel, Max Kahane, and Rudolf Reitler
17. These included Karl Abraham, Max Eitingon, Ernest Jones, and Carl Jung.
18. See www.ipa.world
19. Freud S (1914). The history of the psychoanalytic movement. *Psychoanalytic Review* 3: 406–454. For a more recent history of the IPA see www.ipa.world (accessed 11 November 2017).
20. Fromm E (1975). *La Mission de Sigmund Freud: une analyse de sa personnalité et de son influence [Sigmund Freud's Mission: an analysis of his personality and influence]* (P Alexandre trans). Bruxelles: Laffont.

21. Roudinesco F. (2001). Critique of psychoanalytic institutions. In: Roudinesco E. *Why Psychoanalysis?* (R Bowlby trans). Paris: Libraire Arthème Fayard.
22. See: Makari G (2008). *Revolution in Mind: the creation of psychoanalysis.* New York, NY: Harper Collins
23. Kirsner D (2009). *Unfree Associations: inside psychoanalytic institutes* (updated ed). New York, NY: Jason Aaronson.
24. Reich WR (1973/1942). *The Function of the Orgasm.* London: Souvenir Press (p125).
25. http://www.europsyche.org
26. See www.worldpsyche.org/cms-tag/125/world-council-for-psychotherapy
27. Aron & Starr (2013) (p129).
28. See: Rangell L (1954). Similarities and differences between psychoanalysis and dynamic psychotherapy. *Journal of the American Psychoanalytic Association 2*: 734–744.
29. Aron & Starr (2013) (p2).
30. Freud S (1959/1926). The question of lay analysis: conversations with an impartial person. In: Strachey J (trans & ed). *The Standard Edition of the Complete Psychological Works of Sigmund Freud, vol 20.* London: Hogarth Press (pp183–250).
31. Wallerstein I (1998). *Utopistics: or historical choices of the twenty-first century.* New York, NY: The New Press (p49).
32. Aron & Starr (2013) (p131).
33. Macleod A, McSherry B (2007). Regulating mental healthcare practitioners: towards a standardised and workable framework. *Psychiatry, Psychology and Law 14*(1): 45–55.
34. As identified by: Clarkson P (2000). *Ethics: working with ethical and moral dilemmas in psychotherapy.* London: Whurr.
35. The distinction between the two is well illustrated in an exchange between two characters in the film *Pirates of the Caribbean: the curse of the black pearl* (2003, directed by Gore Verbinski) when Elizabeth Turner (who has been captured by pirates) quotes their code to Captain Barbossa:

    Elizabeth: Wait! You have to take me to shore. According to the Code of the Order of the Brethren…

    Barbossa: First, your return to shore was not part of our negotiations nor our agreement so I *must* do nothing. And secondly, you must be a *pirate* for the pirate's code to apply and you're *not*. And thirdly, the code is more what you'd call 'guidelines' than actual *rules*. Welcome aboard the *Black Pearl*, Miss Turner.
36. Morice MP (2003). *Towards a Māori Psychotherapy. The therapeutic*

relationship and Māori concepts of relationship: a systematic literature review with case illustrations. Master's thesis. Auckland: Auckland University of Technology. These principles are also articulated in: Morice MP, Woodard W, with Came H (2017). Māori psychotherapy and the Health Practitioners' Competence Assurance Act 2003. In: Tudor K (ed). *Pluralism in Psychotherapy: critical reflections from a post-regulation landscape.* (The revised and expanded edition of *The Turning Tide*). Auckland: Resource Books (pp115–126).

37. In the Māori world, a *kaitiaki* is a spiritual guardian, a trustee who holds responsibility for certain resources or domains.

38. Hahn H (2004). F***ing, failing and finding out. [Review of the book *Disgrace* by JM Coetzee]. *British Journal of Psychotherapy* 18: 537-542 (pp539–540).

39. Macleod & McSherry (2007).

40. Freud S (1959/1926). The question of lay analysis: conversations with an impartial person. In: Strachey J (trans & ed). *The Standard Edition of the Complete Psychological Works of Sigmund Freud, vol 20.* London: Hogarth Press (pp183–250) (p234).

41. See Mowbray R (1995) *The Case against Psychotherapy Registration: a conservation issue for the human potential movement.* London: Trans Marginal Press. Also, most recently: Tudor K (ed) (2017). *Pluralism in Psychotherapy: critical reflections from a post-regulation landscape.* (The revised and expanded edition of *The Turning Tide*.) Auckland: Resource Books.

42. Tudor K (2017). Recognition, regulation and registration. In: Tudor K (ed). *Pluralism in Psychotherapy: critical reflections from a post-regulation landscape.* (The revised and expanded edition of *The Turning Tide*.) Auckland: Resource Books (pp29–46).

43. Füredi F (2004). *Where Have All the Intellectuals Gone? Confronting 21st century philistinism.* London: Continuum (p152).

44. Kaye J (1999). Towards a non-regulative praxis. In: Parker I (ed). *Deconstructing Psychotherapy.* London: Sage (pp19–38).

45. Aron & Starr (2013) (p28).

46. Quoted in: Carey B (2005). Psychotherapy on the road to... where? *New York Times*; 27 December. www.nytimes.com/2005/12/27/science/psychotherapy-on-the-road-to-where.html (accessed June 2017).

47. The others being psychotherapy *in* politics, the politics *of* psychotherapy, and politics *in* psychotherapy – see Totton N (2000). *Psychotherapy and Politics.* London: Sage.

48. All these topics have been the subject of articles in – and, in the case of neoliberalism and austerity, and of global transformation, the subject of special themed issues of – *Psychotherapy and Politics International.*

49. A number of these topics reflect the subjects of articles that have been published in the past couple of years in *Psychotherapy and Politics International* (http://onlinelibrary.wiley.com/journal/10.1002/(ISSN)1556-9195).
50. Browne MN, Keeley S (1993). Conversation. In: Esterle J, Cluman D (eds). *Conversations with Critical Thinkers*. San Francisco, CA: The Whitman Institute (pp71–89) (p80).
51. See: Schmid P (2014). Psychotherapy is political or it is not psychotherapy: the person-centred approach as an essentially political venture. *Psychotherapy and Politics International 21*(1): 4–17, and the rest of the special issue of the journal on the theme.
52. Fay J (2008). Conservative, liberal and radical psychotherapy. *Forum* [the Journal of the New Zealand Association of Psychotherapists] *14*: 103–110.
53. Tudor K (2010). Transactional analysis: a little liberal, a little conservative, and a little radical. *The Psychotherapist 46*: 17–20.
54. Akhtar S (2005). *Freud along the Ganges: psychoanalytic reflections on the people and culture of India*. New York, NY: Other Press (p11).
55. Akhtar (2005) (p13).
56. A phrase coined originally in 1963 – see also: Szasz T (1984). *The Therapeutic State: psychiatry in the mirror of current events*. Buffalo, NY: Prometheus Books.
57. Szasz T (2001). The Therapeutic State: the tyranny of pharmacracy. *The Independent Review 5*(4): 485–521 (p515).
58. See: Tudor K (2017). The question of regulation and registration. In: Tudor K (ed). *Pluralism in Psychotherapy: critical reflections from a post-regulation landscape* (The revised and expanded edition of *The Turning Tide*). Auckland: Resource Books (pp179–211).
59. Füredi (2004) (p126).
60. Aron L & Starr (2013) (pp8–9). See also: Stepansky PE (2009). *Psychoanalysis at the Margins*. New York, NY: Other Press.
61. Larner G (1999). Derrida and the deconstruction of power as context and topic in psychotherapy. In: Parker I (ed). *Deconstructing Psychotherapy*. London: Sage (pp39–53) (p51).
62. Eagleton T (2005/1984). *The Function of Criticism*. London: Verso (p7).
63. Paul R (1993). Conversation. In: Esterle J, Cluman D (eds). *Conversations with Critical Thinkers*. San Francisco, CA: The Whitman Institute (pp91–101). Here, Paul is citing the work of Sumner WG (1940/1906). *Folkways: a study of the sociological importance of usages, manners, customs, mores, and morals*. New York, NY: Ginn & Co.

NAME INDEX

A

Akhtar, S 36, 75, 96, 110, 127, 138, 256, 263
Albee, G 67, 77
Alexander, R 25, 68, 77, 87
Allan, H viii
Allan, R 240
Anderson, R 241
Angyal, A 52, 57, 71, 73
Arden, J 54, 72
Aron, L 3, 9, 65, 69, 74, 76, 137, 138, 143, 224, 244, 249, 250, 251, 254, 257, 259, 261, 262, 263
Arroyave, F 93, 109
Asay, TP 69, 71
Asch, SE 21, 38
Atkinson, M 206
Autton, N 86, 107

B

Baker, DB 44, 71
Barkham, M 204
Barnes, G 15, 36, 69, 70, 71, 105, 114, 119, 120, 133, 134, 135, 136, 137, 139, 140
Barrett-Lennard, GT 40, 111
Barrow, G viii, 209, 227, 237, 240
Bassman, R 236, 241
Bates, Y 77
Bazzano, M 6, 10, 101, 108, 111
Benjamin, J 57, 71, 73

Berlin, I 125, 137
Bernard, J 155, 156, 169
Berne, E 15, 16, 20, 36, 38, 39, 44, 64, 69, 86, 88, 89, 108, 110, 116, 119, 120, 134, 135, 138
Bernstein, J 133, 140
Beutler, LE 65, 167, 199, 201
Bohart, AC 107, 190, 203, 204
Boisvert, CM 201
Borders, LD 171
Braud, W 241
Brogan, MM 202
Brookfield, S 32, 41, 97, 104, 112
Brown, S 34, 35, 36, 241
Buber, M 52, 71, 237
Bulkeley, K 72
Burrell, G 204, 259, 260

C

Came, H viii, 12, 21, 33, 62, 121, 123, 155, 192, 236, 238, 262
Caplan, E 75
Carkhuff, R 100, 101, 111
Carper, B 204
Carr, W 205
Carroll, M 156, 169, 171, 183
Casement, A 233, 241
Casement, P 24, 32, 39, 41, 159, 171
Casemore, R 107

Cautin, RL 74
Chaffee, J 41, 112
Cieszkowski, A 112
Clarkin, JF 201
Clarkson, P 65, 75, 76, 102, 111, 160, 171, 261
Coase, RH 211, 238
Cocks, G 38
Collens, P viii, 70
Connell, R 16, 35, 37, 131, 139
Cooper, M 5, 10, 39, 40, 43, 66, 175, 178, 179, 180, 199, 201, 204, 237, 243
Cornell, WF 20, 22, 37, 38, 158, 170
Corsini, RJ 75
Cousins, D 42, 68
Cozollino, L 72
Craig, I 74
Cramer, D 118, 136
Cronbach, LJ 201
Cunningham, I 206
Cushman, E 68, 205

D

Damasio, A 31, 41, 45, 69
Darongkamas, J 170
Dawkins, R 27, 40
Deacon, B 199
Denzin, NK 137, 205, 206, 225, 228, 239, 240, 241
DiClemente, CC 182
Dollard, J 184, 202
Dona, G 206
Dreyfus, H 110
Droysen, J 107
Duncan, BL 69, 71, 72, 116, 118, 135, 139, 185, 193, 196, 203, 205, 206

E

Eagleton, T 11, 33, 134, 140, 258, 263

Egan, G 100, 101, 111, 202
Eisner, D 68, 70, 77
Eitingon, M 154, 167, 212, 215, 238, 260
Elliott, R 199, 204
Ellis, C 108, 212, 241
Embleton Tudor, L vii, 73, 237
Evans, B 31, 41
Eysenck, H 9, 67, 76

F

Fay, J 126, 128, 137, 138, 235, 241, 256, 263
Feltham, C 9, 14, 35, 68, 74, 77, 111, 179, 218, 238
Fenichel, O 138
Ferenczi, S 17, 51, 52, 66, 71, 84, 106, 109, 142, 154, 212, 247, 260
Ferrando, F 76
Fischer, HJ 137
Fleming, P 81, 82, 105, 106, 158, 171
Fonagy, P 114, 135, 202
Fordham, M 57, 73, 136
Foucault, M 15, 24, 36, 39, 132, 133, 139, 140
Fox, NJ 140
France, A 68, 75, 77, 81, 105
Frank, JD 21, 68, 113, 185, 203, 210
Frawley-O'Dea, M 153, 168
Freire, ES 190, 194
Freire, P 205, 2066
Freud, S 45, 46, 50, 51, 52, 63, 64, 67, 68, 69, 70, 71, 73, 74, 75, 76, 77, 105, 106, 107, 108, 109, 110, 123, 124, 125, 126, 127, 136, 137, 138, 141, 142, 200, 225, 226, 238, 239, 243, 244, 247, 248, 249, 260, 261, 262, 263

Friedrich, CD 53, 137
Fruzzetti, AE 169
Frymer-Kensky, T 138
Füredi, F 111, 210, 223, 238, 239, 254, 257, 262, 263

G

Gabbard, GO 200
Garfield, S 167, 184, 200, 201, 203
Geuss, R 9
Ghandi, M 37
Glaser, B 136
Glass, CR 200
Goldfried, M 75, 185, 200, 203
Goldstein, K 69
Goulding, MM 139
Graham, H 15, 44, 69, 137, 210
Gramsci, A 33, 112
Grencavage, LM 186, 203
Grimmer, A 166, 167

H

Hahn, H 233, 234, 241, 253, 262
Harari, YN 49, 70
Harbour, R 203
Hare, AP 85, 106
Hargaden, H 38, 74, 138, 170
Harrison, J 90, 108
Hartmann, H 54, 73
Hassan, I 136
Hawkins, P 159, 170, 171
Hegel, GWF 78, 105
Herink, R 75
Herlo, D 168, 209, 237
Heron, J 89, 92, 108, 206
Heuer, G viii, 36, 68, 69, 70, 71, 73, 106
Heyward, C 68, 77
Hillard, RB 200
Hoch, P 116, 135
Hogan, RA 158, 170
Holland, S 66, 139, 202

Holloway, E 169, 171
Holmes, J 34, 192, 205
Horney, K 15, 66, 173, 199
House, ER 190, 204
House, R 16, 36, 65, 76, 190, 204, 260
Houston, G 39, 199, 237
Howard, KI 179, 201, 203
Hunsley, J 183, 202

I

Illich, I 229, 240
Illsley Clarke, J 118, 136

J

Jackson, C viii
Jackson, SW 68,
Jacobs, A 21, 23, 27, 38, 39, 40
Jacobs, D 115, 169
Jacoby, R 75
Jahoda, M 138
Janesick, V 206
Jaramillo, N 136
Jenkins, P viii, 160, 164, 171, 172
Jones, E 125, 137, 247, 260
Jung, CG 17, 46, 48, 54, 56, 57, 66, 70, 71, 73, 74, 84, 106, 119, 136, 247, 260

K

Kabat-Zinn, J 89, 108
Kadushin, A 157, 170
Kaplan, EA 124, 137
Kapp, A 39, 237
Karpman, S 121, 136
Kellerman, S 107
Kelly, G 49, 70, 135
Kelman, HC 22, 38
Kernberg, O 117, 135, 167, 210, 221, 222, 223, 224, 225, 226, 228, 229, 237, 239, 240, 246

Keyes, CLM 57, 73
Kierkegaard, S 80, 105
King, L 238, 240
Kinsella EA 206
Kitzinger, C 206
Klein, GS 52, 72
Knowles, MS 25, 39, 237
Kourkouta, L 74
Kovacs, AL 70
Kramer, R 118, 136

L

Labriola, A 112
Ladany, N 163, 172
Lake, F 113, 134
Lao Tse, 26, 40
Larner, G 91, 108, 258, 263
Lask, J 168
Lecours, S 135
Leichsenring, F 180, 201
Levitt, B 107
Lewes, GH 70
Lewin, K 118, 135
Lewis, T 3, 102, 107, 183, 212
Liese, BS 169
Lincoln, TS 37, 137, 205, 206, 225, 228, 239, 240, 241
Loewenthal, D viii, 37, 204
Lomas, P 25, 39
López, S 102, 111
Lowen, A 87, 107

M

MacLennan, N 75
Macran, S 166, 167
Maluccio, AN 200
Marx, K 6, 10, 52, 60, 71, 74
Maslow, AH 57, 73
Masson, J 67, 77
Mazzetti, M 169
McLeod, J 119, 136, 167, 173, 174, 175, 199, 200, 236, 241

Mearns, D 29, 30, 41, 110, 117, 135, 146, 167, 202
Merry, T 28, 40, 166, 172
Meyer, B 155, 169, 202
Mill, JS 227, 240
Miller, N 184
Miller, S 69, 71, 72, 116, 139, 185, 193, 196, 202, 203
Mingers, J 14, 36
Minikin, K 34
Mitchell, J 36, 129, 138
Mohr, DC 199, 201
Moncayo, R 38
Moravia, A 24, 39
Moreno, JL 13, 27, 40, 66, 106, 244
Morgan, S 117, 135, 188, 204, 259, 260
Morice, MP 235, 241, 251, 262
Morrall, P 37, 68, 77
Morris, DG 20, 37
Morrow-Bradley, C 199
Mowbray, R 47, 70, 262
Murphy, D 140, 143, 152, 166, 167

N

Naughton, M 241
Neville, B 98, 100, 111, 126, 137
Newnes, C vii, 10, 34, 37, 91, 108, 138, 203
Nicholls, D viii
Norcross, JC 74, 75, 166, 167, 186, 200, 203

O

O'Connor, N 39
Ogden, T 59, 74
Onions, CT 37
Orange, D 97, 109, 110, 138
Orlinsky, DE 179, 201, 203
Owen, IR 37, 56, 157, 170, 256
Owen-Pugh, V 157, 170

P

Page, S 149, 171
Paglia, C 207, 237
Parker, I 10, 16, 34, 37, 95, 108, 109, 193, 205, 262, 263
Paul, R 14, 35, 40, 45, 50, 64, 68, 71, 85, 97, 116, 139, 155, 259, 264
Phillips, A 79, 105, 106
Piaget, J 57, 73
Pihama, L 206
Plummer, K 206
Pohatu, TW 206
Porter, JE 205
Pound, E 129, 138
Prasko, J 170
Prochaska JO 182, 202
Proctor, B 157, 170
Proner, BD 93, 109
Prouty, GF 110, 202

R

Ramana, CV 138
Rangell, L 114, 115, 117, 118, 121, 134, 135, 136, 261
Rawn, ML 166
Reich, W 15, 22, 38, 62, 64, 66, 74, 87, 107, 138, 249, 255, 260, 261
Reiff, P 113, 134
Renik, O 56, 72
Richards, G 137, 170
Ricoeur, P 97, 137
Riebel, L 20, 38, 118, 136
Robinson, WL 40, 77, 102, 111
Rodgers, B 203
Rogers, CR 34, 73, 83, 85, 87, 88, 93, 94, 95, 96, 97, 98, 105, 106, 107, 109, 110, 111, 113, 114, 116, 117, 118, 134, 135, 136, 137, 138, 184, 185, 202, 203, 204, 208, 209, 237
Rogers, N 85, 106
Rosenzweig, S 18, 37, 72, 110, 183, 202
Rowan, J 24, 39
Rowland, N 204
Rubin, H 206
Russell, P 73, 139

S

Sacks, H 206
Sahlins, M 71
Salzberg, S 31, 32, 41
Samuels, A 6, 9, 10, 65, 76
Sanders, P viii, 9, 34
Sands, A 68, 77, 81, 105
Sarnat, J 154, 165, 166, 169, 172
Sartre, J-P 45, 49, 51, 52, 69, 70, 71, 80, 105, 123, 137
Saunders, MK 15, 36
Schmid, P 39, 40, 88, 108, 110, 203, 237, 263
Schmidt, M 73
Schore, A 12, 35, 128, 138
Schott R 206
Schwartz, J 38
Searles, H 155, 169
Seeley, K 105
Segal, ZV 108
Sève, L 36, 138
Shakespeare, W 1, 9, 59, 73
Shedler, J 64, 75, 180, 183, 201, 202
Sherrard, E vii
Siegel, D 115, 135
Singer, MT 38, 40
Singh, J 34
Slife, BD 35
Smail, D 67, 77
Smythe, E viii
Socrates, 112
Solomon, M 105, 106
Souto-Manning, M 206
Speierer, G-W 131, 139

Spinelli, E 106
Standal, S 95, 109
Stark, M 61, 74, 165, 168, 172, 224
Starr, K 65, 123, 143, 210, 224, 244, 249, 250, 251, 254, 257
Steiner, C vii, 12, 33, 38, 40, 66, 74, 104, 112, 139
Stern, DN 12, 34, 89, 108, 115, 135, 159, 171
Stevens, JO 73
Stevenson, L 72
Stewart-Harawira, S 36
Storr, A 138
Strauss, AL 107, 136
Strupp, H 203
Stubbs, JP 184, 203
Summers, G 34, 38, 53, 69, 72, 108, 140, 210, 238
Szasz, TS 24, 39, 67, 77, 131, 139, 257, 263

T

Taft, J 42, 44, 64, 68, 94, 95, 109, 260
Tavris, C 32, 41, 210, 238
Taylor-Sanders, M viii
Te Pou o Te Whakaaro Nui, 9
Thomas, J 24, 59, 67, 131, 205, 257
Thompson, C 109
Thorne, B 29, 30, 41, 70, 108, 111, 167
Torrey, EF 76
Torrey, RA 40,
Totton, N 4, 6, 9, 10, 107, 132, 139, 247, 255, 260, 263
Troyna, B 241
Tryon, GS 201
Tudor, K 9, 34, 36, 37, 38, 39, 40, 69, 72, 73, 74, 75, 76, 106, 107, 108, 110, 111, 134, 137, 138, 139, 140, 168, 169, 170, 171, 172, 203, 205, 237, 238, 240, 241, 262, 263

V

Vallance, K 170
van Deurzen-Smith, E 50, 71, 243, 244
Van Werde, D 110, 202
Viljoen, B viii
Von Haenisch, C 167

W

Wallerstein, RS 155, 169, 225, 239, 240, 261
Wampold, B 179, 201
Watkins, CE 111, 136, 158, 169, 171
Watson, JB 63, 75, 176, 200
Watson, N 202
Webb, J 6, 10, 90, 101, 108, 111
Wheeler, S 167, 170
Whelton, WJ 128, 138
Wilberg, P 80, 105
Winnicott, DW 24, 38, 39, 52, 71, 72, 256
Wittgenstein, L 15, 36, 40, 108
Wogan, M 166
Wood, JK 96, 110, 113, 116, 134, 135
Woodard, W 69, 195, 206, 262

Y

Yalom, I 57, 73
Yellow Bird, M 13, 35
Yontef, G 169

Z

Zalcman, MJ 158, 170

SUBJECT INDEX

A

abuse 17, 37, 47, 121, 257
adaptation 24, 57–8, 80
alienation 59–60, 120, 130, 194, 231
analysing 77, 80, 83, 90–2, 155
andragogy 25, 211, 222, 224
andragogic(al) 166, 209, 220
attitudes 7, 21, 28, 79, 89, 92–6, 98, 100, 184, 198, 200
authenticity 47, 59, 80, 94, 127

B

body, 35, 45, 49, 53–4, 57, 87

C

certainty 18, 26–7
codes of conduct 251
competencies 92–3
conditions 29, 79, 83, 85, 92–4, 96–100, 124, 175, 184
conformity 18, 21–2, 24, 27, 208
    see also 'non-conformity'
confronting 80, 88–92
connection 57, 80, 236
counselling 2–4, 66, 80, 99, 101, 143–5, 160, 171–5, 198, 243, 245, 250
    psychology 2, 4, 12, 174, 198, 243, 245, 250
critical

influences on psychotherapy theory 122
research methodologies and methods 192
thinking 11, 13, 31–3, 79, 97, 104, 176, 210, 220–21, 225, 234–35, 256, 259
criticism 11–17, 32–3, 60, 122, 131, 134, 164, 242–43, *see also* 'social criticism'
critique v, 11, 13–16, 24, 27, 58–9, 119–20, 132, 164–65, 192–94, 216, 220–21
    of authority 16, 21, 122, 192
    of objectivity 16, 193
    of rhetoric 15, 42, 193
    of tradition 15–16
cure, 47, 56, 58, 62, 80, 116, 120

D

development
    continuing professional, 7, 103, 141, 232–34, 241
    of psychotherapy 15, 63, 93, 175, 246
    sustaining, 207–237
directing, 80, 84–86, 91–2, 146
discipline viii, 5, 7, 16–17, 24–5, 81, 173–74, 227–28, 242–59

dogmatism 11, 18, 26, 216–17
doubt 14, 31–32

E

education 6–8, 12, 19–20, 22–3, 25–6, 99–103, 141, 146–47, 160, 166, 198, 207–36, 246
 apprenticeship model of, 141, 207, 211
 continuing, 141, 150, 231, 234–35
 models of, 207–9, 222, 224
educational theory 209
empathising 80, 87–8, 91–2, 95
empirically-supported treatments 186, 188
empiricism 188, 244
the Enlightenment 7, 49, 114, 122–23, 128, 134
evidence 20, 33, 64, 67, 144, 146, 174, 176–80, 186–89, 191–93
 levels of, 176, 187, 204
 practice-based, *see* 'practice-based evidence'

F

fundamentalism 11, 18, 27–8, 30, 190

G

Gestalt therapy 1, 45

H

healing 42–6, 57, 62, 83, 132, 144, 185, 243, 245–47, 250, 259
health 43–5, 53, 61, 120, 124, 127, 130, 132–33, 233, 247, 257
holiness 44–5, 55
holism 44–5
homo-
 ludens 10, 53, 72
 politicus 51
 sapiens 49, 114
human 8, 31, 49–54, 57, 59, 76, 80, 83, 86, 120, 123–24, 126–27, 129–30, 132–33, 188–90, 215–16, 257
 beings 49–50, 57, 123, 126, 129–30, 132, 227
 nature 5, 8, 45, 49–53, 86, 120, 123, 126–27, 129, 132–33, 189
humanistic psychology 12, 16, 56, 59, 124, 127, 156
humility 44, 95, 252

I

individuation 56–7, 80
insight 56, 80, 94, 104, 141, 178
intolerance 28–30

K

kaupapa Māori
 research methodology 194–95

L

learning 21, 26, 155–56, 177–78, 184, 207–11, 221
 experiential, 142, 151,
 theory 99, 102
liberation 59–60, 80, 247
listening 79–83, 90–2, 94, 99, 175, 178, 183
 levels of, 81

M

medicine 25, 43, 46, 62–3, 176, 186, 192, 225, 243, 246–47, 250, 257

methodology 11, 78, 85, 88, 186, 192–95, 197–99, 217
mind 49–51, 53–4, 57, 61–2, 81, 83, 88, 90, 115, 120, 123, 126, 133
minding 80, 89–92
modernism 7, 28, 122, 128–29, 131

N

non-conformity 23, 30

O

outcome studies 174–76

P

personality 19, 26, 48–9, 54–5, 57, 89, 94, 98, 117, 133, 181, 183–84, 246
personal therapy 6–7, 99, 141–54, 213, 219–20, 236
  arguments for, 144
person-centred 19, 29–30, 88, 95–8, 100, 145–46
  approach 3, 10, 29–30, 45, 96–7, 100, 145–46
  psychology 12, 28, 82, 87–88, 98
  therapy 45, 79, 95–8, 113, 117, 145–46
postmodernism 7, 16, 114, 122, 131–32
power 12, 15, 17, 24, 26, 84–5, 90–1, 129, 131, 153–55, 194, 196, 231, 235, 252
  abuse of, 17
practice 2–8, 12–15, 32–3, 78–105, 113–17, 119–22, 160–66, 173–78, 186–88, 213–23, 242–43, 245–47, 250–53
  -based evidence 80, 117, 188, 193

supervised, 91, 147, 161, 213, 217–20
praxis 78–105, 107, 193, 216, 254
priesthood 18, 24–5
principles 28–30, 184–85, 188, 192, 194–95, 251–52
  fundamental, 28, 30
  rigid adherence to, 28
profession 7, 17, 63, 97, 142–43, 173, 183, 227–28, 232–33, 242–59
professional development 7, 94, 103, 141, 145, 147, 150, 153, 158, 231–33, 235, 249
  continuing, 7, 103, 141, 150, 207, 231–35
  sustaining, 7, 141, 233–35, 241
professionalisation 12, 153, 232, 242, 247, 249, 251, 253
psyche 42–68, 83, 133, 227, 235
  the nature of, 7, 42, 48, 58
psychoanalysis 2–4, 20, 22, 24, 51–2, 55–6, 63–6, 116, 121–24, 130–31, 154, 167, 211–12, 215, 224–26, 246–50
psychology 2, 46, 48–9, 54–7, 63, 66, 124–29, 165, 176, 186–87, 215, 243, 245–48, 250
  counselling, *see* 'counselling psychology'
  humanistic, *see* 'humanistic psychology,
psychotherapy
  as an academic discipline 245
  as an art 223, 242, 244
  critical, 8, 258
  critiques of, 66, 183
  the discipline of, 48, 243
  education and training 6–7, 25, 147, 166, 179, 186, 207–8, 211, 213, 220, 234, 236

models of, 207–8
the organisation of, 220
the field of, 16, 25, 30, 66, 160, 173, 245, 249–50
overview of, 42, 61, 66
as a profession 7, 228, 242–43, 246–47
the profession of, 7, 23, 183
radical, 12–13, 42, 52, 59, 65–6, 192, 197, 229, 256, 258
as a science 113
as social criticism 242, 254–55
purity 18–20, 28, 208

Q

qualities 7, 79, 92–3, 95–6, 177, 186

R

research 7–9, 97, 116–19, 170, 173–99, 216–18, 225–26, 228, 230, 236, 244–46
case study 174–76, 192, 196–97
client factors 174–75, 179–81, 184–85
common factors 97, 174–75, 179, 183–86
empirical approach to, 191
methodologies 174, 176, 189, 192–95, 197, 225, 236, 245
critical, 174, 176, 192–97, 225
Romanticism 7, 114, 122, 125–26, 128

S

secularism 28, 30
service 42, 44, 47, 94, 205, 227, 229, 247
skills 7, 78–9, 85, 92–3, 99–102, 113, 120–21, 179, 208, 217, 222

social 12–13, 51–2, 60–1, 65–6, 104, 124–25, 128–30, 133–34, 242–43, 245–47, 249–51, 252–59
criticism 5, 7, 12, 17, 60, 134, 242–43, 245, 247, 249, 251, 252–59
purpose 57, 60–1
spirit 2, 35, 48–9, 53–4, 57, 78, 100, 122, 130, 151, 225
supervision 6–7, 37–8, 141, 143, 145, 147, 149–51, 153–66, 212, 214–15, 217–20, 234–36
brief history of, 154
cultural, 161, 234–35
and responsibility 157, 217
scope of, 161

T

theory 12–16, 18–23, 64–7, 78, 92, 97–100, 102–3, 113–34, 194, 196–99, 213–18
criteria for, 23, 114, 118, 188
critical influences on, 122
nature and purpose of 114
problems with, 114, 120
psychotherapy, 2, 4–7, 14–16, 79, 113–14, 118–24, 126–30, 197–99, 213–14, 216–17, 245
and skills 102, 208
Southern, 16, 131–32
therapeutic outcome 44, 51, 90
therapy 6–10, 42–68, 78–9, 83–5, 90–2, 94–100, 132–4, 141–57, 166, 175–77, 179–86, 191–93, 250
the nature of, 7, 42, 48, 58
personal, 1, 6–7, 67, 141–55, 157, 159, 161, 163, 165–66, 173, 219–20
thinking 11, 13, 27, 31–3, 53–7,

95–7, 103–4, 158–59, 210,
 233–35, 256, 258–59
  critical, 11, 13, 31–33, 65, 97,
   104, 192, 197, 210, 225,
   234–35, 256, 258–59
  free, 18, 27, 229, 245
   threats to, 18
touching 80, 86–87, 90–92
training 12–13, 20–26, 101, 103–4,
  141–49, 151–52, 154–55,
  161–63, 165, 207–27,
  229–31, 233–36
  institutes 101, 207, 212–15,
   217, 219, 222, 225, 230
transactional analysis 12, 15, 20,
  22–23, 25, 114, 116–19,
  213–14

U

uncertainty 27, 30, 32–33, 50, 131,
  209

V

value orientation 8, 113, 160

W

Western intellectual tradition 8, 43,
  53, 122, 194
  also 'Northern' 131, 235